Family Interaction
and Transaction

Family Interaction and Transaction

The Developmental Approach

ROY H. RODGERS
University of Oregon

Prentice-Hall, Inc., Englewood Cliffs, New Jersey

Library of Congress Cataloging in Publication Data

RODGERS, ROY H.
    Family interaction and transaction.

    Includes bibliographies.
    1. Family.   I. Title.
HQ728.R569   301.42   73-389
ISBN 0-13-301879-2

PRENTICE-HALL SERIES IN SOCIOLOGY
Neil J. Smelser, *Editor*

10 9 8 7 6 5 4 3 2 1

PRINTED IN THE UNITED STATES OF AMERICA

Prentice-Hall International, Inc., *London*
Prentice-Hall of Australia, Pty. Ltd., *Sydney*
Prentice-Hall of Canada, Ltd., *Toronto*
Prentice-Hall of India Private Limited, *New Delhi*
Prentice-Hall of Japan, Inc., *Tokyo*

Acknowledgments

The author gratefully acknowledges permission to reprint excerpts from the following works:

Cicourel, Aaron V., "Fertility, Family Planning and the Social Organization of Family Life: Some Methodological Issues," from *The Journal of Social Issues*, 23:4 (October 1967).

Dubin, Robert, *Theory Building* (New York: The Free Press and London: Collier-Macmillan Limited). © by The Free Press.

Hill, Reuben et al., *The Family and Population Control* (Chapel Hill, N.C.: University of North Carolina Press, 1959).

Rainwater, Lee, *Family Design* (Chicago: Aldine Publishing Company, 1965); copyright © by Social Research, Inc., 1965. Reprinted by permission of the author and Aldine-Atherton, Inc.

Zigler, Edward and Irwin L. Child, "Socialization," in Gardner Lindzey and Elliott Aronson, eds., *The Handbook of Social Psychology*, 2nd ed., Vol. III (Reading, Mass.: Addison-Wesley Publishing Co., 1969).

Contents

3
Three Facets of Family Dynamics 23

4
Operationalizing the Theoretical Approach 71

5
Family Careers— Interactional Analysis: 85

Recruitment, Maintenance of Biological Functioning, and Socialization

Preface

Doing sociology is an active pursuit. In many ways, it resembles a detective solving a mystery. It involves getting an idea or a clue about the explanation of some aspect of human behavior and going to work to see if the explanation solves the mystery. Most of the time, though, books in sociology do not reflect this activity as much as they reflect the results of it. Consequently, they do not tend to give the reader a sense of the thrill of the chase. I am convinced that, to some extent, this is why some people find sociology rather dull. The books they read seem to have answered all of the questions they raise and, quite often, do not even let the reader in on very much of the process of finding the answers. The truth is, of course, that there really have been very few "answers"—final ones, at least—to the thousands of questions sociologists have asked over the years; that is, we still actually know very little about why people behave the way they do. And, so, there ought to be a lot of good sociological mystery books around.

Back in 1956, I was introduced to one such sociological mystery story in its relatively early stages. I became intrigued with it and have maintained a continuous interest in it ever since. The mystery had to do with family behavior and how we could explain what we observed from the establishment of a family to its final dissolution. The particular approach to solving these questions has become generally known as the "developmental approach" to the family. Over the years, this approach has made a certain amount of progress toward some explanations, but it has a long way to go. After I began teaching, I found that students were particularly intrigued with this approach and one of the reasons for this fascination, it appeared, was because all of the answers were not there already. Just as I had found genuine pleasure in making some contributions to solving the mystery, they also enjoyed the opportunity to become part of the process. After all, since the answers had not been found yet, their attempts were every bit as legitimate as anyone else's. They could follow a clue and could find out whether or not it led them to a solution or just down a blind alley.

This book is an invitation to others to join the quest. It is addressed to students in the broadest sense of this term, that is, to anyone who enjoys the intellectual pursuit of answers to unsolved problems. But, be forewarned. *This book is unfinished.* There are many loose ends, unpursued clues, and unidentified suspects. Undoubtedly, even some of the proposed approaches to answering some of the questions will turn out to be blind alleys. But, every sociologist who has *done* sociology is used to this experience.

I have tried to write the book in an order that will bring the reader along as far as the approach has gone to date. After briefly discussing how I view theory, I present in relatively complete form the developmental theoretical approach as I see it today. This perspective provides the basic conceptual equipment for pursuing the mystery further. I then discuss how one puts the conceptual tools to work in research and some of the problems encountered in this process. The remainder of the book consists of a series of chapters on how research has been done or how it may be attempted if the developmental theory is going to become a better one than it is now. In doing this examination, I review research which was carried out with a conscious developmental perspective but also research which—though not consciously—gives developmental insights.

I hope that readers of this book will gain several things. First, I expect that they will have a clearer understanding of what a developmental analysis of the family is. Second, I hope that they gain some new understandings of the structure and of the functioning of the family by seeing it from the developmental perspective. Third, I anticipate that they will learn a bit more about how sociologists go about their work in theory and in research. Although I have assumed that readers will have some basic understanding of the sociological study of families and of the general sociological perspective, one does not have to be deeply interested in the technical problems of theory and of method to achieve these objectives. The book should be of interest to readers at a fairly basic level as well as to advanced professionals who have not encountered the developmental approach before. I also hope that workers in the helping professions—medicine, health education, home economics, counselling, social welfare, and other community service activities—will find some profit in its pages.

Books like this one are always the product of a whole set of relationships with a great many people. As I have said, this book actually began for me in 1956. I can not possibly remember all who have made a contribution over the years. Certainly, many colleagues and students have stimulated my thinking by asking the "nasty question" for which I had no answer. Specifically, I am especially grateful to Robert Dubin who, as a former colleague at the University of Oregon, asked a number of such questions but also helped with some answers. Reuben Hill—teacher, colleague, and friend—asked such questions the first time I ever talked to him in 1955 and has not ceased doing so. The margins of a copy of the original manuscript I sent him are filled, and much that is found on the following pages has been influenced by those questions. I know that they will trigger a whole new set from him, even though I have not responded satisfactorily to all of the first ones! Among my colleagues at the University of Oregon, Ted Johannis has provided constant encouragement and interest in this project from the beginning. The E. C. Brown Center for Family Studies, where he is Director, provided a financial grant to aid me. I owe a debt to Mr. Edward Stanford, Sociology Editor of Prentice-Hall, who, though a relative newcomer to the project, arrived at a critical time and gave an impetus that was sorely needed. The University of Oregon granted me a six-month sabbatical leave in 1969–70, when I was able to complete the initial draft of the manuscript. Finally, only authors know how very much they owe to their families in such ventures. Ginny, Mike, Debbie, and Steve have been vital to this project.

Eugene, Oregon   ROY H. RODGERS
February 10, 1972

1

Explanation—the Goal
of Theory
and Research

This book deals with a theory of the family that focuses on two processes: interactions among family members and their transactions with members of other organizations in the society. The theory attempts to treat interactions and transactions as they change in character over the life history, or *career*, of the family. For this reason, it has been termed *the developmental approach*.

This body of principles is not the only theory of the family, nor is it necessarily "the best" one. To reveal its strengths and weaknesses is one of the major goals of this book; however, before we can judge the quality of this theory adequately, it probably is necessary to understand something about what a theory should do. Why have theories in social science at all? Isn't it much simpler just to study families, that is, to read about them or to do research about them, and then to analyze what we have learned? The objective of this chapter is to provide at least partial answers to these questions.

ALTERNATIVE VIEWS OF THEORY

"You know, I've got a *theory* about that. The way I see it. . . ."
"Oh, that's just a *theory*. Nobody really knows. I'll bet that. . . ."
"You know how he is—always *theorizing*. He hardly ever gets down to practical everyday things."

"The *theory* shows that two out of three Americans are likely to. . . ."

"Now that we have gathered this information, we have developed a *theory* based on our findings which. . . ."

All these statements use the word *theory*, but in each one it has a slightly different connotation. Although students in the behavioral sciences are used to hearing theory discussed in their course work, they are not always sure what the term means. Indeed, it seems to signify different intentions depending on who is using it and on the context in which it is being used, in some cases, even by the same person. The examples above imply such diverse meanings as having a hunch about something, possessing a vague idea concerning a situation which apparently can't be "known," daydreaming, making a declaration of statistical findings concerning some phenomenon, and setting down conclusions based on some empirical findings.

Aside from the slightly differing connotations that the statements communicate, there are variations in attitudinal content. Some of the statements convey an element of scorn for the theorizer. Others give an impression of a slipshod approach to concerns. Still others have a no-nonsense, "let's get down to the facts" quality. Many individuals hold one or more of these attitudes toward theory, whereas others are just not very interested in it because it is so "abstract," "impractical," or "ambiguous."

Yet, all of us must be concerned with theory since we use it in our daily lives. Furthermore, we do so in much the same way that this book is going to treat the term. All the statements above, in spite of their differences in connotation and attitudinal content, have a common theme. All of them in one way or another attempt to *explain* a set of events or some other kind of phenomenon. And that effort, quite simply, is what theories are all about. Whenever we try to explain something, we are theorizing. Of course, when we begin to look for *scientific* explanations, we are doing a special type of theorizing.

SCIENTIFIC THEORIES AS EXPLANATIONS

A quick survey of the literature on scientific theories may suggest that theories generally are intended to describe, to explain, and/or to predict some phenomenon. The position I am going to take is that to ask only for a *description* is too little to expect of a science, and to ask for a *prediction* is probably too much to expect—at least for social science in its present state of development.

Although it is very important to know as precisely as possible what the characteristics of a phenomenon are, description tells us very little about how and under what circumstances the event occurs. In the early development of a science, a great deal of effort is expended in developing techniques for making accurate and precise observations so that phenomena may be detailed adequately. This stage is certainly a prerequisite to any real understanding, but it is not the same as explanation (Dubin, 1969:85, 226–28). To describe the structure of the human body, for example, is not to explain how that human body functions; one must move from anatomy to physiology in order to accomplish this objective. Zetterberg (1963:7) applies the term *taxonomy* to a description of phenomena. Taxonomies are not explanations, that is, theories.

To *predict* means to have such an accurate and complete explanation and such a precise definition of the phenomenon as to leave no unknowns. Understanding through prediction is simply not the present state of affairs in the social sciences. Their subject matter is so complex, their variables so numerous, and their unknowns so many, that these disciplines fall far short of any such lofty goal.

Dubin (1969:14–18) notes an interesting paradox. He cites the fact that in much of their research, social scientists quite successfully have predicted *outcomes* without being able to state how they were produced, that is, without understanding the underlying process causing them. Dubin (1969:17) remarks:

> The precision paradox may be summarized as follows: It is possible to achieve high precision in predicting *when* changes in system states will occur and *what* states will succeed each other, without possessing knowledge of how the system operates. Furthermore, we can predict individual values of variables without knowing the connection between the forecasting indices and the outcome predicted.

It is clear that ability to predict does little for ability to theorize, since no explanation of how the forecast came about is offered.

Furthermore, there is some question in my mind about whether prediction is really the business of science at all. Although prediction and observation of what was forecast is a method for *testing* a theory, prediction also provides the basis for the manipulation of phenomena. At this point, science clearly is not involved. Science's goal is to find out what *is*. It remains for engineers of various kinds to take up the task of using that knowledge to change what is to what *ought to be*. Any attempt to manipulate a state of affairs involves some conception of its relative merit as opposed to some presumed better or worse condition. Science simply has no criteria for making such value judgments. These issues are ethical and moral. It is a frequent practice, of course, for scientists experimentally to manipulate aspects of phenomena under analysis in order to test a theory. This type of control is not done to determine which of two states is more desirable. Indeed, there are some clear ethical considerations which, in order to avoid interference with the lives of their subjects, scientists must take into account before deciding to manipulate a situation experimentally. Thus, on at least three grounds—that the state of the social sciences is not well enough developed, that prediction of outcomes does not necessarily explain their underlying process, and that the manipulation of phenomena involves ethical decisions outside the realm of science—I hold that the goal of prediction is not a necessary one for science.

But what of theory as explanation? I see this activity as more suitable than description, although explanation is more limited and objective than prediction. This fact does not suggest that explanation is less difficult than either description or prediction. An explanation consists of a set of statements about the relationships between the various elements comprising a phenomenon and about relationships existing between that phenomenon and others in its universe. Often it is assumed that, if such a statement of relationships is complete, we have a *causal* explanation. However, this fact is not necessarily the case and, in the social sciences, usually is not so. As Dubin (1969:94) states, "Empirically relevant theory in the behavioral and social sciences is built upon an acceptance of the notion of relationship rather than of the notion of causality." This subtle yet important difference must be kept in mind as we develop a theoretical model. (For an excellent discussion of this issue, cf. Dubin, 1969:89–95.) A truly causal statement accounts for all of the observed phenomenon in terms of some other phenomenon or set of phenomena; however, even though we often use the word *cause* in our explanatory statements, for example, "Broken homes cause juvenile delinquency," a more careful look at the data from which a statement is derived shows that a more accurate statement is phrased, "A greater-than-chance proportion of delinquents comes from broken homes" (Dubin, 1969:94–95). It is quite clear that it is neither true that *all* delinquents come from broken homes nor that *all* broken homes produce criminal children. Thus, the statement of a limited relationship between broken homes and delinquency is the more accurate one and is not a complete explanation of delinquency. Indeed, much more analysis will be necessary to determine the variables accounting for this greater-than-chance occurrence. Perhaps, in some behavioral science utopia of the future, it may be possible to develop theoretical models which will be total explanations and, thus, it may be possible to provide causal explanations. It seems more productive for the present, however, to live with the reality of our situation and to concentrate on more limited statements of relationships with circumscribed explanatory properties.

Dubin points out that even in cases where restricted explanatory theories have been developed, however, there has been a real weakness in our ability to predict outcomes. He calls this shortcoming the *power paradox* (Dubin, 1969:23):

> The power paradox may be summarized as follows: A theoretical model that focuses on the analysis of processes of interaction may contribute significantly to understanding. This understanding may be achieved by limiting the system being analyzed, by simplifying its variables and/or the laws of interaction among them, and by focusing on broad relationships among variables. Understanding of process, when achieved, does not *necessarily* provide the basis for accuracy of prediction about the reality being modeled by the theoretical system.

This inability to predict outcomes, however, is not as serious as the inability to explain process as identified in the precision paradox. If the goal of science, as I have maintained, is to provide explanations of phenomena, then for the time being it is preferable to develop reasonable and logical explanations from which predictions may be possible later, rather than to continue to develop predictive models which yield little or nothing in the way of explanation. Therefore, in the following chapters describing the developmental theory, I want to focus attention on the qualities of the model which allows us to explain what we observe, even though we will frequently be unable to predict outcomes on the basis of that model.

THE RELATIONSHIP OF THEORY AND RESEARCH

In the first section of this chapter, I stated that a theory was an attempt to explain a phenomenon. Moreover, I pointed out that a *scientific* theory is a special sort of theory. It is unique because it postulates a systematic relationship between the abstract explanation developed and the empirical phenomena observed. There exists an inextricable tie between the theory and the empirical research used to test it. Few scientists are satisfied simply to develop a model which they intuitively believe fits reality. To complete their work, they systematically gather data to which they apply their theory to determine whether it is valid or true. Several years ago in a lecture, Professor Roy G. Francis made a statement which has remained with me. He pointed out that in empirical science, the world *is*, that is, it is neither true nor false. The work of the scientist is *to make statements about that world which are true*, that is, which accurately reflect reality. The only way the scientist can determine the truth of his statements is to gather data to test them.

Once again, Dubin (1969:234–37) is very instructive by helping us to understand the significance of this essential scientific activity. He points out that the best theoretical models fall short of perfection. And, although a scientist may take as his reason for gathering data the proof of his theory, more is gained if he takes the alternative of *improving* his theory. That is, the scientist compares his data with his theoretical explanation and then attempts to restate the theory to coincide more closely with his data. Dubin asserts that all one can hope to learn by taking the proof stance is whether his theory is or is not an accurate statement of the facts—and it is likely not to be. However, if he takes the *improvement stance*, the scientist gains in two ways. First, he is able to marshal all the data which he has gathered in testing his theory. He is not forced to discard information that contradicts the theory, as in the "broken homes cause delinquency" statement above. Rather, he is able to use the data to reformulate his theory so that it becomes a more complete explanation of the empirical world. Second, Dubin points out that frequently the most interesting data do not "fit" the explanation; that is, the factors which *disprove* the theory, rather than those which prove it, provide new insights. To lose this important opportunity to explore data further works against the ultimate goal of explaining the phenomenon being studied.

This important point applies to the theoretical model I am presenting. The model is in no sense complete, which is one of the most intellectually exciting characteristics about it. There are many inadequacies in its formulation; indeed, the major purpose of this book is to provide a basis for thinking through some of them in order to point to possible improvements. As Dubin (1969:236–37) puts it,

> . . . if all the propositions of a model are worked out, the theorist has nothing more to learn from his model. The job of theory building is complete, and there remains only the task of either testing the theory to see if it accurately models reality or leaving this task for someone else. With an orientation to improve a model, the theorist-researcher may tinker with the model in order to determine whether, with minor changes, it will generate different propositions. One of the theorist's prime sources for ideas about tinkering with a model is the empirical world that is supposed to be described by the model. Thus, attention on improving a model makes the theorist constantly on the alert for those disconfirming ideas or data that constitute a signal for redoing the theory.

Merton (1957) also has discussed the close tie between theory and research. In two chapters which have become classics in sociology, he points out that theory may broaden the scope of generalizations derived from research findings, may provide for a cumulation of propositions derived from research, may reformulate empirical generalizations into theoretical statements, may furnish ground for prediction of empirical data, and may give logically coherent explanations of empirical findings. Research, on the other hand, initiates theory when unanticipated information is encountered, precipitates the recasting of theory to take into account new data, refocuses theoretical interest as new research methods are devised, and helps to clarify concepts in order to apply them to empirical phenomena. In summary, the complete scientific approach to explanation inevitably involves moving back and forth between two essential activities: forming a theory and the testing it through research.

In conformity with this posture, the text of each chapter will refer frequently to those aspects of the model which inadequately explain the phenomenon under analysis. Since research specifically oriented toward testing the developmental theory is relatively limited, there will be sustained emphasis on ways of examining the model and reference to research which appears to do so, even if such research was carried out primarily for some other purpose.

SUMMARY

The point of view of this book will be that theories are explanations of phenomena, rather than either descriptions or attempts at prediction. Since I am concerned with scientific theory, I shall be referring continually to the research applicability of the theory. An adequate scientific theory must conform in some degree to the empirical world to which it refers. The purpose of an interest in research will be to gain whatever is possible for the improvement of the theoretical model.

In this chapter, I have not attempted to mention all aspects of theory and theory building. Such a discussion comprises a book in itself, and there are several excellent ones readily available to anyone who wishes to focus on this matter. Some of them are listed in the references at the end of this chapter.[1] Rather, I have attempted to provide a rudimentary view of the goal of theory in social science and to indicate the stance that will be taken in this book. I hope that the discussion of theory itself has provided some idea of the issues involved in building a body of principles and has detailed its particular characteristics.

[1] It should be obvious that I have found the volume by Dubin (1969), which I cite frequently in this chapter, to be a most stimulating one. As a former colleague, I had the opportunity to discuss with Professor Dubin my concerns about the inability of the developmental theory to adequately predict findings in some of my own research. It was in these discussions prior to the publication of his book, that he mentioned to me the distinctions which he makes between ability to predict outcomes and ability to explain process. I owe him a considerable debt for his contributions to my thinking in this area.

REFERENCES

DUBIN, ROBERT
    1969   *Theory Building*. New York: The Free Press.
MERTON, ROBERT K.
    1957   *Social Theory and Social Structure*, rev. ed. Glencoe, Ill.: The
        Free Press, Chapters 2 and 3.
ZETTERBERG, HANS L.
    1963   *On Theory and Verification in Sociology*, rev. ed. Totawa, N.J.:
        The Bedminster Press.

An Introduction
to the Family
Development Schema

The purpose of this chapter is to provide a general overview of the theoretical framework of family development. Since there have been in sociology various ways to view the family, we will look briefly at them to determine what issues or problems each attempts to explain. No attempt will be made to deal in great detail with the alternative approaches, since the article by Hill and Hansen (1960) is the classic statement on the theories most frequently used in family sociology. A conceptual framework which has been devised to handle these phenomena will be presented. In the following chapter I will then examine in detail the family phenomena to which the developmental theory addresses itself. The remaining chapters will analyze in detail the research applications and the methodological problems which arise from it.

FAMILY THEORIES—AN OVERVIEW

The Institutional Approach

Reduced to the bare minimum, sociology has approached the family in two basic ways (Kirkpatrick, 1970; Kephart, 1971). Probably first, historically, are theories which analyze the family as an institution. They deal with the family as a cultural pattern or one of the major structures of the society and analyze the family in terms of its relationships with other major structures such as religion, education, government, and the economy. The primary concern of these theories is the way the family pattern is related to these other configurations and, thus, to the place which it takes in the overall structure of the society. There is frequently a heavy emphasis on the *functions* which the family carries out for the society and on the way the family avails itself of the functions performed by the other institutional structures of the society.

In such an approach, individuals in families and single family units receive little or no attention. It is frequently the case that the generalizations made are so broad that they fail to deal with alternative institutional patterns followed by subcultural groups in the society. In addition, little attention is paid to changes which may occur over short periods of time, in favor of the analysis of changes which occur in broader historical periods. Thus, there are analyses of The American Family which deal with the patterns which existed during Colonial times, during Westward expansion, during the late nineteenth and early twentieth centuries, and during post World War Two. Comparisons are made between how the family is related to the other institutions of the society in these various periods. Frequently there is little or no recognition of differences in family patterns which have existed in various regions of the country or in the numerous ethnic, religious, or other subcultures. Although it is certainly true that there probably has been a dominant American family pattern over the history of the United States to which all families conformed to some extent, it is also true that there have been some significant minority patterns which explain a number of phenomena in American family life (Anshen, 1949; Kephart, 1971).

Such an approach has both advantages and disadvantages. It provides a very clear way to trace the origins and development of certain phenomena over broad expanses of time and frequently can furnish explanations of the kinds of strengths and weaknesses which have existed in the family structure in various periods. This approach also offers interesting ways to explain alternative social structures when the family systems of two or more societies or two or more periods of history are compared. On the other hand, only partial explanations can be given to the phenomena of differing behavioral patterns in specific subgroups of the society at any given point in time, and little can be found to explain how families change during their own individual histories. In addition, little can be accomplished toward explaining behavior observed in specific families and between particular members of those families which does not follow the broad institutional patterns of the dominant society. Thus, because the institutional approach is so macroscopic, another viewpoint becomes necessary to deal with problems of explanation at a more minute level.

The Interactional Approach

The general term *interactional approach* can be applied to a number of theoretical systems which have developed to deal with a microscopic analysis of families. In these approaches, the general focus becomes the way individuals or sets of individuals relate to one another within the family, which becomes a system of dynamic interaction between actors (Waller and Hill, 1951:25). The matter of the cultural or subcultural setting is frequently taken for granted as known, it is specified, or it becomes an issue to be explored through derivation from the interactions observed. Relationships between members of the family or between members of the family and other groups in the society are treated by looking at the interactions which the actors carry on. Differing patterns of interaction in a family or in a set of families within the same culture or subculture are identified and are explained by the kinds of expectations for interaction set up in that family or in that set of families.

In the interactional approach, then, it is possible to gain a great deal more information about the family differences that exist within a large society possessing a similar institutional pattern. Individual actors or sets of actors come to the forefront, and patterns of interaction become the focus. This emphasis means that some of the broad sweep of time is lost. It becomes less possible to deal with changes which occur over more than a few brief and not too distantly separated time periods. At the same time, however, the processes of interaction are delineated much more clearly than in the institutional approach. A frequent method of dealing with the time dimension is to limit analyses to families composed of similar membership groupings, such as recently married couples, families with young children, or families in retirement. Sometimes the interactional patterns of two or more of these types will be compared, and processes of change will be inferred.

To summarize the two basic theoretical approaches most frequently used, the institutional approach satisfactorily handles broad patterns of family structures and major sweeps of time. The interactional approach deals very well with the internal dynamics of families and makes it possible to analyze the behavior of individuals and sets of individuals in the family and their conduct relating to other organizations within the society. The ability to handle the time dimension, however, is limited to short spans and to comparisons between them.

Contained in the discussion above are several key problems which arise whenever a particular theoretical framework is applied to family analysis. These may be put in three general categories: (1) the levels at which family behavior is analyzed; (2) whether the analysis deals with internal or with external family behavior; and (3) the degree to which the framework can handle the time dimension. The developmental framework has been addressed rather consciously to each of these problems. Since a number of different theorists have been involved in this work over several decades, each had his own particular concerns. In the discussion to follow, I am going to try to bring these scattered efforts together. I am not going to present them in the order of when they were developed. However, I am going to discuss them in a way I hope will make clear how developmental theory deals with issues. For this reason, I am going to start with time. Then I am going to present the set of concepts which have been produced over the years. Finally, I shall return to the matters concerning the levels of analysis and internal-external behavior.

FAMILIES HAVE HISTORIES

"The unique contribution of the family development approach to family theory has been its attempt to deal with the dimension of time in the analysis of the family as a small group association." (Rodgers, 1964:263) As I stated before, the institutional theories handle the time dimension in broad sweeps which do not capture adequately the changes occurring in families over their own life histories. The interactional theories, on the other hand, are able to treat time only in short spans, which is done mostly by comparing two or more sets of events and by implying the processual aspects from their changes. The developmental approach begins with the basic idea that families are long-lived groups with a history which must be taken into account if the dynamics of their behavior are to be explained adequately. Elements of the time perspective may be applied to a number of different aspects of family behavior. Let us look at two elements of the time perspective and their relationships to family behavior.

The first element of the time perspective is historical time. One of the major contributions of the institutional approach has been its ability to show how the family institution has changed over the history of humanity. There is no question, then, that the historical time in which a given set of families is situated has effects on its behavior. It is impossible to ignore the impact of the depression of the 1930s or World War Two on American family life (Angell, 1936; Cavan and Ranck, 1938; Komarovsky, 1940; Koos, 1946; Hill, 1949). Aside from these more dramatic societal historical periods with their particularly stressful influence on families, subtle changes occur in the institutional norms for family life. Since a family has a history which may span as much as half a century or more, the modifications of institutional norms are bound to provide some of the change which may be observed in a family. Consequently, we cannot explain all change by variables within the family group alone.

Another dimension of historical time is the fact that the normative expectations for family behavior are not the same for all periods of the family's history. This truth is not simply a function of chronological time but is more accurately a function of social process time (Moore, 1963:7). By *social process time* I mean the periods comprised in the life space of a group or individual with a given process. For example, when we say, "He is getting an education," we are not referring to a chronological period. Rather, we are talking about a processual period. The institutional norms defining the behavior of young marrieds differs from those for couples with infants, from those with teen-aged children, from those who no longer have children at home, and so on. This time element is directly related to the idea of *family life cycle stages*, which is so closely identified with the developmental approach. We shall have more to say about this idea later. It is important to emphasize, however, that the life-cycle stages comprise only one aspect of the attempt of the developmental theory to deal with the time dimension.

The idea of social process time, as distinct from chronological time, becomes even clearer when we are looking at a specific family. The structure of the group changes during its history; and, given the varying structure and the opportunity to develop a set of normative definitions of its own, the interactional patterns change during the life of the group. As members interact with one another over a variety of matters happening in the group, a whole set of learned and shared experiences develop which become precedents for further interactions. Although many of these experiences are unique, a great many are related to the normal and inevitable issues that arise in living together. Recently married couples must work out a set of relationships which are mutually satisfactory concerning many matters. Once established, however, the relationships do not remain constant but change subtly or perhaps dramatically because of later events, which may occur in the family or outside it. The happenings may be the birth of a child, a change in employment, the marriage of a child, or the divorce of close personal friends. These occurrences are not abnormal but are the stuff of which a family history is made. Many happenings are anticipated and prepared for, whereas many are unexpected—though not peculiar to that family alone. Thus, though each family's history is unique, it is also common. Furthermore, it has a certain quality of inevitability though not necessarily of predictability as to exact time or circumstance. The developmental approach does not seek to explain family dynamics in terms of its unique elements but in terms of the common quality of its experience over its history. There exist many more events that are common than are unique.

Individuals in families highlight still other factors related to historical time. The most obvious is the physical and psychological maturation process, seen most dramatically in children but no less important in adult members of families. It would be easy to divert our attention to those individual aspects of physical and psychological maturation. In developmental theory, however, these matters are significant for their impact on the social relationships which occur in the family group as a consequence of these particular changes. The newly found physical ability to walk—or at the other extreme, the loss of some physical ability—has important implications for the relationships which exist in a family. Furthermore, the family develops expectations with respect to its individual members according to their maturational level. "Big boys don't act that way" is a clear statement of a set of normative expectations attached to maturational level. The society, as well, has a great many *age-graded* norms, which are in actuality maturationally based. This truth is most easily seen in the fact that cultures which do not place the stress upon chronological age as our own culture does nevertheless have *rites of passage* which are associated with maturational levels.

The second and somewhat less obvious element of time perspective is associated with the behavioral history of individuals. Members of families develop characteristic ways of behaving which become precedents for later behavior. The "personality development" of a member of the family is strongly influenced by these precedents, and an individual is frequently locked into a particular mode of behavior by the family. In all probability, conventions have little to do with the original genetic makeup of the individual, though it would be naive to completely ignore this element. For the developmental approach, genetic elements in personality formation are taken primarily as limiting factors which place some sort of boundaries around the possible personality outcomes. The primary focus remains on the influence of the behavioral history of an individual member on the family dynamics over time.

In summary, then, the developmental theoretical framework approaches the explanation of family phenomena in a way which accounts for both chronological and social process time. The concepts which have been brought together as tools of analysis are designed for this purpose.

A CONCEPTUAL SCHEMA EMERGES

The developmental theoretical approach has a relatively short history. Though Rowntree (1903) used the idea of the life cycle of families just after the turn of the century, the systematic development of the framework spans less than four decades. It is not my purpose to provide a historical narrative here, since it has been done adequately in other works (Hill and Rodgers, 1964; Duvall, 1971).

A Definition of the Family

I have left undefined until now the basic term with which we are dealing, namely, *family*. Any textbook dealing with the subject will provide a definition, but it soon becomes clear that there exists considerable divergence between definitions. There is little point in listing a series of definitions, since they would not bring us any nearer to the goal of understanding. It is important, however, to determine why the divergence occurs. Then it becomes clear that the definitions which various writers develop are closely related to the kind of theoretical orientation they follow, that is, the kind of explanations they seek to make concerning the family. Writers making institutional analyses tend to emphasize the organizational characteristics of the family in their definitions, whereas writers with an interactional orientation emphasize dynamic behavioral characteristics. It is not the case that some definitions are right and that others are wrong. Rather, the theoretical orientation leads a writer to one sort of definition as opposed to another (Bell and Vogel, 1968:1–3; Kephart, 1971:2–11; Winch, 1971:3–29; Christensen, 1964:3–5; Zelditch, 1964:465–69).

Since the developmental approach attempts to explain the family in both its institutional and interactional context through the history of that family, the definition of the family used should reflect this perspective.

> The family is a semiclosed system of actors occupying interrelated positions defined by the society of which the family system is a part as unique to that system with respect to the role content of the positions and to ideas of kinship relatedness. The definitions of positional role content change over the history of the group.[1]

The first part of this definition, "a semiclosed system of actors occupying interrelated positions," deals with the interactional aspect of family dynamics. It can be traced directly back to the work of Ernest W. Burgess (1926) and of Reuben Hill (Waller and Hill, 1951:25–36), both strongly associated with the school of social psychologists known as *symbolic interactionists* (Stryker, 1964 and 1968). This portion of the definition also points to the place of individuals in the family in its reference to "actors." The second section of the definition, "defined by the society of which the

[1] This definition represents a modification of one I developed earlier (Rodgers, 1964: 264). I am indebted especially to Reuben Hill for his comments and his suggestions concerning this definition and for ideas he presented in a recently published paper (Hill, 1971).

family system is a part as unique to that system with respect to the role content of the positions and to ideas of kinship relatedness" stresses the institutional nature of the family system. It points to the family as one institutional structure in the society which has a peculiar place in that society and that the positions assigned to that institutional structure are not duplicated in their role content by any other positions in any other system. The final portion of the definition, "The definitions of positional role content change over the history of the group," emphasizes the changing character of the system through time.

It should be noted that this definition is essentially contentless; that is, it does not specify which particular combination of positions constitute a family, nor does it indicate which particular functions the actors must carry out in order for the system to be termed a family. These omissions free the definition from the difficulty frequently encountered with other definitions which do specify the content and which exclude patterns clearly constituting the family system in some societies. The definition, then, is sufficiently general to account for various structures but is specific enough that it considers the structure unique within the society where it is found.

Important Concepts

Given the definition above, we can turn to the concepts which provide the additional analytical tools for the theory. The ideas to be discussed are so interrelated that it is difficult to follow a logical order in their presentation. I shall begin with the least general concept and, as nearly as possible, shall progress to increasingly more general ones.

Norm. In any group, certain common expectations for behavior of actors develop. Bates (1956:314) has stated that a norm is "a patterned or commonly held behavior expectation. A learned response, held in common by members of a group." This definition places norms in a structural context as a basic building block for groups. This structure is abstracted from the observations of the interactions of groups. To some extent, therefore, such a distinction is one of analytical significance only; that is, it is impossible to separate in reality the interactions which take place in groups from the structure of that group.

Role. Roles are simply combinations of norms related to each other. As Bates (1956:314) has asserted, roles are "a part of a social position consisting of a more or less integrated or related sub-set of social norms which is distinguishable from other sets of norms forming the same position." The significant point about this definition of role, as opposed to some others which are frequently used in sociology, is that it makes role a structural concept. A role is a set of *expectations* for an actor in a group, not a set of *behaviors* of the actor. This analytical distinction is quite critical, since there is frequent confusion between these two very different phenomena. A third concept deals with the behavioral response to roles.

Role Behavior. Role behavior is the concept applied to what an actor in a group actually does in the group in response to role expectations. Gross et al. (1958:64) state the idea in the following way: role behavior is "an actual performance of an incumbent of a position which can be referred to an expectation for an incumbent of that position." Since it is quite obvious that members of groups do not always behave in the way they are expected to behave, it is important to be able to analyze both kinds of phenomena.

Sanction. There are limitations on the degree to which groups will allow individual occupants of roles to deviate from their expectations for behavior in those roles. Indeed, there are specific kinds of behaviors which are intended to encourage individuals to perform in the expected manner and which demonstrate disapproval if the individual strays too far from these expectations. "A sanction is a role behavior the primary significance of which is gratificational-deprivation" (Gross et al., 1958:65). This role behavior arises from norms which call for certain gratification or deprivation in response to the role behavior of some other actor in the group. Thus, there is an intricate system of expectations, behavior in response to these expectations, and further normative expectations bringing forth further role behavior in a continuous interactive process.

Position. When all the roles which belong together and which refer to one potential actor in a group are combined, a position has been formed. A position is a "location of an actor or class of actors in a system of social relationships" (Gross et al., 1958:48).

Group. Finally, as the preceding definition implies, a group is a system of interrelated positions.

Bates (1956:315–17) is very helpful by providing insight into how the concepts above are related to one another. He points out several significant characteristics possessed by this set of ideas:

1. In any given culture, there are a limited number of roles making up a limited number of positions.
2. Each position contains dominant and recessive roles.
3. A role is always paired with a reciprocal role of another position.
4. In a pair of related positions, there is always at least one pair of reciprocal roles composed of reciprocal norms requiring certain kinds of expected behavior.

If these observations are applied to the American family, it becomes clear that there are, indeed, a limited number of positions defined as appropriate. They include husband-father, wife-mother, son-brother, and daughter-sister.

Any other positions which may appear in a given family are extraordinary to some extent. It is always viewed as "out of the ordinary" for married couples to live with either set of parents. If an aging parent is located in a given family, this parent is viewed as an "extra" person in that family. Other persons who may be found in a particular household are similarly viewed as being outside the "normal" situation, and, frequently, people will go to great lengths to explain the presence of unexpected constituents. Furthermore, each of the normal positions of the family group contains its dominant roles. Husband-fathers are expected to be the wage earners, among other roles which they may possess. Wife-mothers are the home-makers. When a wife-mother is employed outside the home, as occurs often in American society, this role is not viewed as her primary responsibility. The recessive role of her position has been made manifest, but it remains defined differently than the wage-earner role of the husband-father. Finally, it is quite apparent that there is an intricate reciprocity in the roles of the various positions.

This set of concepts deals with the family as it can be observed both in its institutional and in its interactional context. The positions, roles, and norms are both societally based and group founded. The role behaviors and sanctions which occur also have both societal and group sources. Now let us examine the time dimension of these concepts.

Role Sequence. In examining a given role in a system, it will be seen that the normative content of that role changes through time. This effect may be due to the changing characteristics of the individual expected to occupy that role in the system, to the changing character of the system, or to changes which take place in the society. The disciplinary role of father, for example, does not have the same normative content in relation to an infant as it does with respect to a teen-ager. This fact is due both to the changing role of the child and to the modified characteristics of the father, for example, his own increasing maturity and the experience he gains as a father. Furthermore, the societal expectations for the role content of the father position may well vary during the time a particular individual occupies that role. Irwin Deutscher (1959:18) has identified this phenomenon when he states: "As an individual moves through the life cycle he is called upon to play a series of roles *sequentially*, in distinction to the may roles he may play concurrently at any one period of his life." Within any social position, then, the norms associated with a particular role change over time. When the norms are modified, for analytical purposes, we have a somewhat new role. Linking these changing roles together produces a *role sequence*.

Role Cluster. A position is the sum total of all the roles occupied by a given actor in a system. In order to distinguish between the general concept of position which exists in a group over time and the specific set or roles which make up a position at one particular point in time, Deutscher

(1959:24) uses the term role cluster. A role cluster is the set of concurrent roles which are the content of a position at any particular point in time in a given group. Over the life of a position in a group, this content will vary, with some roles being dropped and others being added while others merely change in normative content.

Role Complex. Since roles are reciprocal, the changing contents of a particular position has implications for the contents of the other positions in that group. The role clusters of two or more positions in a system at any given point in its history is a *role complex* of that system; that is, two or more sets of role clusters which are held concurrently by two or more actors or occupants of positions in an interlocking system at one point in time is a role complex (Rodgers, 1964:266).

Positional Career. The linking together of all the role clusters which occur in a given position sequentially during its life in the group is called the *positional career*. Farber (1961) has done some interesting analyses of the family in terms of the interrelatedness of positional careers, and I am indebted to him for the use of the term in this way.

Family Career. Finally, linking the role complexes, i.e., all the role clusters which exist at any one point in time concurrently, together sequentially over the life of the group constitute the *family career* (Rodgers, 1964:266). This final concept provides the most general statement of the dynamics of the family over time. Family career encompasses a very complex process since it ultimately refers to three different levels of family analysis as well as to both internal and external family behavior for the entire history of any family system. Let us examine these two remaining issues.

REFERENCES

ANGELL, R. C.
  1936 *The Family Encounters the Depression.* New York: Charles Scribner's Sons.
ANSHEN, RUTH
  1949 *The Family: Its Function and Destiny.* New York: Harper and Brothers.
BATES, FREDERICK L.
  1956 "Position, role and status: a reformulation of concepts." *Social Forces* 34 (May): 313–21.
BELL, NORMAN W. W., AND EZRA F. VOGEL, EDS.
  1968 *A Modern Introduction to the Family,* rev. ed. New York: The Free Press.

BURGESS, ERNEST W.
1926 "The family as a unity of interacting personalities." *The Family* 7 (March): 3–9.

CAVAN, RUTH S., and KATHARINE H. RANCK
1938 *The Family and the Depression.* Chicago: University of Chicago Press.

CHRISTENSEN, HAROLD T.
1964 "Development of the Family Field of Study." Pp.3–32 in Christensen (ed.), *Handbook of Marriage and the Family.* Chicago: Rand McNally & Company.

DEUTSCHER, IRWIN
1959 *Married Life in the Middle Years.* Kansas City, Mo.: Community Studies, Inc.

DUVALL, EVELYN M.
1971 *Family Development,* 4th edition. Philadelphia: J. B. Lippincott Company.

FARBER, BERNARD
1961 "The family as a set of mutually contingent careers." Pp. 276–97 in Nelson Foote (ed.), *Consumer Behavior: Models of Household Decision-Making.* New York: New York University Press.

GROSS, NEAL, ET AL.
1958 *Explorations in Role Analysis.* New York: John Wiley & Sons., Inc.

HILL, REUBEN
1949 *Families Under Stress.* New York: Harper and Brothers.

———, and DONALD A. HANSEN
1960 "The identification of conceptual frameworks utilized in family study." *Marriage and Family Living* 12 (November): 299–311.

———, and ROY H. RODGERS
1964 "The developmental approach." Pp. 171–211 in Harold Christensen (ed.), *Handbook of Marriage and the Family.* Chicago: Rand McNally & Company.

KEPHART, WILLIAM M.
1971 *The Family, Society, and the Individual,* 3rd edition. Boston: Houghton Mifflin Company.

KIRKPATRICK, CLIFFORD
1967 "Familial development, selective needs, and predictive theory." *Journal of Marriage and the Family* 29 (May): 229–36.

———
1970 *The Family: As Process and Institution,* 3rd edition. New York: The Ronald Press Company.

KOMAROVSKY, MIRRA
1940 *The Unemployed Man.* New York: Dryden Press.

KOOS, E. L.
1946 *Families in Trouble.* New York: King's Crown Press.

MOORE, WILBERT E.
1963 *Man, Time, and Society.* New York: John Wiley & Sons, Inc.
RODGERS, ROY H.
1962 *Improvements in the Construction and Analysis of Family Life Cycle Categories.* Kalamazoo, Mich.: School of Graduate Studies, Western Michigan University.

―――――
1964 "Toward a theory of family development." *Journal of Marriage and the Family* 26 (August): 262–70.
ROWNTREE, B. S.
1903 *Poverty: A Study of Town Life.* London: MacMillan.
STRYKER, SHELDON
1964 "The interactional and situational approaches." Pp. 127–63 in Harold Christensen (ed.), *Handbook of Marriage and the Family.* Chicago: Rand McNally & Company.

―――――
1968 "Identity salience and role performance: the relevance of symbolic interaction theory for family research." *Journal of Marriage and the Family* 30 (November): 558–64.
WALLER, WILLARD, and REUBEN HILL
1951 *The Family: A Dynamic Interpretation,* rev. ed. New York: Dryden Press.
WINCH, Robert F.
1971 *The Modern Family,* 3rd ed. New York: Holt, Rinehart & Winston, Inc.
ZELDITCH, MORRIS
1964 "Cross-cultural analyses of family structure." Pp. 462–500 in Harold Christensen (ed.), *Handbook of Marriage and the Family.* Chicago: Rand McNally & Company.

3

Three Facets
of Family Dynamics

The behavior of families is a very complex whole. Any analysis of it necessarily takes a particular perspective and, in the process, ignores other possible ones. If someone were inspecting a cut diamond with its many facets, each turn of the diamond would reflect a different character, though the stone would always be the same one. Undoubtedly, there exist many facets to family dynamics. The developmental approach focuses its particular attention on three of them.

Much family behavior has its origin in the society's expectations concerning what family ought to be. There always exists a certain set of institutional norms which govern family behavior. And, so, throughout a family's career there is a *societal-institutional* facet to its conduct. What is equally true is that many activities occurring in families arise out of expectations which develop within the groups themselves concerning the appropriate rules for interaction within them. This evolved aspect can be called the *group-interactional facet.* Finally, every group is made up of individuals with their own physical-psychological makeup. The unique qualities of individuals also determine to some extent the kinds of interaction which take place in families. This last level may be labeled the *individual-psychological facet.*

In recalling the two basic theoretical approaches discussed earlier, it becomes clear that the institutional perspective deals primarily with the societal-institutional facet of family analysis. The interactional approach handles most adequately the group-interactional facet and, somewhat less adequately, the individual-psychological one. One of the problems to which the developmental approach addresses itself is a more adequate way of dealing with analysis of families in all three facets. Each level has something significant to tell us about how families behave. The more information we include in our theoretical approach about each of these aspects, the greater explanatory power of the theory. The developmental approach has attempted to incorporate into its theoretical framework concepts which will deal adequately with each of the facets and also concepts which will tie the three facets more closely into an integrated whole. Let us take a closer look at each of the facets.

THE SOCIETAL-INSTITUTIONAL FACET

Every society develops a fairly systematic and conscious set of expectations concerning what it considers right and what it deems wrong about the way families should be formed and function (Sirjamaki, 1948:464–70). In American society there are expectations that individuals should possess a certain maturity before they enter into a marriage, that sexual relationships should occur within wedlock, that husbands should be the primary providers, that husbands should be the "heads of the household," and many others. Although these expectations generally are recognized in the society, it also is quite clear that there are ranges of conformity to them which vary in different cultural groups of the society or in certain regions of the country. For example, it is much more likely that a girl will marry younger if she lives in the Southeastern part of our country, if she lives in a rural area, if she is Negro, or if she is from a low-income family. Although husbands are the primary providers, middle-class wives with high educational attainment frequently are employed at occupations which rival or exceed the income of their spouses (Varga, 1965:100–103). Similarly, low socioeconomic status families often find it necessary to have both husbands and wives employed in order to have sufficient income to survive. Nevertheless, as one observes family life throughout the American culture, one finds a clear common thread of behavior running through it that is based on societal-institutional expectations about which all members of the society know and to which they conform to a considerable degree.

The developmental theoretical approach deals with the societal-institutional facet from two perspectives. One view treats the family as a major social system in the society. This approach stresses how the family system is interrelated with the other structures of the society as a functioning whole. The other standpoint deals with the structuring of the family institution in terms of a broad range of cultural values and goals. In a very real sense, the primary emphasis of the social system aspect is on the role of the family within the larger society, whereas the institutional perspective emphasizes the influence of the larger society on the family structure. These distinctions are primarily analytical ones which help us to clarify the complex interrelationships which exist. In the day to day functioning of the society, they are not so clearly distinguished.

Functions of the Family System for the Society

Social system theorists usually have talked about the functions of a system for the society or, alternatively, about the development of structures to carry out certain duties the society considers necessary. Several sets of these "necessary" functions have been developed by various writers (Reiss, 1965; Bell and Vogel, 1968:7-34). One such set, which seems to capture the functions most adequately, was presented several years ago by Bennett and Tumin (1948:49). They include: (1) maintenance of biological functioning of group members; (2) reproduction or recruitment of new group members; (3) socialization of new members; (4) production and distribution of goods and services; (5) maintenance of order; and (6) maintenance of meaning and motivation for group activity. Although there has been a great deal of controversy in sociology over the issue of *functionalism* (Aberle et al., 1950; Davis, 1959), it remains clear that every society does make some provision in its structure for each of these services to be carried out. As a convenient way of classifying group activity, it does seem useful to examine the family relationship in light of these functional prerequisites.

Robert Bierstedt (1963:341) has defined an institution as an organized procedure for carrying out some societal task; that is, an institution is the set of rules which defines the way in which something ought to be accomplished. If we tie this idea of an institution to the functional prerequisites of Bennett and Tumin, we can see that there are major institutional structures, that is, organized procedures in the society, which are designed to meet each of these necessary tasks. Or, putting the point another way, every group either has such a procedure as a part of its own system of roles or has available to it some other group or system to carry out these tasks. The family may be seen as an institution of the society which carries out some of these obligations. Exactly which functions are handled by the family depends on the structure of a given society. For American society, reproduction and a great share of the socialization function are the responsibilities of the family structure. In an earlier period of American history, when the society was largely agricultural, it is probably true that the family had a larger responsibility for several other functions than now. Other structures have taken these over to a large degree, however, as the society has grown larger, has become more industrialized and more urbanized, and as the family has changed from an extended to a nuclear form. Indeed, Reiss (1965:448–49) argues that universally the family has only the common function of "nurturant socialization" assigned to it. The essential point is that part of the family system's position and role structure will carry out whatever functions are its responsibility in the society and, at the same time, will provide those functions for its own family members.

Reproductive Roles. In most societies, reproduction is a family function with some very cleary defined roles specifying how it is to be carried out. There is, first of all, the limitation on entry into the function which is usually handled by a minimal age specification before which reproduction is viewed as inappropriate. There may be puberty rites or defloration rituals which indicate that a person is eligible for the reproductive role. There may be certain designated ages when the individual is viewed as eligible for marriage and when he is considered not eligible. These ages may be very formally specified in laws or may be informally formulated.

The second kind of normative structure encourages individuals who have reached eligibility for reproduction to begin to have offspring. In American society, young married couples who delay childbearing find increasingly that their associates and kin begin to raise questions concerning the imminence of their "starting a family." As a matter of fact, the term typically applied to a married pair without children is more likely to be *couple* than it is to be *family.* Having children, not simply being married, becomes the significant criterion for qualifying as a family. Couples who find that they are biologically incapable of having children also feel pressures placed upon them to adopt children to attain family status. There is a quality of evaluation toward childless couples which implies that they have not totally fulfilled themselves until they have reproduced. In other societies, similar behaviors are noted—even to the extreme of legitimizing divorce on the grounds of the failure to bear children or of the failure to bear children of a given sex.

Patterns appear in many societies which put pressure on single persons to get married. These configurations may consist of elements such as frequent questioning of single individuals about their plans for marriage, thinly veiled matchmaking, terms concerning marriage-eligibles which have negative connotations, or economic aspects which encourage families to marry off their children or to stimulate individuals to marry. All these are expressions of norms designed to influence people occupying positions in which reproductive behavior is defined as desirable to demonstrate the appropriate role behavior.

The third aspect has to do with the exit from the reproductive role. There are often negative norms which discourage individuals who have reached a certain point in their career from having any more children. Especially in societies which emphasize the nuclear family pattern, older couples—especially older men—may be discouraged from reproducing, since they may not live long enough to care for the children to maturity. The nuclear family system has little provision for the care of orphaned children and, therefore, they place a special burden on the system.

From a developmental point of view, then, the reproductive role contains clear time elements. There are periods when reproduction is appropriate and is encouraged, and there are periods when it is inappropriate and is discouraged. These periods usually are tied to the role sequences of positions in the family system in a way that designates when reproduction is fitting in the sequences and how it should occur. These indications by the society may be communicated formally and informally.

Maintenance of Biological Functioning. The human infant has one of the longest periods of dependency on others for its nourishment and shelter needs. Societies do not always assign this function to the family system as the case of the Israeli Kibbutz system demonstrates (Spiro, 1956 and 1958). But it is also clear that a great many societies have placed this responsibility within the family system. Reciprocal role complexes are incorporated into the role structure of the family careers requiring certain actors to provide for the protection and the sustenance of the young and for persons at all age levels above childhood.

The assignment of the biological maintenance function is highly variable. The familiar Western pattern of the wife-mother having primary responsibility for the domestic activities of food preparation and for personal care, while the husband-father is accountable for physical protection and for obtaining the food and other goods to be utilized in physical maintenance, is only one type of approach to this task. Some societies turn these matters over to actors other than the mother or father of the child. Older children may be assigned the responsibility of child care so that the mother and father are released to carry out some other role, such as working in the fields to produce food or other desired products. An older female, a grandmother or aunt, may have this role as a part of her position in some extended family systems. Still another common pattern is to wean the child early from the mother's breast or to transfer the nursing of the infant to another individual, not necessarily a family member, which allows the mother to meet other role expectations. Indeed, the nursery school of American society, often involving children as young as two years, has this last function.

There are a number of legal aspects to the maintenance function which appear in American society. Child support laws require fathers to provide for their minor children in cases of divorce, separation, and out-of-wedlock reproduction, even though the mother may have remarried. There are also laws dealing with child neglect by which parents may be criminally prosecuted for failing to provide adequate maintenance for their offspring.

In American society, however, there is considerable ambivalence and ambiguity found in the role definitions of the wife-mother concerning her responsibility for the care of the young. Although it is generally viewed as highly desirable that a mother care for her own young, and mothers who society thinks neglect their children in favor of other roles are frequently negatively evaluated, the industrialization of the society has developed alternative roles for women which compete with this traditional family role. The data on the behavior of American women indicates that there are periods in the role sequence of mother when it is less obligatory for her to play the child-care role. Mothers of infants and preschool children are less likely to be found among the ranks of the gainfully employed, implying some sort of role prescription which keeps them in the home, but an increasing number of mothers go to work as the ages of the children increase (Nye and Hoffman, 1963:3–16). There is, however, evidence that employed mothers frequently experience guilt feelings about their jobs and the possible negative effects their so-called neglect of the children may have (Nye and Hoffman, 1963:25, 96, 148, 317). The norms for American women appear to have strong moral implications in favor of the child-care role for mother, though the society finds great use for these women in outside employment.

The evidence shows a clear developmental quality to the maintenance function norms which ties the maintenance role to certain periods of the role sequences of actors in the system. Although we have focused on the child care period, similar data exists with respect to the care of individuals throughout the family career.

Socialization of New Members. Data similar to that just discussed appears for the socialization function. Societies differ in the amount of socialization assigned to the family system, the roles it is allotted, and the various segments of the role sequences in which the function is concentrated. However, Reiss (1965) argues that this is probably the single function found universally attached to the family system. He does not analyze to any great degree the developmental character of this function, though it is implied in much of his discussion.

The characteristics of the socialization function are reflected in both the objects of socialization and in the roles of the socializers. Some societies, expecting that children will receive a great share of their total socialization experience within the family system, assign the roles of socializer to the positions of the mother, the father, and/or the older siblings. Other societies assign this function to the family only in certain portions of the role sequence of the child, turning over major portions of the socialization experience to other systems of the society. The Kibbutz, for example, places a heavy burden upon child-care units with professionally trained individuals who specialize in socializing all of the children from infancy to adulthood.

The parental socialization role becomes one narrowly confined to a kind of emotional nurturance role, similar to the grandparent role in American society. Parents do not have responsibility for the discipline of the children in the American sense but spend time with children in recreation and holidays, when the quality of the relationship is considerably more expressive than it is instrumental (Spiro, 1956, 1958).

In contrast, American society concentrates the socialization function in the roles of parents in the early years of the role sequence of the child but divides the responsibility between the family and the school system in later childhood until, finally, the school becomes the primary socialization experience in late adolescence and young adulthood.

Another side of the socialization function is seen in societies which have given a considerable amount of the duty to the elders of the society, often segregating the sexes, with the elder of the same sex as the children teaching them their appropriate roles. In such a system, an adult male or groups of males, not necessarily the parents of the boys, will teach appropriate masculine skills to the entire group of boys who are of the suitable developmental level. Meanwhile, the adult women will be providing appropriate experience for the girls of the society.

Frequently, the society sets up finely divided age-graded experiences, with special rites of passage accompanying the movement from one category of socialization experience to the next. Our own society, though it places some emphasis on the movement from school grade to school grade (especially on the transition from grade school to junior high school, from junior high to senior high school, and graduation from senior high school) generally focuses less on this kind of ceremonial occasion than other societies. There is considerable blurring of the movement through the role sequences and their attendant socialization experiences. Even such fairly significant events as reaching the age of twenty-one, with its supposed symbolism as the attainment of adulthood, do not change sharply the role relationships which the individual experiences. The role sequences in American society are considerably more continuous in nature than the disjunctive character of role sequences in some other societies. Nevertheless, by the time the child reaches the later portion of his role sequence in the family career, his socialization experiences with respect to the family are rather minimal, and the parents are not expected to treat their offspring as "children" at this point in life.

All the examples above have more of an informal quality to them, though some have strong moral aspects which place them in the general area of the mores of the society. Examples of legal definitions of socialization functions are not as frequent in this area as is some others. In American society, aside from laws which deal primarily with the maintenance function, most statutes tend to limit the socializing responsibility of the family by placing obligations on the parents to turn their children over to the school system. A number of court decisions and interpretations of law have ruled that even parents who are formally trained and certified as school teachers may not attempt to educate their own children but must send them to the public schools or to approved private schools for this experience.

The major developmental aspect of the socialization function appears in the way the socialization experience is tied closely to the maturational level of the child. Indeed, the role of socializer is almost always defined by the role sequence of the recipient of socialization. Thus, the age and developmental status of the socializer may vary from a relatively young person with only minimal adult status for himself to that of a quite aged senior person with many adult responsibilities. Yet, their socialization roles in the same society with respect to a child of the same developmental status will be quite similar. This example is a particularly good one of how the role obligations of a given actor are defined by the reciprocal role and contain little discretionary behavior.

Production and Distribution of Goods and Services. Industrialized societies usually place little responsibility on the nuclear family for this function. Even the agricultural activities of such societies are highly developed technologically so that the farm family unit is less important than having a few trained workers to operate the complex equipment utilized in agricultural production. Furthermore, only a minority of the population of an industrialized society is involved in farming. Most productive activity is located in highly complex industrial organizations which deal with the individual as a working unit, rather than being situated in a family which constitutes the unit of production. In such a societal setting, the family contributes individual workers to the productive system, but the family unit is a consuming, not a productive one.

The productive role in the American family is focused on the adult male husband-father position as provider, which is closely associated with the maintenance function. Likewise, the adult female's productive roles are devoted to preparation of food, to provision for personal needs, and occasionally to production of items of wearing apparel, which are also more identified with the maintenance function than with the productive responsibility. For the male children of the family, the productive role appears primarily in anticipatory socialization. It consists of pointing them toward adulthood, when they will be expected to take on a provider role in their future position as husband-father, rather than with respect to any current role that they might be expected to play. Female children may experience very little normative pressure either of an anticipatory socialization kind or with respect to any current productive expectations. It is probable, though, that American girls begin to experience quite early some of the ambiguity which was noted above over the conflict between domestic and productive roles in their future positions as adult women in the society.

Societies which do assign productive roles to the family members may do so in a variety of ways. Some societies place no productive expectations on occupants of the young-child positions but suddenly may inject normative anticipations into the position at a given developmental level. Others attach expectations very early with increasing responsibility as the child matures. Similarly, the wife-mother position may have productive roles associated with it. These may vary depending upon whether she also is expected to bear and to care for young children or whether she is released quickly from the child-care role in order to meet productive role expectations. Though not universally true, the adult male position in a great share of all societies appears to have the most clearly defined expectation for productive activity and for the direction of the other members of the family in carrying out their productive rules.

Another aspect of the production-and-distribution function relates to how productive roles are assigned *within* the family group. Family division of labor has been researched heavily in the United States. There exists a very strong age-sex element exhibited in the data which shows that certain kinds of tasks are clearly "man's work" or "woman's work." Although the equalitarian model tends to be highly valued in American society and, indeed, there is considerable evidence of some sharing of certain tasks, the sex designation of a great part of the family activity remains. A similar pattern is exhibited in the tasks assigned to the child positions. Male children tend to be expected to participate in the so-called masculine kinds of activity —lawn mowing, trash handling, and the like—whereas female children are assigned the domestic duties involved in food preparation, washing, ironing, and cleaning the house (Blood and Wolfe, 1960:47–74). Non-American cultures also tend to have strong age-sex definitions of family division of labor.

Maintenance of Order. Two types of order maintenance are of concern to the developmental approach. There is internal regularity, which focuses on the way authority and decision-making roles are defined within the family. Some characteristics of order maintenance are seen in patterns of patriarchal, matriarchal, equalitarian, and democratic authority structures. For the American society, although the dominant value orientation appears to be a democratic or equalitarian one, there is considerable evidence to indicate that the entire range of patterns is present in family behavior (Blood and Wolfe, 1960:11–46). The strong tradition of patriarchy, probably rooted in Puritan patterns of the Colonial era and in the period of Westward expansion, remains a very real force in modern American families. Even very middle-class households, when pressed to indicate who should make the final decision on a given issue, tend to respond that the husband is the ultimate authority. Both upper- and and lower-class families tend to select patriarchal authority as the standard value orientation more frequently than their middle-class counterparts. Developmental researchers try to emphasize how increasing amounts of authority for decision making may be incorporated into the role sequences of the child positions and how the relative weight of authority in family positions would shift over the family career.

Both European and Asian cultures still represent the patriarchal tradition. Japanese family life exhibits a pattern of giving more authority in the family to males, even down to the youngest male child, before any amount of power is given to female members of the family (Queen and Adams, 1952, Chapter 5; Vogel, 1963). This culture is particularly interesting developmentally because it provides an excellent opportunity to analyze a modern industrial society which still holds to many extended family patterns in the midst of a major and rapid urbanization and industrialization transition.

The major sources of authority and decision-making patterns are found in the more informal folkways and mores of most societies. There are some formal legal aspects, such as laws which give American parents major control over the behavior of their children until they reach the age of majority. Children apparently hold some rights as indirectly indicated in the laws of inheritance. These laws often provide for the division of an estate in proportions which may leave the widow with as little as one-third to one-half of the family property where no will has been executed, even though the children may still be below the age of majority. In contrast, traditional Japanese law provides for all kinds of power for the patriarch and upon his death, for the passing of this power to the oldest son. Thus, distinctions between the amount of authority granted to male children versus female children and the division of authority between the husband-father position and the wife-mother position over the career of the family may be found in a variety of societal normative structures.

Another area of interest is what the society expects of the family for maintaining external order. It is clear that the more urbanized societies assign less responsibility to the family, placing the function in the hands of the government. Punishment of family members for violations of societal laws falls less to the family than to the courts in most of these systems. On the other hand, less urbanized societies (present and past) expect considerably more of the family in order maintenance. A classic example is the ancient Judaic society, in which the family system was the primary source of order in the society with the patriarch holding almost absolute power, even to the point of death, over family members. Traditional Japanese and Chinese societies exhibited a similar pattern of strong control by the family, as did our own early American culture. In each of these, there were clearly defined roles associated with authority which were as-signed to familial positions and which changed as the occupant moved through his positional career in the family system. This power continued to be exercised over members long after they had reached adulthood, since they were still members of the extended family where power was located. The power was expressed in both formal legal and informal moral codes of conduct.

Maintenance of Meaning and Motivation. This function has to do with the issues often treated under the heading Religion or Philosophy in Societal Life. The degree that the society assigns the task of providing the basic meaning in life to the family system is the basic focus of this section. In one sense, we may view the matter under consideration as discerning societies which are to a greater or lesser degree "familistic" in their orienta-tion; that is, some societies or subcultures place great emphasis upon the family system as the primary source of meaning in life. Once again, the ancient Judaic, Japanese traditional and Chinese traditional societies are excellent examples. In these societies, a great share of all the role definitions for individuals have their source in their particular position in the family system; to be cut off from the family system is to be cut off from a place in the society in general. This means, that developmentally, throughout the life of the individual, a basic reference point for the various role sequences in his career is his family position. The legal systems of Judaic, Japanese, and Chinese societies all carry heavy family aspects in them.

In contrast, our own American society tends to see the family more as a center from which the *individual* operates. As Sirjamaki (1948:470) pointed out, "Individual, not familial, values are to be sought in family living." This orientation takes place during the socialization process, when basic values are taught to the child. These values do not tend to be familistic in their focus, but individualistic. The child is taught to find meaning for himself as an independent actor, not necessarily in the context of the family system. The American legal system reflects this encouragement by how it treats the individual as an independent actor. Family law demon-strates this orientation both in treating marriage as a contract between two individuals and divorce as based on offenses of one individual party toward the other. In addition, a well developed religious institutional structure exists where a great deal of responsibility is placed by the society for inter-preting the basic meaning of life. In American society, the legal separation of church and state has the effect of reserving to the church certain matters concerning individual meaning in life.

The consequence of these facts for the developmental approach is that nonfamilistic societies have few clearly defined family role sequences related to meaning and to motivation. In familistic societies, a great many role sequences as defined by the society are directly concerned with this function.

Summary. The functional prerequisites just discussed show that the family affects the society in a number of ways, even in modern industrialized settings. Developmental theorists have been attempting to identify the way positional and familial careers are structured with respect to various functions. This work is not fully developed by any means. What I have tried to describe in this section are some of the possibilities which exist when the societal-institutional facet of the family is approached from the developmental vantage point. There remains the analysis of how the society affects the family during its career.

The Impact of the Society on the Family System

A major impact of the society on the family system has already been treated in the discussion of the societal definitions of roles designed to carry out societal functions. No further elaboration of that aspect is necessary. In addition, there are the major relationships which exist between other systems of the society and the family. Although there are many such relationships which could be cited, the discussion to follow will be restricted to some of those intersystem relationships which influence the family over its entire career. This area is not one which has had a great deal of attention from developmental analysts. Therefore, as above, the discussion is intended to provide some indication of the possibilities which exist more than of the accomplishments attained.

Government and Family. One way that the governmental institution has a strong influence on the family system is through its legal authority. In societies with highly developed formal legal systems, there are many aspects of those systems which bear directly upon family structure and functioning. Matters dealing with meeting the qualifications for marriage, property rights, care of children, inheritance laws, divorce, and a host of others all influence the family at various points in its career (Rheinstein, 1965; Goldstein and Katz, 1965; Mencher, 1967).

Another way the government affects the family system is through the various facilities which are developed and may take the form of direct or indirect services to family units. For example, the entire social welfare effort of many societies is directly intended to provide for family stability. In the early and middle years of the family career, this aim may take the form of financial aid for the welfare of children or the provision of food, clothing, and medical care through governmental financing. In the later years of the family career, programs for the aged such as social security and medical care for the aged are provided. Throughout the family's career, programs to provide housing or financing for housing may be made available. Other types of governmental service deal with the production and consumption activities of the family. In the United States, the Departments of Agriculture and of Commerce are particularly concerned with these activities.

More indirect in their effect, though no less real, are the many services associated with the provision of streets, sewers, street lights, parks, police protection, fire protection, postal service, and so on. To cite one illustration, the massive system of state and interstate highways has made possible the distribution of goods and services in a more efficient and less expensive manner than before. These same roadways have allowed families to move about more easily, which accounts in part for their increased spatial mobility, while at the same time the transportation system makes possible contact between various units of the extended family even though they are widely separated.

Of course, a major governmental impact on families is its taxing power. The U.S. federal income tax system uses the family as a major taxing unit, and the family has differing tax statuses at various points in its career. The provision for dependency exemptions and for deductions for items essential to family life, such as excessive medical expenses and interest payments on mortgages and consumer purchases, is a recognition of the impact of the taxing power on the family. Similarly, provisions for special tax considerations for the aged and disabled are also recognitions of the pervasive effect of this governmental authority.

Finally, there is the military function of the governmental system, which has a great effect on the family system. Families with children approaching the age of military eligibility are acutely conscious of this governmental relationship. During times of national emergency, the husband-father may be called to military service, providing a severe impact on the family system. Once again the military system recognizes its important relationship to the family structure through its provision for dependency allotments, medical care for dependents, certain kinds of exemptions from military service related to the dependency status of the eligible individual or exempting the "sole surviving son" from military service.

The developmental approach recognizes the intricate relationship which the family has with the government in numerous phases of its career and attempts to take these into account where they appear significant.

Education and Family. I have already mentioned that many societies turn over a great share of the socialization function to agencies other than the family. Educational systems of various cultures are structured in many ways; but regardless of their unique characteristics, they are a major factor in the life of the families of the society. One of the more obvious facts concerning the educational system is that it removes members from the family setting for major periods of time and exposes the members to new ideas and to fresh ways of behaving which they may not have known before. The outcome is that these members may adopt ways of thinking and acting which may vary with those considered appropriate within their family. Although parents may value highly the educational experience, there most likely exists some ambivalence in their response to the effect that it has on their offspring. In a society like the United States, with its high value on education as the route to success, the educational system may produce some fascinating conflicts in the family's role relationships. The educational system is a major factor to deal with through a large portion of the family career as it envelopes much of the life space of the children and, reciprocally, as it involves the parents to a high degree.

The economic factors associated with education also have considerable importance. Even in societies with "free" public education, there exist some major economic burdens related to taking advantage of the educational opportunities provided. This fact becomes particularly true where college education is involved. Many families invest a large proportion of their economic resources in providing the formal education of their children, which cannot help but to have profound effects on other areas of their life together.

A third consequence of the educational system is the mobility in the social structure which it may provide. Children may enter new socioeconomic classes as a result of their experience in school. Their relationships with the parental family may be affected so that they find it more difficult than before to relate to their parents in the roles they had played as young persons or in the roles which their parents believe to be appropriate. College students are frequently heard to remark that they can no longer find a common ground with their parents because of their educational experience. As this process is extended into the kind of life style to which they and their parents may have aspired, the ability to relate to their mothers and fathers from their new positions becomes increasingly difficult.

The developmental consequences of the educational system are long term, carrying far beyond the schooling years in the effects that they have on the later positional careers of family members.

Economy and Family. In societies with a highly developed economic system, the family is involved with this structure in two distinct ways. As already noted, the family becomes the unit which supplies occupants for all manner of positions in the economic system. The occupational roles have a heavy influence on the way in which they are able to carry out their familial roles. From the period that children begin to enter this system as part-time workers through the span when they as adults play a full-time worker role, they are constantly having to balance off the demands of the work setting with those of the family. In a family with which I am familiar, a sixteen-year-old son took a summer job in a grocery super market. Almost immediately, a number of family activities were affected. Mealtimes were adjusted to fit with the work schedule of the son, even to the extent of modifying the work schedule of the father so that common meals might be taken occasionally. The family found itself taking weekend trips and other excursions without the son, whereas these had always been family group experiences before. Adjustments were made in the division of labor in the home, with the assigning of tasks formerly carried out by the oldest son to the other two children in the group. The new-found economic "independence" of the oldest son provided him the opportunity to be more active in extrafamily events which further separated him from the family. The relatively recent affluence of the oldest sibling also provided some pressure on the parents from the other two children as they recognized his ability to make expenditures beyond their ability. In these and a number of other ways, the oldest son's participation in the economy directly affected the family's role structure. Another effect was a kind of anticipatory socialization experience for all of the members of the family. They began to recognize the ultimate fact that he someday would be totally outside the household structure. More than once, the remark was made, "Well, I guess we'd better get used to the idea that he won't always be with us." The long-term consequences of participation in the economy were recognized, even though the complete break with the family would not occur for a number of years.

Another major impact of the economy, shown by the example above, is the place of the family as a major unit for the consumption of the goods and services produced. One need only analyze the advertising media to recognize the importance of the family unit in the functioning of the economy. Although much advertising is directed to individuals, a great share of it emphasizes the family unit as its target. Family themes are appealed to in sales techniques, and family values are frequently utilized as a means for making a given product appear attractive. A widely advertized cold salve carried out a campaign which emphasized the parent-child unity which could be achieved through the use of the preparation as opposed to the so-called impersonal quality of decongestant pills. Children were pictured as receiving the loving attention of their mothers as the salve was rubbed on their chests at bedtime. Similar approaches have been used to sell all kinds of products. Thus, the family becomes a major target of the business world, and marketing techniques are developed to appeal to families at various points in their careers. There exists a very real reciprocal relationship between these two societal systems, since it is true that the family finds its needs for certain kinds of products vary at differing points in its career (Clark, 1955; Foote, 1961; Hill, 1965).

Religion and Family. The long history of the Judaic-Christian traditions reflects a continuing close relationship with the family system. In early

Judaism, of course, the family and religion were essentially coterminous with the patriarch of the family, who also had the role of religious elder. With the institutionalization of Judaism as a separate system complete with its own independent priests and other officials and later, with the coming of the rabbi, the emphasis on the family character of the religion was not lost. Thus, in modern Judaism the most important religious observances, such as Passover, are still family observances. Furthermore, depending to some extent on the particular branch of modern Judaism, the day-to-day life of the family is strongly affected by its religious tradition.

Similarly, though Christianity emphasized the faith of the individual believer to a much greater extent than Judaism, the Christian church has maintained a strong tie with the family unit. The New Testament frequently uses family themes and, indeed, the apostle Paul likens the relationship between husband and wife to the affinity between Jesus Christ and the church. American Christian churches have been family-unit oriented from the earliest days; and, significantly, one of the major problems of the contemporary Christian church has been dealing with the changing family structure. Urbanization and the individualization which has resulted has made it increasingly difficult for the church to meet the needs of the family as a unit. Older traditions, such as daily family devotions, have almost vanished in all but the most conservative families. With this disappearance has gone the participation of the family as a whole in many of the church activities. One major denomination has abandoned an approach to religious education which emphasized the joining of the parents in home study with their children because it became clear that the great share of families were not utilizing the materials made available for use in the home. This experience and others has caused the denomination to initiate an intensive study of its relationship to its member families along a number of dimensions of church programs including worship forms, educational activities, and various smaller group programs.

Catholicism, of course, has a long history of influence on the family. In terms of the basic issues of reproductive behavior, the validity of marriage, the naming of children, the grounds for divorce, and many other considerations, the Catholic Church has clear ecclesiastical legal positions. Indeed, the Sacraments of the Catholic Church are in a very real sense a series of rites of passage in the life cycle of the individual. Although they are not related directly to the family for the most part, they nevertheless have great significance in the life careers of family members and in the career of the family itself.

Religions outside the Judaic-Christian tradition vary in the extent of their involvement in the family. Some, such as Confucianism in classical China or Shintoism in Japan, are strongly family oriented and have a great impact on the family career. It is interesting that, in both China and

Japan, Buddhism is also quite strong. This extremely philosophical and individualistic religion often is practiced at the same time as the worship of ancestors. Taoism in China is also considerably more philosophical and individualistic in focus than Judaism or than Christianity. Hinduism has some strong family influences due especially to its caste structure. Finally, Islam has very strong familistic principles. In fact, a great deal of Muslim law deals with family matters.

There exist, of course, a great many sects and cults both within and outside Judaic-Christian traditions some of which have strong family influences and others which have little or no family implications. Thus, for example, the Old-Order Amish are strongly familistic, as is the Church of Jesus Christ of Latter-Day Saints (the Mormon Church). On the other hand, there appears to be very little familistic quality to Christian Science (Church of Christ, Scientist). The Oneida Community, which was founded about 1840 by John Humphrey Noyes, was in one sense a reaction to traditional Calvinistic and other ascetic Protestant religious philosophies. The Oneida Community developed its own philosophy of Perfectionism, a central point involving communal living which included an extensive group-marriage system. Ultimately the sect failed around 1880, though it survives in the name of a famous brand of silverware. Another such cult, the Shakers, also had difficulty because of a rather basic family attitude that it held—a strong prohibition against sexual intercourse. Lacking any biological means of reproduction, the Shakers ultimately were unable to recruit enough members from the outside society to flourish. Recent attempts at revitalization are not meeting with great success.

In summary, we can see that there are wide variations in the degree of relationship between religious systems and the family. Some of these structures have extremely strong effects on the family from its initiation to its dissolution. Others seem to have little or no impact at all.

Other Systems and the Family. The four systems which we have examined appear to be the most frequently encountered in a broad range of societies. There are other structures, but they do not appear as universally. Thus, for example, the system of recreation in American society undoubtedly has a major influence on the family. Increasingly, as the time devoted to productive labor is decreased, nonwork time becomes an important element in the life of the American family. A whole new area of sociological concern is developing around this factor in modern industrialized societies. As a greater body of research and theoretical literature is developed, it may soon become possible to indicate in greater detail how this important area affects the family career.

Likewise, we may cite effects of the system of health maintenance on the family. Medicine, nutrition, and sanitation are all well developed areas in the more technologically evolved societies. Indeed, one of the most significant single factors in the changing demographic characteristics of the "developing societies" is health maintenance. The impact of this area on the birth-rate and the death-rate characteristics of a society are massive. Inevitably, the family system is caught up in the resulting changes.

I have mentioned these two additional areas only to indicate the additional possibilities for analysis of the relationships which may exist between the family and the broad society. In any developmental examination, these factors play an important part in a satisfactory explanation of the family phenomena being studied.

Explanations Available in the
Societal-Institutional Facet

As was mentioned in the first chapter, the ultimate goal of theory is explanation. In concluding this section let us attempt a brief identification of the kinds of explanations of behavioral phenomena made possible by attention to the societal-institutional facet in the developmental approach.

A review of the kinds of issues identified in this section should show that the societal-institutional facet is quite helpful in explaining patterns of familial role structures that may be found in a given society; that is, analyses in this area are going to be most productive in showing the dimensions of the structural boundaries within which familial behavior takes place. It will be possible to point out the sources of basic intrafamilial relationships in the broadest terms as the kinds of positional and role structures appropriate for a given society are identified. Explanations for the types of transactive relations which are observed between the family group and other groups in the society, as well as between individual positional occupants in their nonfamilial positions, may also be discovered. In a very genuine way, the societal-institutional facet provides the explanation for the themes observed in familial behavior. On this basis, it is possible to explain the *variations* on the themes which may be observed. Certainly the identification of the basic boundaries for familial behavior is a significant foundation for the explanatory process; however, much will remain unexplained if the analysis is carried no further.

THE GROUP-INTERACTIONAL FACET

Each individual family group plays its own variations on the theme of the societal-institutional expectations for family life. These modifications may have their source in a particular tradition which one or the other of the marital partners brings from his or her parental family, in some combination of such customs, from some unique set of circumstances which develop and solidify into a normative pattern in the family's own history, or from some other internal or external source. Whatever the origin, it is clear that families do develop their own distinctive style of operation which, when viewed by the outsider, may seem deviant to a greater or lesser extent from the dominant family expectations. It is probably true that the degree of individual variation is related to the kind of societal setting in which the family is located, with the more traditional or authoritarian societies providing less opportunity for deviation than the less rigid ones. These distinctive styles are of considerable significance to the theorist who tries to account for a variety of outcomes in family behavior in his research. The degree of patterning or systematic development of these variations is also a theoretical problem of considerable importance.

In defining the family from a developmental point of view, we found that part of the definition dealing with the unique quality of the positional and role definitions in a given society actually represents a set of boundaries for the family. Now in turning to the group-interactional facet of development, we shall select only that part of the definition which treats the familial behavior incorporated within its boundaries. In other words, we shall analyze both the way in which the interrelated positions and roles are structured to result in the semiclosed system of actors and how this structure changes through time.

But already a roadblock looms, and we must clarify a difficult, though common, analytical distinction in sociological analysis. In sociological work, there exists a continuing tension between the *structure* and the *dynamic process* of social groups. They are inseparable; we cannot observe family behavior outside the family. Observed behavior provides the raw data from which the structure is abstracted, but this structure must already exist as a concept in the minds of the actors or no orderly behavior will take place. Therefore, we must oscillate back and forth between the structural concepts of norm, role, position, and so on and the role behaviors related to and partially explained by these structural concepts.

The Family as a Semiclosed System

The central core of the developmental theory lies in the view of the family as a *system*. Sociologists have given extensive attention to this concept over many years (Parsons, 1951; Buckley, 1967 and 1968), and many theorists (Hill, 1971) have applied it to the family. Superficially, it seems easy enough to define a *system* as a set of parts structurally tied together, but then we have only examined the tip of the iceberg. Below the surface, we find that a system also involves a process of feedback, in which changes in one part of the system activate changes in another element or elements of the same system. Ben Franklin's old potbellied stove is a good example. Neither it nor our grandfather's original central heating furnaces with their heat ducts, registers, and dampers were heating systems in the technical sense. (And they were not very effective in the practical sense.) There were no automatic changes due to feedback except on the human level; when the temperature dropped, someone had to rush to the basement to refuel the furnace. A heating system was created only when thermostatic controls were linked to an automatic fueling device, such as a mechanical coal stoker. Then people could relax. When the temperature rose by a certain number of degrees, the stoker stopped. The system was interconnected so that changes in one part triggered changes in another part.

When we shift our attention back to the family, we see that it is more than just a complex set of related roles and positions. It is a *system,* and when changes occur in the roles of one position, it changes the roles of other positions. And to further refine the point, the position itself is a system to a certain degree, since a change in one role of a position often means that other roles of that position are also effected.

But why a *semiclosed* system? Most discussions of systems involve some notion of their boundaries. We have seen that the societal-institutional facet tends to identify the confines of the family. The definition of the family we have used states that the content of the positions and the roles assigned to the family are unique to the family structure. This assertion is a way of setting limits. But there also are notions of kinship in the family which do not apply to other systems of the society. These facts notwithstanding, all behavior which occurs within families is not motivated by other family behavior, and all behavior of family members is not directed toward other family members. The system of the family "opens and closes" to deal with other systems, to be influenced by them, and to allow certain actors to act in other structures both as family representatives and without any reference to their family status. Therefore, *some* change and *some* behavior in the family is related to outside factors, i.e., the system is semiclosed.

Another look at our definition of the family will illuminate a critical difference between the developmental approach and other sociological approaches. "The family is a semiclosed system of actors occupying interrelated positions defined by the society of which the family system is a part as unique to that system with respect to the role content of the positions and to ideas of kinship relatedness. The definitions of positional role content change over the history of the group." If our definition ended with the first sentence, it would be quite time bound. But, as we have seen, the great advantage of the developmental approach is that it does not limit itself to the narrow time dimension of the interactional perspective but instead tries to explain the dynamics of change in family behavior through family history. The historical perspective makes the developmental approach unique. Previously we used one set of descriptive terms with the static structure, namely, norm, role, position, and group, as well as another set for changing structure, that is, role sequence, positional career, and family career. In addition, the terms *role cluster* and *role complex* are utilized as bridging concepts (Hill and Hansen, 1960:301); they provide a method of reflecting the time element in the static structure. At any given time, a specified position will be composed of a set of roles which will differ from the roles in that position in another period. Using the idea of *role cluster* allows us to make this distinction. Similarly, the reciprocal roles of a given group will change at various times; so, we may use the term *role complex* here. (We are using *position* and *group* as generic terms, whereas we are using role cluster and role complex to specify a content for these general terms at a given point in time.) The concepts of *role behavior* and *sanction* provide us with a way of dealing with the behavioral expressions of the normative structure, and most essentially, with a way of accounting for the changes due to the interactional experience of the family members. These concepts are now our operational tools, and they will enable us to examine minutely the structural characteristics of the system they describe.

Structural Conditions

Structure initially is defined normatively by the cultural expectations of a given society. In a structure, there are a specified set of positions with given role content. These roles also are defined by a stated set of norms. In one sense, this structure is the ideal family group. Although this model varies from society to society, the perfect Indian family is much larger than the ideal American family and even may have subcultural variation, it is always possible to find both a core structural definition for the family and a number of conditions which provide for change in the family structure.

Excess and Deficit in Structure. An amusing anecdote from some of the initial attempts of American technological experts to aid the Indian government's efforts to control the population growth, will illustrate this idea: The specialists used colorful before-and-after pictures as one of their methods. The before picture showed a large, badly undernourished family that wore tattered clothing, whereas the after picture showed a three-child family, two girls and a boy, who were considerably healthier and wore much better clothing. The caption read, "WHICH WOULD YOU CHOOSE?" Unexpectedly, the widespread reaction was in favor of the larger family. Most people said of the smaller family, "Look how poor that man is. Only three children and only one boy at that!" According to Indian family values, this group was incomplete in structure. Not only were there too few children, but the highly valued male child was nearly absent. This father was a failure. The Indian family structure demanded not only a certain number of children but also a number of boys in the ideal family. If either expectation is unfilled, the family has a deficit structure.

A deficit structure raises a number of implications for familial behavior. Most obvious is the fact that certain roles may be shifted to other positions in the family organization, may be played by nonfamily members, or may not even be played at all. We all have heard comments made about households in which one or the other parent is absent: "She has to be both mother and father to the children." "His oldest daughter was like a mother to the other children." These statements simply describe the shifting of certain roles from one position to another; however, the consequence of this kind of shifting causes a change in the so-called normal characteristics of the related roles in the other family positions. Clearly, while an older daughter may act like a mother in a family, she cannot play the role exactly as a mother would play it. Neither her role relationships with her siblings nor with her father are the same as those of a real wife-mother. Her roles as a daughter-sister modify the wife-mother roles to a considerable extent. Her father cannot play the same type of reciprocal role that he played with his wife, nor can the children play their reciprocal roles as sons and daughters in the power manner when their mother is missing. Certain roles of the wife-mother, such as sex partner, cannot be shifted to some other position in the family, or, in this society, even to some outside member. Other roles, though moved to a new position, are modified as a result of the presence of other role expectations normally a part of this position. Occasionally, there exists some tension between the normal expectations of the roles constituting the original position and the new expectation of the shifted roles. For example, an outside male may attempt the father role for a set of fatherless children, but the roles of his own position as outside male may cause some problems which will undercut the adequacy of his function as a father-substitute. He cannot always be both father-disciplinarian and objective pal. Thus, a deficit structure modifies both the internal and external patterns of the family.

At the other extreme, there may be actors present in the family for which there normally are no designated positions. In the American nuclear family system, the presence of an aging parent or an unmarried sibling of the husband or wife disrupts the usual structure. Although the roles of grandparent and aunt or uncle form a part of the extended family system in American society, the neolocal characteristic of the system provides no place for such a position *within* the nuclear family. When such an actor is present, the position may be almost devoid of any role content. A grandmother, while allowed to play an affectional role toward her grandchildren, would be infringing on the role content of the wife-mother if she disciplined them or if she took over certain housekeeping duties. Thus, in this type of excess in structure, there is also a necessity for a reallocation of roles to the position of the extra member. No societal norms currently exist for dealing with the situation. Each family must solve its own problems.

There are other types of excessive structure which have various implications. A daughter's illegitimate child is one example. The moving in of a young married couple with either set of parents is another. The failure of a grown child to leave the parental home is another. In each case, the presence of additional actors, for whom no position is defined normatively, leads both to a reallocation of roles within the family structure and to a change in the interactional patterns of the group.

These excessive and deficit structures have longitudinal implications; that is, they dramatically change the role sequence and positional careers of all the family members, and sometimes their effects last long after the superfluity or the lack has disappeared.

Plurality Patterns. The impact of size on group functioning is so obvious that often it is taken for granted. Everybody knows that large families are different from small ones. Years ago, Bossard (1945:293) pointed out the mathematical quality of family size with the formula $X = \dfrac{Y^2 - Y}{2}$.

In this formula X is the number of paired interpersonal relations, and Y is the number of persons. Thus, in a family of five people there are ten pairs of relationships, whereas in a family of eight, there are twenty-eight combinations. The formula only begins, however, to capture the complexity of size. There are also possibilities for coalitions of three persons, four persons, and so on up to the maximum size of a given family. Kephart (1950) attempted to deal with this problem. According to his method, a family of five has a potentiality of from four to ninety different interpersonal relationships.

However, neither Bossard nor Kephart's formulas deal with a very important aspect of size as it relates to the family, which fluctuates in such a way that the additions and the subtractions from membership precipitate notable and far-reaching reorganizations to the role and positional structure of the group. This result brings up three additional structural factors: spacing patterns, sex patterns, and age patterns, all intimately tied to the plurality issue, all interrelated and conveying implications of their own.

Spacing Patterns. A common American folksaying goes, "The first pregnancy takes any amount of time; all the rest take nine months." Although humorous, this pithy saying does contain a kernel of truth. The first child may be conceived premaritally, but after that the minimum biological limit is nine months. Exceptions to this fact are premature births, multiple births, and adoptions. Maximum theoretical spacing involves the birth of the first child early in the marriage, with the second child not appearing until shortly before the onset of the mother's menopause. This extreme pattern is not as common as other ones, and there exists an almost infinite set of possibilities. It depends on the number of children in the family, but they may be bunched close together early in the marriage; they may be clustered at some other time during the childbearing period; they may be distributed rather evenly over a portion of the childbearing period or over the entire span; they may be concentrated in two or more periods; they may be concentrated at one point with one or more children born during earlier or later isolated periods, and so on.

It is probably true that there are some societal and group normative expectations concerning child-spacing patterns, although I am aware of no studies which have dealt with normative issues and relatively few which have presented data on this subject (Christensen, 1960). In a study of three-generation families carried out in the late 1950s (Rodgers, 1962; Hill, 1970), the spacing patterns of the grandparent and of the parent generations who were presumed to have completed their childbearing were tabulated. In a total of 854 individual births in 182 nuclear families which ranged from one to sixteen births per family, arrangements covering from less than one calendar year to over nine calendar years occurred. The model for grandparent families spanned 24–35 months, whereas the one for parent families extended over 12–23 months; however, the overall spread in the distribution of the data made it difficult to determine what normative patterns may have governed the child spacing of these two groups. Regardless of what normative patterns there may be, a given spacing pattern places certain important structural influences on the developing role structure of the family. As in the case of plurality patterns, the longitudinal impact of a given spacing configuration has its most profound effects on the interactional experience of the family.

Sex Patterns. As might be expected, a family of all female children has a remarkably different set of role characteristics than one composed of all males. Various combinations of the two sexes provide for additionally interesting variations in role structure. Here again is an area where very little research has been done, although the sexual composition of a family is highly significant, as is the influence of sex on role expectations. To date, developmental research tends to ignore the element of sex, treating role development as if it were the same regardless of the gender of the child. This view is surely inadequate.

Age Patterns. Role structure is further modified by the existent pattern of ages which prevail at any point in the family career. This factor is tied closely to the spacing, the size, and the birth order of the children. There is a considerable body of research on certain factors related to the birth order of the children, but it basically is oriented to the personality variables of the individuals or with variables essentially treated as an extension of a particular personality, such as the impact of ordinal position on occupational preference (Clausen, 1966; Kammeyer, 1967; Sampson, 1965; Tomeh,

1969; Hendershot, 1969). Most of the research done deals with the characteristics of the roles of the oldest and youngest children and ignores all the middle ones. Furthermore, the impact of the change in roles associated with a change in the relative position resulting from the birth of additional children remains relatively unexplored.

Another important factor concerning age is the relative gap between the ages of the parents and the ages of the children. Middle-aged parents with young children do not have the same role relationships as young parents with young children. Placed in longitudinal perspective, these differences continue throughout the family career; parents who delayed having children still have their offspring at home in their later years, whereas parents who had children soon after marriage find themselves childless at a relatively early age. In the late sixties and in the early seventies, the concern and the anguish that people felt about the generation gap may be explained partly by a systematic analysis of this kind of age differential between parents and children. This section concludes our highlighting of the key structural conditions necessary for an interactional analysis of a family; the fact that they must be seen in dynamic terms has significant implications for the whole set of role sequences and of role complexes which develop over the family career.

Change in the Family System

During our discussion dealing with the important areas of change in the family structure over a period of time, we shall begin with the nature of change, shall move to a treatment of the interactional alteration arising from varying normative content of positions, and shall conclude by examining the modifications springing from societal sources. Remember we shall separate these three factors only for analytical purposes. In reality, they are not distinct entities.

The Nature of Change. Western industrial cultures measure change in terms of chronological time; that is, we talk and think about periods—years, months, days, hours, and minutes. Close examination reveals that chronological divisions are imposed on the process of change. Frequently, these units break a process of change into artificial elements which are inadequate reflections of what is happening. Any college student knows that midterms occur in a spread which may begin in the third week of a ten-week term and which may not end until the eighth week; or, if they do take place at midterm, there is frequently an awkward division of the course material which has little to do with logical units of time. Similarly, the job hours of a day may impose an awkward break in the work process, with certain tasks remaining incomplete. On other days, all work may be done before quitting time, and the employee finds himself trying to appear busy when there is nothing to do. In other words, social processes and chronological time do not necessarily coincide.

This point is very important to understanding the developmental view of change and of time. The focus of the developmental analysis is on processual not on chronological time. Thus, a developmental period is identified by a distinctive processual character which may be separated from another span of a different character, regardless of the chronological time dimension. The chief criterion for a given developmental period is the identification of a distinctive role complex structure. Therefore, we speak of divisions in family development as the "Establishment Stage," the "Childbearing Stage," the "Childrearing Stage," the "Launching Stage," the "Postparental Stage," and so on. These periods are identified not because they have the same chronological length nor because they occur during the same chronological era in all families, but because they have a distinctive role structure which separates them from other periods in the family career. Thus, they are measured in processual time.

It is important to understand qualitatively the process of change as well as the nature of the alteration of time. Some of the variations in social structure are precipitious, unanticipated, and almost revolutionary in essence. Others occur in a much slower evolutionary manner. The former type of change has been termed *disjunctive*, since it involves a radical and sudden reordering of the role structure of the system. The latter type of change may be seen as *continuous*, including considerably less disruption of the system and allowing for a somewhat more leisurely adjustment of the structure.

There are certain specific problems in dealing analytically with these two kinds of change. At first glance, it may appear relatively easy to distinguish between them. When we begin to think of examples of disjunctive changes, however, it becomes clear that we must deal with a more or less disjunctive quality. Some examples may be marriage, the birth of a child, the departure of a member, the death of a member, or the sudden disability of a member. On close examination, it becomes possible to see a continuous quality to most of these events. The courtship process is in actuality a period during which a couple gradually takes on marital roles. In a very real sense, the marriage ceremony symbolizes what has already occurred to a great extent—the couple already has taken on the marital roles. The situation is analogous to academic commencement exercises. The granting of a diploma or of a degree represents what a person has *become* over a period of time. He does not reach the platform as an uneducated person and does not suddenly become educated when he is handed his diploma. Neither do the great share of couples approach the marriage ceremony in our society totally devoid of marital roles and, upon pronouncement of the marital vows, suddenly incorporate these combinations of norms into their role complex. The couples have been in the process of taking them on for some time. Of course, it is true that they continue to modify and to adjust the normative content of these roles during the postceremony. This practice occurs, however, throughout their marital history, not simply during the "period of adjustment." Similarly, birth is preceded by pregnancy, which carries with it the beginning of a readjustment of roles anticipating the addition of the new member; departures of members are often anticipated and role relationships subtly adjusted; even death is frequently anticipated.

Probably there are some relatively pure cases of disjunctive change. It is also most likely, however, that a great many of the changes which appear disjunctive at first contain a clear, continuous element. Furthermore, some changes, such as the entry into adolescence, often are thought of as disjunctive but in actuality are continuous in nature. Artificial "benchmarks" expressed by a given chronological age may be established in a given culture. They, however, frequently are inadequate indicators of the actual role situation. But this fact does not mean that they are insignificant. Indeed, they may serve to explain a given kind of behavioral phenomenon in which certain role expectations are focused on an actor and in which he is unable or is unwilling to incorporate the new roles into his position. Some of the problems of American society associated with adolescence, reaching adulthood, and retirement may be explained in these terms.

Yet another kind of difficulty occurs that has to do with how the analyst can determine when enough change in a role structure has taken place so that he is justified in stating that a "new" role structure exists. If the analyst compares the role structure which exists between parents and a child of age seven and the one which exists between these same parents and their child at age eleven, he can see some clear differences in the two systems. But *when*, that is, at what point in the process, is he justified in stating that an analytically genuine change has taken place in periods of a considerably shorter length? In American society, there are no rites of passage during this time that mark a dramatic shift in role expectations, but they do occur. Clearly, it is theoretically unjustified to treat the role complexes at the two periods as identical, but it is also difficult to ascertain empirically when the shifts take place. This fact is generally the case with continuous change situations (Strauss, 1962).

Changing Normative Content of Positions. Within the interactional facet of analysis, there are four key sources for the change in normative content of positions over time. The first source is a variation in structure. When this change occurs, adjustments in the normative content of positions follow. Normative change is implied where there exists an excess or deficit in structure, in plurality pattern changes, in spacing patterns, in sex patterns, and in age patterns. It would be redundant to carry our discussion of these effects any further than we have above.

The second source of change, the shifting importance of roles, can be explained best by referring to Bates' (1956) article on the concepts of position, role, and status. He points out that in each position there are both dominant and recessive roles, which also can be called obligatory-discretionary or manifest-latent roles. Each variation provides us with the conceptual equipment to account for various kinds of change in the interactional patterns of the family. Throughout the family career, roles change. Dominant ones become recessive, and recessive ones become dominant. The role of the wife is certainly dominant at the beginning of the marriage. With the onset of children, however, it must compete with the role of mother, and, thus, the role of wife becomes recessive. The same result occurs when the husband becomes a father. At a later point, these parental roles become less dominant as the children become more independent of their parents. This example also provides us with an excellent case if a latent role, the parental one, becoming manifest, and when the children leave home, it returns to a relatively latent state. Both the parent and the spouse roles are obligatory, but other ones are discretionary. For example, the wife may be a wage-earner. In early marriage, before the children arrive, she may work in order to obtain material goods or to build up some savings. Then, too, when the children are older, she may return to work. Nothing in the societal-institutional norms, however, defines such a role as obligatory, unless the husband should die or the couple should separate. Then the role of wage earner may become obligatory. Although the family changes in its career, it is possible to analyze the resulting variations in roles from the perspective of the dominant-recessive, latent-manifest, and obligatory-discretionary natures they possess, and this kind of approach becomes a powerful tool in examining the changes.

The third source, involving the concept of *developmental task* has been closely associated with the type of examination mentioned above and has been a major focus of developmental material almost from the beginning. Robert J. Havighurst (1953:2) defines developmental task in the following way:

> A developmental task is a task which arises at or about a certain period in the life of an individual, the successful achievement of which leads to his happiness and to success with later tasks, while failure leads to unhappiness in the individual, disapproval by the society, and difficulty with later tasks.

Later work in developmental theory seems to call for a modification of Havighurst's definition. In an early analysis (Rodgers, 1962:54–55), I concluded that in reality the developmental task phenomenon is only a special case of the incorporation of a given role into the role cluster of a position at some given point in the role sequence of a positional career. Viewed another way, it is the process of making manifest one of the latent roles of a position. I therefore redefine the developmental task phenomenon as follows:

> A developmental task is a set of norms (role expectations) arising at a particular point in the career of a position in a social system, which, if incorporated by the occupant of the position as a role or part of a role cluster, brings about integration and temporary equilibrium in the system with regard to a role complex or set of role complexes; failure to incorporate the norms leads to lack of integration, application of additional normative pressures in the form of sanctions, and difficulty in incorporating later norms into the role cluster of the position.

Thus, one explanation for a certain kind of interactive process in the family may be associated with the actors in the system imposing normative pressures on one of the members to take on a certain role at a particular point in his positional career. These influences usually are associated with age and sex norms which provide the broad pattern of the positional career in the system. Thus, when infants reach a certain age in a given society, normative pressures are brought to bear with respect to the basic drives of food intake and elimination. Children are weaned and are switched to culturally appropriate foods. Children are "toilet-trained" in a certain manner. Later they are the focus of normative pressures to take on particular roles which may be associated with the division of labor in the family or with some set of roles which they may be expected to play in the larger society. As the developmental task concept notes, this process has a cumulative character. If the role is incorporated inadequately, it has implications both for the role complexes in which the actor is involved and for the role sequence of his own career. The process we have been describing here is, of course, socialization within the family. Broom and Selznick (1968:86–87) divide socialization into four elements: (1) concern with the basic physical and emotional disciplines—eating, elimination, control of emotions, sexual drives, sleep, and so on; (2) imparting the culturally accepted aspirations; (3) acquisitions of the necessary cultural skills; and (4) learning the appropriate social roles. Elements of this process involve the kind of focused normative pressure at a given point in the positional career identified in the developmental task concept. The first and third elements probably are most easily identifiable in this respect. The second and fourth elements probably are associated with a more continuous kind of role development, and the kind of heightened normative pressure points involved in developmental tasks is not observed readily.

There is a danger in associating developmental tasks only with the child positions in the family system, for socialization clearly is a life-long process, and developmental tasks can be identified in the adult positions. Developmental tasks, however, are less likely to be so dramatically obvious as in the concentrated socialization experience of the child positions. Certain aspects of the husband-father position, particularly those associated with his role of supporting the family, have strong developmental task implications as his occupational career unfolds. Similarly, the wife-mother roles, such as those identified with the shift from the primary focus on mothering as the children leave the nuclear family, have equally strong developmental task associations. The movement into the postparental period, the movement into retirement, and similar major shifts in the role clusters of the adult positions are possible points of emphasis of a developmental task type.

Finally, there is another aspect of the developmental task that deals with certain points in the family career when major role shifts involve the entire family role complex. Here, instead of stressing one role in the system, the entire organization constitutes the unit of emphasis. Duvall (1971:150) states: "Family developmental tasks are those growth responsibilities that must be accomplished by a family at a given stage of development in a way that will satisfy its (1) biological requirements, (2) cultural imperatives, and (3) personal aspirations and values, if the family is to continue to grow as a unit." Although these major role adjustments may be precipitated by the developmental state of one position in the system, their impact is so widespread that it involves a radical reorganization of the role structure of the system. Obviously, such a radical role change has dramatic effects on the interactional patterns of the family. These radical role changes can explain the phenomenon of a total reorientation of a family in their interactional experience, which often is observed in research but is difficult to explain.

The fourth major source of change in the normative content of positions is related to the day-to-day interactional experiences of the family. In contrast to the kinds of normative shifts tied to particular points in the career of a position or linked to the family as a total system, these normative changes occur out of a given interactional experience. The experiences may be idiosyncratic to a specified family. They may be treated in a general fashion, however, by noting that in all social systems certain normative structures are established as a result of the interactional history of each system. A certain circumstance or event may arise in the family experience in which the normative structure that prevails proves inadequate. The sociological term to identify such a situation is anomie—normlessness. There are several types of anomie: (1) a situation in which there are no norms to guide the actors in their behavior; (2) a situation in which the norms are ambiguous so that it is unclear what behavior is called for; (3) a situation in which there are conflicting sets of norms requiring mutually exclusive kinds of behaviors; and (4) a situation in which more than one set of appropriate norms are acceptable. Thus, in any of these types of circumstances, a series of interactions must take place which will serve to define the norms for the roles of the actors. Such a series of interactions may then serve as a precedent which will guide future behaviors in similar situations and, thus, will incorporate a new role into one or more role clusters in the system.

A crisis provides a conspicuous example of anomie. (We must be cautious not to think that anomic situations occur only in obvious interactional experiences.) If a crisis arises which the family has never faced before and for which there seem to exist no clearly defined roles, modifications are made in the role expectations of one or more positions in the family. Thus, the family equips itself to meet the situation when it arises again. Similarly, but often at a less emotionally charged level, a certain set of expectations involving two or more reciprocal roles may prove inadequate in meeting the kinds of goals which those role definitions were intended to serve. As a result, subtle or more obvious redefinitions of the roles will take place to deal more satisfactorily with the situation in the future interactional experience. Such role shifts may involve reassigning certain areas of responsibility in the division of the labor of the family system or in the decision-making process. The areas of responsibility may include such mundane matters as who takes out the trash or some major issues such as who allocates the money. Regardless of the sphere to which they refer, the essential point is that these normative changes arise from the interactional experience itself, which is how a relatively unique family subculture is built and is modified over the family career. Old agreements concerning role relationships are abandoned, and new ones are reached in order to carry out more satisfactorily the day-to-day operations of the system.

We have identified the four major areas of changing normative content of positions: the structural changes of the family system, the manifest-dominant-obligatory nature of certain roles, the developmental state of a position or of the total family system, the interactional experience of the actors in the system. We turn now to another area of potential variation in the normative structure of the family—societal change.

Societal Change as a Source of Familial Change. We already have pointed to the way societal norms set boundaries for family interaction. One obvious source for an explanation of change in family interaction is a variation in the character of the boundaries, for example, as a result of the direct and sometimes dramatic effects of historical changes. Our goal here is not to detail the kinds of modification that have occurred in a particular society but simply is to sensitize ourselves to the fact that one explanation

for the change in internal dynamics of families is historical in its nature.
Thus, both the long-term historical changes involving industrialization,
urbanization, and the like, and the short-term historical events involving
wars, economic depressions or inflations, disasters, and so forth, have an
important impact on interactional patterns and the variations which may
occur. As we noted in our discussion of the societal-institutional facet, these
matters are not central to the developmental process per se, but they may
so change the thematic content of the family so as to divert the developmental process in a new direction which can be explained in no other way.

**Explanations Available in the
Group-Interactional Facet**

Although the societal-institutional facet depends on an analysis of the
basic characteristics of the society, an analysis of the family group provides
the explanation of behavior in the group-interactional facet.

First, the fact that the family is not a closed system explains some
familial behavior. Roles and positions occupied by family members in other
social systems affect the conduct of these same members in their household
positions.

The second point is derived from the various aspects of the structural
characteristics of the family. Some proportion of the variance in behavior
can be accounted for by analyzing families according to common sets of
structural characteristics.

The third point is derived from the process of change which is an inherent characteristic of the family system. These changes can be disjunctive
or continuous. One explanation of a particular kind of interactional phenomenon is related to the quality of change. Another explanation is related to one of four major kinds of change: (1) those associated with
structural conditions; (2) those associated with the dominant-recessive,
manifest-latent, and/or obligatory-discretionary character of roles; (3) those
associated with changes arising at a critical period in a family, which we
called developmental tasks; and finally, (4) those arising from the interactional experience of the family.

The fourth point providing the explanation for interactive characteristics
of families is related to long-term societal change and to particular short-
term historical events which change the thematic quality of family roles.

THE INDIVIDUAL-PSYCHOLOGICAL FACET

Students in the behavioral sciences often despair of ever making any
scientific generalizations because of the unique quality of the individual

human personality. This quality is certainly a powerful influence on the functioning of most groups. Certain combinations of personalities found within a group probably determine to a considerable degree the nature of group interaction. It also must be noted that the group provides considerable influence on the development of individual personality, so that we see a complex process involving the group and the individual. Ignoring either group or individual influence reduces the explanatory power possible. Sociologists frequently have been guilty of neglecting individual influences. Psychologists often fail to take account of group effects. This fact is one major reason for the rise of interest in the social-psychological perspective in the behavioral sciences. Indeed, the developmental approach is explicitly social-psychological, since it includes individual, as well as group, concepts in its framework.

In turning attention to the individual-psychological facet of analysis of family careers, we become most acutely aware of the incomplete character of the developmental theory. Although some family development theorists have identified this aspect as a necessary element in the overall theory, they have paid very little concentrated attention to creating the necessary conceptual scheme to reflect processes occurring at this level. The essential bridging concepts which would tie this facet to the other two also have received little effort. There are several interlocking reasons for this neglect: The great share of theorists have their primary expertise and interest in the sociological aspects of the developmental approach. Consequently, they have neither the necessary scholarly background nor the interest in the kinds of problems typically associated with individual-psychological matters.[1] Those theorists who have the necessary professional background have tended to be more concerned with the strictly individual developmental problems than with the group context of these issues. Finally, a review of some of the most recent literature indicates that there exist a great many unresolved issues in psychological developmental theory (Goslin, 1969; Inhelder, 1957).

The goals of this section, then, are considerably more limited than the objectives of the two immediately preceding divisions. All that will be attempted is an identification of the kinds of problems which the individual-psychological facet must handle, some possible concepts to deal with these difficulties, and some of the kinds of explanations which may result from an adequate analysis of the individual-psychological facet.

In their article on family conceptual frameworks, Hill and Hansen (1960:309) state five assumptions of the developmental approach. Three of these assumptions are relevant here:

[1] I fully recognize my limitations in this respect and take full responsibility for the inadequacies in the treatment of this area which others with greater expertise are sure to find. In my opinion, however, one way to stimulate work in a field is to present it in its incomplete state so that others may see what needs to be done.

3. The human is actor as well as reactor.

4. Individual and group development is best seen as dependent upon stimulation by a social milieu as well as on inherent (developed) capacities.

5. The individual in a social setting is the basic autonomous unit.

Perhaps the implications of these three assumptions may be stated best as follows: The developmental theory does not view human behavior as a simple and automatic stimulus-response chain but posits between stimulus and response an intervening step in which characteristics of the individual come into play to process the stimuli as well as to add new elements resulting in a unique response. In addition, the individual himself may be the source of new stimuli to which others respond in the same manner (Kohlberg, 1969; Rheingold, 1969).

The Individual as Actor—Impact of the Individual on the Family

Earlier we distinguished between the concept of *role*, the group expectations for behavior, *and role behavior*, the way a given actor carries out the expectations. The disparity between the expectations for behavior and the actual behavior of the individual is one reason why a simple stimulus response model is inadequate to explain human conduct. We shall look for these explanations in the characteristics of the individual.

Each individual is born with a unique genetic makeup. The implications of this fact are far-reaching. It is apparent that no two individual human beings are exactly alike in their physical or psychological composition. Yet, it is equally apparent that there exist many physical and psychological similarities among all humans. For purposes of illustration, we know that the ability to see is generally alike in all human beings, though we also know that it has a range, with some people having better sight than others. On a purely physical level, then, the ability to sense light stimuli emitted from a book page is essentially similar among individuals, though there is a scope of ability around this likeness. Furthermore, evidence exists that the genetic makeup of some individuals gives them special talents or abilities. Some people seem to have particularly agile muscular coordination, others great aesthetic sensitivity, and still others high intellectual ability. This is not the place to enter into a detailed discussion of all the research on individual differences which has been carried out over the years, nor is it the spot to get involved in a nature-nurture controversy over the degree to which such abilities are inborn versus learned. Both influences are involved. The elementary fact is that there exist certain genetically based individual differences which must receive some weight in explanations of familial behavior. The essence of the debate (and a question as yet unanswered) is, "How much weight?"

Returning to the family setting and to the occupant of a position in the family, we already have seen that each occupant has certain roles assigned to his position. When persons holding reciprocal roles pressure an individual to behave in a particular way, we observe a particular kind of role behavior. Rarely is this conduct precisely that prescribed by the role. It may be very close, but it may also be at wide variance. There are three possible reasons for this variation between the expected and the actual behavior: First, the actor may not have grasped fully what was expected of him. Second, although he may have comprehended what was expected, he may have been unable to respond in the anticipated way. Third, having understood what was expected, he may not have desired to respond in the anticipated way.

Assuming adequate communication of clearly defined normative expectations, if the actor fails to understand them, he is unlikely to respond in a satisfactory manner. His lack of comprehension may result from his inability to receive adequately the full range of stimuli addressed to him, from his inability to process these stimuli in sufficient manner, or from his reaching a set of conclusions concerning the stimuli which bring a behavioral response other than the one anticipated. In this latter instance, it is apparent that an element of *anomie* is present, since it is assumed that the stimuli have been received and have been processed adequately; but it is still possible to come to more than one conclusion concerning the appropriate behavioral response. Summarizing this first source of deviation between role and role behavior accounted for by characteristics of the actor, we see that they result either from inadequate reception, processing, or interpretation of the expectations by the actor. Concepts developed for the individual-psychological analysis should be able to take account of these various types of "slippage" in the interactive process.

Turning to the second situation, we shall assume that the expectations have been fully grasped but that the actor is unable to respond appropriately. Inability to act in the anticipated manner may result from the failure of the actor to have incorporated the necessary repertoire of behavioral skills into his role, that is, from the lack of success in achieving certain prerequisite developmental tasks or from some basic lack of physical or psychological ability. In the first case, we can assume that the potential ability is present to behave in the appropriate manner but that the individual has not yet developed the suitable skills for the conduct. There are situations in which expectations may be placed on an individual before he has developed physically and/or mentally to a point of being able to accomplish a particular act, for example, asking for a level of hand-eye coordination which is beyond his developmental level. In the second situation, we assume that the individual simply is incapable of behaving in the expected manner due to some inadequate physical and/or psychological equipment. These are elements of mental or physical retardation or disability which affect the capacity to respond appropriately. In either circumstances, the role behavior deviates somewhat from the role expectation.

In the third situation, we posit a mental process in which the role occupant chooses to act in a manner other than what he concludes is expected of him. There may be various explanations for this decision. Among them may be a desire on the part of the actor to avoid an experience which he has found unsatisfactory in previous circumstances. He may have responded appropriately at some time and may have found that the consequences were displeasing to him. Thus, he fails to respond as expected since he wishes to avoid the same distasteful situation. Or, perhaps, although he has no particular aversion to the kind of behavior expected of him, he envisions an alternative which he anticipates will be even more satisfactory. Another possibility may be that, while recognizing that a particular kind of behavior is called for, he also understands that it will result in certain responses from those in reciprocal roles which he does not want. Therefore, he may react in some other way that gains a response which is more satisfactory to him. The case of deviation between role expectations and role behavior calls attention to the social time element in human interactions. In responding to expectations, actors take into account both past interactive experience and anticipations of future experiences.

Three types of situations which may account for deviations between role and role behavior have been identified. It is improbable that they ordinarily occur in their pure form. It is likely in the day-to-day interactive process that these situations will occur in combination with one another. We can anticipate situations in which inadequate reception and/or processing are combined with unwillingness and/or inability to respond in the manner which the actor concludes is expected. The analytical problem is a very complex one. It is amazing that we find as much correlation between role and role behavior in daily experience as we do, given the many possibilities for variation!

What are the consequences for the family of the individual as autonomous actor in the system? The behavior of a role occupant may be the source for initiating new role expectations, for modifying existing ones, or for eradicating them all together. If a given actor consistently fails to play his role as defined by those in the reciprocal roles, the possibilities for response by the reciprocal role occupants are limited to four: (1) to continue to persist in placing the same expectations on the actor, even though he does not conform to them; (2) to modify the expectations in the hope of gaining conformity; (3) to cease to place the expectations on the actor; or (4) to adopt a set of expectations that the role occupant has indicated are desirable to him. Any of these reactions represents a modification of the normative structure of the system.

Further complicating the situation is that those in the reciprocal roles may misinterpret the actions of the role occupant. They may assume that he is unable to respond when, in fact, he has not understood their expectations or has been unwilling to respond. Any of the other combinations of misunderstanding also may occur. The character of the response to the actions of the role occupant will be quite different depending on how the meaning of his actions is interpreted.

What has been analyzed is not a matter of the role occupant as *reactor*. Instead, what has been highlighted is the fact that the actor in a role does not simply react but that he introduces new elements into the situation as a result of his own genetic characteristics and social experience. A child who says to his parents, verbally or behaviorally in some nonverbal fashion, "I can't," or "I don't want to," or "I don't understand," or "I'd rather do this," is not *reacting*, but *acting*. The child has introduced a new element into the system which instigates a response on the part of the parents. Although the normative expectations placed on the child by the parents has triggered the sequence of events, the youngster's behavior is not a simple reaction but would be only if a fully conforming response took place. The actor plays a most important part in the role sequences of the reciprocal roles as well as of his own role, and he plays a most important part in the family career as an entire system. The phenomenon of central interest is not the unique case of a failure of role behavior to conform to expectations. This topic is of interest when the failure leads to a modification of expectations and a new direction in the role sequences and positional careers of the family.

What makes these processes *developmental?* First, they are more likely to occur at points in the positional career where societal or group norms place new role expectations on the occupants of positions. An actor is more likely to introduce his own particular characteristics into a *new* or into a *revised* situation than into one that has been in force for some time. Although he may certainly change his behavior with respect to a relatively stable role, there is greater opportunity to act autonomously when new role expectations are placed upon him. New role expectations have not been set into a habit pattern in which all parties act in a more uncritical manner. In the very situations where the occupants of reciprocal roles are most conscious of the actor, the actor is also most conscious of the expectations being placed upon him.

These new role expectations often occur in a family career context which already may be encountering other modifications, either in the roles of the other family members or in a general alteration of the system. For example, while a child in his late teens is dealing with increasing independence in his role behavior the following may be happening: The wife-mother actor may be facing playing the roles of middle age; the husband-father may be trying to adjust to leveling off his career aspirations; and a younger sibling may be facing the first experiences of adolescence. If one or more of these actors tends to reject or attempts to modify the expectations placed upon him by the other actors in the system, this behavior only adds to the complexity of an already changing situation.

The individual-psychological facet does not isolate the processes associated with an individual actor in a family position. Rather, the analysis is carried out in relation to the processes occurring in other sectors of the system. It is, therefore, a *social* psychological, not an individual psychological, approach.

The Individual as Reactor—Impact of the Family on the Individual

The other side of the individual-psychological coin turns attention back to the family group. As opposed to the previous discussion in which the concern was with group characteristics and how they affected the group career, the attention focuses now on group characteristics as they affect the positional career. Many of the same elements are relevant here. The factors of excess or deficit in structure, plurality patterns, spacing patterns, sex distribution, age distribution, ordinal position, the various change elements associated with the system, and those changes associated with the society all call for reactions from the actors in the various family positions. There are, however, some additional factors. The features to be discussed arise out of widely observed, though not universal, characteristics of the interactive and normative styles of individual family systems.

Families sometimes assign to particular positions in the family special definitions which have little association with the characteristics of the actor or with the position itself. The occupant of the oldest-son position, for example, may be designated as the one to carry on the family business, not because the occupant has demonstrated any particular ability or any interest in this goal but because the oldest son is considered the appropriate one to head the organization. As a consequence of this general expectation a great many specific role expectations evolve. The response of the role occupant, both active and reactive, may have unique character. In his interactive experience, he does not have a repertoire of role models related to these particular anticipations. His peers may be experiencing some of the same normative pressures related to common roles played by individuals of his particular age and sex. But in this particular role, he has little guidance other than the expectations and behavioral responses of those in his family system; so, the family becomes the dominant influence on the individual.

More closely associated with the actual or assumed characteristics of an actor role occupant are a set of processes which might be best termed *stereotyping*. Labeling a particular actor "the brain of the family," "the queen," "the lazy one," "the athletic one," "the stupid one," or "the scatter-brained one" affects the role definitions of that actor. These assessments may be accurate or inaccurate, but the consequences are real. They demand response from the actor. A body of evidence has been building which indicates, for example, that mentally retarded children who have role expectations placed upon them more applicable to mentally normal children, tend to perform at a level above the one usually observed in their previous behavior. This finding has led some observers to conclude that the mentally retarded child may be responding to role expectations placed upon him by occupants of reciprocal roles who are aware of his slowness. There are also studies which have shown that erroneous information about student's intelligence given to teachers tends to result in the student's performing at the level of expectation set by the incorrect knowledge. One conclusion to be drawn from such findings is that these role expectations have elicited role behavior at variance with the true ability of the child. An alternative explanation is that the teacher's *evaluation* of the performance, rather than the performance itself, has been influenced by the erroneous information. The basic point is that stereotyping demands a response from the actor.

Another impact of the family on the individual results from special patterns of relationship which may develop between one or more actors in the system. There is nothing, generally, in the normative structure of the family which dictates these specific alliances. An exception, perhaps, is the husband-and-wife relationship. Nevertheless, cliques of various types may occur, or a certain actor may become an isolate. Being a member of a particular intrafamilial clique or being an isolate may have a major effect on a given actor.

There are various phenomena with a similar quality which may be called the family's *interactive style*. Jacobsen (1968), in his analysis of family occupational socialization, identified certain "modes of socialization" of families. He noted that some households emphasized verbal approaches with their children; others referred them to sources where information might be gained; whereas still others emphasized the necessity for their children to gain experience. Some families used more than one mode and, indeed, some used all modes. There were certain differing styles typically utilized by families in this socialization area. It seems safe to assume that these approaches also were utilized in other kinds of socialization and that, in general, families develop typical interactive styles associated with certain types of activities.

Other interactive styles may involve focusing by the family on certain principles or values—philosophical, religious, political, economic, or the like. Hill (1961, 1963, 1970) observed that families seemed to follow certain "policies" in their economic decision making. We all know families who hold strong moral or religious values which seem to dominate much of their household life. Or we know families who place a high premium on education, social service, or economic wealth. Such orientations have a major influence on the individual actors and on the way they play the various roles in their positions.

Another family characteristic is the type of psychological or emotional climate which prevails. Such qualities as warmth, coldness, affection, hostility, optimism, pessimism, fatalism, happiness, sadness, acceptance, rejection, and similar attitudes may pervade the general approach to life taken in a family.

Finally, there are a set of characteristics which may be called *facilitating mechanisms* (Rodgers, 1966). The presence of such material things as books, tools, magazines, or the like may aid an actor in playing a particular role. The willingness to help or to give instructions or to talk about experiences or events which have occurred—or the lack of such willingness—can have a similar impact.

In summary, we have identified general effects a family may have on its individual actors: the special definitions of role occupants, the stereotyping of role occupants, the formation of cliques or isolates, the peculiar interactive styles, the particular psychological or emotional climate, and the presence of various facilitating mechanisms.

Some Concepts for Individual-Psychological Analysis

In determining the concepts needed to carry out family developmental analysis at the individual-psychological level, what criteria should such concepts meet? Our discussion above provides a good guide for developing these criteria.

First, we need concepts to capture the basic psychological processes associated with the apprehension and processing of stimuli from other actors in the system and from the general social environment. Second, we need concepts which handle the physical and psychological capacities to act and to react as a result of the reception and the processing of these stimuli. Third, we must bridge the gap between the individual-psychological facet and the other two facets. Fourth, we must use terms which handle the way actions and reactions of the individual actor are converted into part of the normative structure of the system. Fifth, we should have concepts available to capture the kinds of family characteristics pertinent in their impact on the individual actor. Sixth, and the final requirement, we should choose only concepts that have longitudinal process dimensions.

Sample concepts associated with the reception and processing of stimuli would include *perception* and *cognition*. Perception involves receiving or becoming aware of stimuli taken in through the senses of sight, hearing, taste, and touch. Cognition is the thinking and knowing process with respect to stimuli received from outside and stimuli which arise from within the actor. During cognition the actor places the stimuli into some sort of structure of meaning and identifies possible behavioral alternatives.

To deal with the response to the perceptual and cognitive processes, the term *ability* denotes both the physical and psychological capacities for behaving in a given manner. Two concepts to explain some of the behavior observed are *motivation* and *emotion*. Motivation denotes the elements which arouse or direct a given behavioral response, perhaps as the result of drives or needs of a physiological, psychological, or social origin. Emotion designates a quality of feeling or an affect concerning current perceptions and cognitions as well as toward contemplated behavior. Finally, to signify the autonomous character of certain types of behavior, it may be useful to introduce the idea of *volition*.

There are other classical psychological and social-psychological concepts which also need to be added to the ones suggested. Ideas such as definitions of the situation, values, attitudes, self-concept, internalization, and identification come readily to mind (Stryker, 1968). Beyond pointing out the relevant concepts, there is the more demanding task of determining how they are related to one another. This latter activity is the process of constructing a conceptual framework. Such a foundation should reflect empirical reality as far as possible. To list only a set of possible concepts which may be applied falls considerably short of developing a theoretical base for analysis.

Concepts needed to bridge the gap between the societal-institutional, the group-interactional, and the individual-psychological facets may include a concept such as *concensus* to identify the process by which an individual behavior response becomes accepted as normative by the group. Other ideas must deal with such matters as the relative power or influence a given actor may have in achieving recognition for his particular approach to playing a role. Some of the work in social psychology dealing with exchange theory and balance theory will be valuable in determining other appropriate concepts (Edwards, 1969; Richer, 1968).

In developing concepts to deal with the group characteristics affecting the individual actor, such ideas as *idiosyncratic role, stereotyping,* and *coalition* appear useful. Perhaps *modes of interaction,* to generalize Jacobsen's term, may cover processes involving themes, policies, or orientations which characterize particular families. Similarly, the label *emotional climate* may be applied to the other qualitative style of interaction. The term *facilitating mechanism* seems useful to designate the kinds of aids available to individual actors in their roles in a given family setting.

A word of caution is in order at this point. What we have just done may be a bit deceptive. The underlined terms may or may not be authentic concepts. If each word or group of words refers to clearly identifiable phenomena which possess the same qualities, then it probably is valid; however, it may be only a label grouping together a conglomeration of phenomena which do not share the same characteristics and, consequently, which do not carry the same significance in the analysis of behavior. Determining what is actually the case forms another part of the exacting work of constructing conceptual frameworks for a theoretical system.

Explanations Available in the Individual-Psychological Facet

The explanatory focus of the individual-psychological facet centers on the *role—role-behavior* comparison. If individual actors were observed to conduct themselves in exact correspondence with the societal-institutional and group-interactional normative structure, then no explanatory problem would exist. Interpretations of their divergence are sought in an analysis of the characteristics of the individual actor and of his unique experience in the family setting. Rather than basing these explanations on the *absolutely* "unique personality of an individual," we look for generalizeable characteristics which we expect exist in the makeup of all role occupants. We then may be able to advance propositions stating that in a given set of circumstances, particular actors possessing a specified set of characteristics can be anticipated to behave in a designated way.

In seeking these explanations, we can be guided by the analytical areas identified in this chapter; however, it is not possible to enter directly into such explanatory attempts. The conceptual development for the individual-psychological facet remains incomplete. As work progresses, additional analytical problems may become evident. While this will further the complexity of the theory, it will strengthen its explanatory power.

INTERACTIONAL AND TRANSACTIONAL ARENAS OF BEHAVIOR

Throughout the discussion of this chapter, we have been discussing behavior inside and outside the household, especially in the discussion of the family as a semiclosed system. To distinguish between the internal and external behavior, the terms *interaction* and *transaction* have been developed (Hill and Hansen: 1960). We have, then, two *arenas* in which we may observe family conduct taking place.

In the interactional arena of family dynamics, the emphasis is on analysis of the processes which occur within the family system. Explanations of behavior observed are derived from other behavior or from normative patterns of a particular family. If there is a certain pattern of decision making observed, for example, the explanation for its sources are based on other elements internal to the system, such as normative structure which attributes to some actors authority or expertise in decision making and to others less authority or expertise.

We already have established, however, that the family is only more-or-less a closed system. Many internal processes have their explanations partially, if not wholly, in external elements. In this situation, then, the transactional arena becomes involved. For example, a great deal of discussion and interaction may take place in certain families over how to handle a situation with an aging parent. The norms and expectations governing such an interaction are not found totally within that system. Some of them are derived from expectations based in relationships with other relatives, including the aging parent, or with friends and acquaintances. In addition, there are certain societal norms concerning relationships of this sort. In other words, this particular issue does not exist in the vacuum of the nuclear family system but is involved intricately with other relationships external to it.

There is a broader aspect to the transactional arena in family behavior. A number of components of the internal relationships are almost totally dominated by relationships external to the family. A husband's occupational role strongly will influence a great many areas of his family life. Ability to spend time with family members, some of the recreational pursuits followed, participation in certain types of community organizations, and a host of other elements of his occupational life-space govern his ability or his inability to relate to family members.

Hill and Hansen (1960:301) use a third term *action,* to refer to "behavior of the single unit with itself or another object or unit as referent." This element is certainly an analytically distinct one in family behavior. We are not interested primarily in the individual's behavior except as it has a transactional or an interactional referent. Those aspects appear to be adequately captured by the interactional and transactional arenas, even though there may be merit in certain circumstances for abstracting out the actional element.

SUMMARY

This chapter and the last one contained a comprehensive description of the problems addressed by the developmental theory and a presentation on the structure of the theory. It was emphasized that central to the analytical concern of developmental theorists is the matter of processual time. Specific discussion of the three facets of developmental analysis identified the peculiar characteristics of this theoretical approach. The kinds of concepts which have been derived and those which are still needed were discussed, and the explanatory problems to be solved presented. Throughout the inquiry, the inadequacies, as well as the adequacies, of the theory were identified. Finally, the two arenas of family behavior were treated.

The remainder of the book deals with how the developmental theory has been applied to the empirical world. More importantly, I will attempt to show ways that the analysis may be used to explain familial behavior in areas which have not been researched by developmental theorists to date. I shall not try to cover all of the research, potential or actual. Rather, I shall attempt to cover enough work to give a reasonable basis for demonstrating the strengths and weaknesses of developmental theory as it now stands.

REFERENCES

ABERLE, DAVID F., ET AL.
  1950 "Functional prerequisites of a society." *Ethics* 60 (January): 100–111.
BATES, FREDERICK L.
  1956 "Position, role and status: a reformulation of concepts." *Social Forces* 34 (May): 313–21.
BELL, NORMAN W., and EZRA F. VOGEL, EDS.
  1968 *A Modern Introduction to the Family*, rev. ed. New York: The Free Press.
BENNETT, JOHN W., and MELVIN W. TUMIN
  1948 *Social Life.* New York: Alfred A. Knopf, Inc.
BIERSTEDT, ROBERT
  1963 *The Social Order.* New York: McGraw-Hill Book Company.
BLOOD, ROBERT O., and DONALD M. WOLFE
  1960 *Husbands and Wives.* Glencoe, Ill.: The Free Press.
BOSSARD, JAMES H. S.
  1945 "The law of family interaction." *American Journal of Sociology* 50 (January): 292–94.
BROOM, LEONARD, and PHILIP SELZNICK
  1968 *Sociology*, 4th ed. New York: Harper & Row, Publishers.
BUCKLEY, WALTER
  1967 *Sociology and Modern Systems Theory.* Englewood Cliffs, N.J.: Prentice-Hall, Inc.

1968 "Society as a complex adaptive system." Pp. 490–513 in Buckley (ed.), *Modern Systems Research for the Behavioral Scientist.* Chicago: Aldine Publishing Company.

CHRISTENSEN, HAROLD T.
1960 "Children in the family: relationship of number and spacing to marital success." *Journal of Marriage and the Family* 30 (May): 283–89.

CLARK, LINCOLN H., ED.
1955 *The Life Cycle and Consumer Behavior.* Vol. 2 in the *Consumer Behavior* series. New York: New York University Press.

CLAUSEN JOHN A.
1966 "Family structure, socialization and personality." Pp. 15–27 in L. W. and M. L. Hoffman (eds.), *Review of Child Development,* Vol. 2. New York: Russell Sage Foundation.

DAVIS, KINGSLEY
1959 "The myth of functional analysis." *American Sociological Review* 24 (December): 757–72.

DUVALL, EVELYN M.
1971 *Family Development,* 4th ed. Philadelphia: J.B. Lippincott Company.

EDWARDS, JOHN N.
1969 "Familial behavior as social exchange." *Journal of Marriage and the Family* 31 (August): 518–26.

FOOTE, NELSON, ED.
1961 *Consumer Behavior: Models of Household Decision-Making.* New York: New York University Press.

GOLDSTEIN, JOSEPH, and JAY KATZ
1965 *The Family and the Law.* New York: The Free Press.

GOSLIN, DAVID A., ED
1969 *Handbook of Socialization Theory and Research.* Chicago: Rand McNally & Company.

HAVIGHURST, ROBERT J.
1953 *Human Development and Education.* New York: Longmans, Green and Company.

HENDERSHOT, GERRY E.
1969 "Familial satisfaction, birth order, and fertility values." *Journal of Marriage and the Family* 31 (February): 27–33.

HILL, REUBEN
1961 "Patterns of decision-making and the accumulation of family assets." Pp. 57–80 in Nelson Foote (ed.), *Consumer Behavior: Models of Household Decision-Making.* New York: New York University Press.

1963   "Judgment and consumership in the management of family re-
        sources." *Sociology and Social Research* 47 (July): 446–60.

1965   "Decision making and the family cycle." Pp. 112–39 in Ethel
        Shanas and Gordon F. Streib (eds.), *Social Structure and the
        Family*. Englewood Cliffs, N.J.: Prentice-Hall, Inc.

1970   *Family Development in Three Generations*. Cambridge, Mass.:
        Schenkman Publishing Company, Inc.

1971   "Modern systems theory and the family: A confrontation." *Social
        Science Information* 10 (October): 7–26.

———, and DONALD A. HANSEN
1960   "The identification of conceptual frameworks utilized in family
        study." *Marriage and Family Living* 12 (November): 299–311.

INHELDER, BARBEL
1957   "Developmental psychology." *Annual Review of Psychology*
        8:139–62. Also each year thereafter to the present.

JACOBSEN, R. BROOKE
1968   *Intrafamily Modes of Socialization: Theoretical Development and
        Test*. Unpublished doctroal dissertation. Eugene, Oregon: Univer-
        sity of Oregon, Department of Sociology.

KAMMEYER, KENNETH
1967   "Birth order as a research variable." *Social Forces* 46 (September):
        71–80.

KEPHART, WILLIAM M.
1950   "A quantitative analysis of intragroup relationships." *American
        Journal of Sociology* 55 (May): 544–49.

KIRKPATRICK, CLIFFORD
1967   "Familial development, selective needs, and predictive theory."
        Journal of Marriage and the Family 29 (May): 229–36.

KOHLBERG, LAWRENCE
1969   "Stage sequence: the cognitive-developmental approach to sociali-
        zation." Pp. 347–480 David Goslin (ed.), *Handbook of Socializa-
        tion Theory and Research*. Chicago: Rand McNally & Company.

MENCHER, SAMUEL
1967   "Social authority and the family." *Journal of Marriage and the
        Family* 29 (February): 164–92.

MURDOCK, GEORGE PETER
1949   *Social Structure*. New York: The MacMillan Company.

NYE, F. IVAN, and LOIS W. HOFFMAN
1963   *The Employed Mother in America*. Chicago: Rand McNally &
        Company.

PARSONS, TALCOTT
1951 *The Social System*. Glencoe, Ill.: The Free Press.

QUEEN, STUART A., AND JOHN B. ADAMS
1952 *The Family in Various Cultures*. Chicago: J. B. Lippincott Company.

REISS, IRA L.
1965 "The universality of the family: a conceptual analysis." *Journal of Marriage and the Family* 27 (November): 343–53.

RHEINGOLD, HARRIET L.
1969 "The social and socializing infant." Pp. 779–90 in David Goslin (ed.), *Handbook of Socialization Theory and Research*. Chicago: Rand McNally & Company.

RHEINSTEIN, MAX
1965 "Motivation of intergenerational behavior by norms of law." Pp. 241–66 in Ethel Shanas and Gordon F. Streib (eds.), *Social Structure and the Family: Generational Relations*. Englewood Cliffs, N.J.: Prentice-Hall, Inc.

RICHER, STEPHEN
1968 "The economics of child rearing." *Journal of Marriage and the Family* 30 (August): 462–66.

RODGERS, ROY H.
1962 *Improvements in the Construction and Analysis of Family Life Cycle Categories*. Kalamazoo, Mich.: School of Graduate Studies, Western Michigan University.

——— 1964 "Toward a theory of family development." *Journal of Marriage and the Family* 26 (August): 262–70.

——— 1966 "The occupational role of the child: a research frontier in the developmental conceptual framework." *Social Forces* 45 (December): 217–24.

SAMPSON, EDWARD E.
1965 "The study of ordinal position: antecedents and outcomes." Pp. 175–228 in Brendan A. Maher (ed.), *Progress in Experimental Personality Research*, Vol. 2. New York: Academic Press.

SIRJAMAKI, JOHN
1948 "Cultural configurations in the American family." *American Journal of Sociology* 53 (May): 464–70.

SPIRO, MELFORD
1956 *Kibbutz: Venture in Utopia*. Cambridge, Mass.: Harvard University Press.

——— 1958 *Children of the Kibbutz*. Cambridge, Mass.: Harvard University Press.

STRAUSS, ANSELM
    1962 "Transformations of identity." Pp. 63–85 in Arnold M. Rose
          (ed.), *Human Behavior and Social Processes*. Boston: Houghton-
          Mifflin Company.

TOMEH, AIDA K.
    1969 "Birth order and kinship affiliation." *Journal of Marriage and the
          Family* 31 (February): 19–26.

VARGA, ROBERT
    1965 "Dilemmas of a househusband." *Saturday Review* (January): 100–
          103.

VOGEL, EZRA F.
    1963 *Japan's New Middle Class: The Salary Man and His Family in a
          Tokyo Suburb*. Berkeley: University of California Press.

4

Operationalizing the Theoretical Approach

It is not possible to move directly from a theory to a research project. The concepts of a theory are stated in abstract terms, whereas research problems are always stated in concrete terms of observable behaviors. It is necessary to translate the abstract concepts of a theoretical formulation into the empirically based activities of a research problem. This interpretation is done by systematically moving through each of the concepts of a theory applicable to a particular research problem and by specifying what observable behaviors the investigator will take to stand for these concepts. Redefining an idea in terms of some behavioral phenomenon results in an *operational definition*, and the entire process is usually referred to as "operationalizing the theory." In the chapters ahead, I will be discussing various ways in which the theory has been or may be applied to particular research problems. In preparation for that discussion, there are a number of issues related to the process of operationalization to which I want to give attention. In the inquiry to follow, a basic understanding of the methodological procedures necessary for carrying out behavioral research is assumed. I will not treat, therefore, matters pertaining to sampling, data gathering instruments, statistical or other data-analysis techniques, or similar aspects of basic research methods (for such discussions see Christensen, 1964, Chapters 6–10; Hoffman and Lippitt, 1960).

FORMULATING RESEARCH RELEVANT
TO A PARTICULAR THEORY

The way a research problem is formulated depends to some degree on two factors: The first involves how much may be known already about the problem. If there is at present a considerable body of empirical data in the area, it is possible for a researcher to increase his explicitness and his precision in posing the problem which he intends to explore. If, on the other hand, there is relatively little work to which he can refer, he will probably have to be much more general in the way he designs the study. Second, the degree to which a theoretical framework has been developed also will govern the kind of research attempted. The richer the body of theory available, the more able the researcher will be in specifying the variables which will concern him. In essence, the degree of theoretical development and supporting empirical data influences whether the researcher will be engaged in an *exploratory* or in an *explanatory* research venture.

Exploratory research is generally undertaken to identify the variables of a problem, to discover additional variables, to increase information on the relationships which may exist between variables previously identified, and, in general, to broaden the base of knowledge in a particular area of behavior. On the theoretical side, exploratory research may aid in devising concepts and in suggesting a manner in which these concepts are related to one another. Explanatory research, on the other hand, is called for where enough is known empirically and where there is adequate theoretical development to specify to some extent the anticipated relationships which may exist in a given area. Explanatory research is undertaken to verify and to make more explicit the exact nature of relationships between variables indicated by a theory. This distinction should become clearer in the following discussion.

In the developmental literature on the family, considerable work has been accomplished in conceptualizing the societal-institutional and the group-interactional facets. In addition, empirical work has been done which, though not necessarily carried out from a developmental theoretical perspective, provides us with a good deal of information on the behavioral characteristics of the family in the two facets. In contrast, the theoretical development in the individual-psychological facet is severely limited. Furthermore, although we have much research on the psychological development of individuals, the empirical literature on the relationships of individual psychological characteristics to family behavior is also quite sparse. Therefore, the formulation of research in this latter area will differ considerably from its development in the former two areas.

In planning research focusing on the individual-psychological facet, the investigator is much more likely to begin with general *research questions*. He may, for example, simply ask this broad question: "In this phenomenon of family behavior which I intend to study, what are the key variables operating in the individual-psychological realm, and to which concepts may they be related?" Or, perhaps, having identified what he believes to be the key variables and their conceptual significance, he may ask: "How are these variables related to one another to bring about the phenomenon that I have observed?" At this level, he is exploring the area to gain enough empirical data so that he may build a theoretical framework to account for what he has observed.

If enough exploratory work has been done, the inquiry may take a considerably different form. The researcher may begin with certain theoretical *propositions* (Dubin, 1969: Chapter 7). A proposition is a general statement of relationships between concepts which is derived logically from the theoretical framework. For example, in the theoretical formulation of the family as a social system, the conceptual framework indicates that the system is composed of a number of positions, each of which consists of a set of roles. These roles always have at least one reciprocal role in another position of that system. A proposition derived from this theoretical perspective, then, is that a change in a given role will bring about modifications in the roles reciprocal to it. This reasoning involves simply a logical deduction from the constructed theoretical framework. If the theory has been developed further concerning certain types of change which may take place —perhaps incorporating particular group-interactional and individual-psychological conceptual elements—the logically deduced propositions may be even more specific in stating the kinds of change which may be expected to occur. These propositions, however, remain at a general level and may be applied to a variety of behavioral situations to which they may refer conceptually. Furthermore, since propositions are stated in abstract terms, they must be operationalized before they can be useful for research.

The operationalized form of a proposition is a *hypothesis* (Dubin, 1969: Chapter 9). Hypotheses are always stated in terms of the empirically observable behavioral units which the researcher has constructed to stand for his abstract concepts. Hypotheses are developed to test the propositions of a theory, which in turn verify the theory. For, if propositions logically derived from a given framework are found to be empirically accurate, then the theory from which those propositions are derived must also be correct.

We can illustrate this process of moving from theory to propositions to hypotheses with the classic restatement of Durkheim's theory of suicide made several years ago by Robert K. Merton (1957:97). He set forth the following four statements:

1. Social cohesion provides psychic support to group members subjected to acute stresses and anxieties.
2. Suicide rates are functions of *unrelieved* anxieties and stresses to which persons are subjected.
3. Catholics have greater social cohesion than Protestants.
4. Therefore, lower suicide rates should be anticipated among Catholics than among Protestants.

The first statement in this series is essentially a proposition derived from a theory of social cohesion. Statement 2 is an operationalization designed to empirically measure unrelieved anxieties and stresses. (It should be noted that no direct attempt is made to operationalize anxieties and stresses in order to measure them.) Statement 3 is an assertion concerning the level of social cohesion in two groups to be studied. Actually, the concept of social cohesion would have to be operationalized in some fashion, and higher social cohesion demonstrated empirically among Catholics as compared to Protestants using this operational definition. In this case, however, let us assume that such empirical evidence was already present. Statement 4 is a hypothesis designed to test the general proposition that social cohesion provides psychic support. Notice that there are other possible ways of operationalizing the same proposition and, therefore, other possible hypotheses to test it. For example, two groups of subjects may be compared after it has been determined on some operational measure that one group has higher social cohesion than the other. It then may be hopothesized that the group with higher social cohesion will score lower on a psychological instrument designed to show anxiety and stress. In this case, the operational definition of anxiety and stress becomes the *score* on a psychological test. Another possibility is to select people who show differences in anxiety on some measurement and to hypothesize that individuals high in anxiety will tend to seek membership in groups with tight social cohesion. All these possible hypotheses are derived from the same basic proposition, which is in turn drawn from a general theory concerning social cohesion. It also may be pointed out that there may exist other propositions concerning the relationship of social cohesion to other kinds of behavior. Thus, the proposition may be set forth that social cohesion is related to some political stance, conservative vs. liberal, for example. A number of hypotheses may be generated to test such a proposition.

The test of a hypothesis yields several results. The determination of whether the hypothesis has been confirmed or disconfirmed, of course, is subject to the usual statistical and other methodological standards. If the hypothesis is supported by the data, then backing has been gained for the proposition from which it was derived. Confirmation of several different hypotheses derived from the same proposition can be taken as confirmation of the proposition. And, finally, if a great many propositions derived from a given theory are confirmed, these verifications provide support for the theory. Such a situation, however, is scientific utopia. The more usual experience, especially in the behavioral sciences, is that some hypotheses are supported, and others are rejected. In addition, some hypotheses have higher levels of support than others. Thus, there are usually mixed results from empirical testing.

Mixed results should not cause dismay, however. It will be recalled that I took the position with Dubin that the testing of theories was designed to improve them. The source of the improvement is found in the mixed outcomes of testing hypotheses. Rejection of a hypothesis leads the researcher to find out why it failed. As a result of this search, new variables may be discovered which need to be taken into account. These findings lead to the introduction of new concepts into the theory and to the generation of fresh or refined propositions. Another outcome of the failure to confirm a hypothesis may be the improvement in the operationalization of concepts. This process has the consequence of sharpening the definition of the basic ideas, since the inadequacy of the operationalization of a concept may be due to the ambiquity of the concept itself.

Little can be gained from moving through the various concepts of the developmental theory and from providing operational definitions for them. Operationalization is carried out with respect to a specific research problem designed to explore clearly stated research questions (in the case of exploratory research) or carefully formulated hypotheses drawn from logically deduced propositions of the theory (in the case of explanatory research). In the chapters ahead, a number of possible or actual research problems will be examined. There are two matters, however, to which I want to direct attention because they have been consistently a part of the history of family developmental work. Each of these is related directly to the process of operationalization.

TWO IMPORTANT
OPERATIONAL MATTERS

Two ideas were mentioned earlier, developmental tasks and family life cycle stages. One cannot spend much time with literature in the developmental area without encountering these two concepts. Both provide an opportunity to illustrate some of the experiences encountered in operationalizing the developmental theory.

Developmental Tasks

In Chapter 3, I discussed the classic definition of developmental task first presented by Havighurst (1953:2), and I presented my redefinition of the idea using the concepts of this theory (Rodgers, 1962:54–55). I stated that the developmental task may be conceptualized as a special case of the latent role becoming manifest in a role cluster at a particular point in a positional career. Now I want to go one step further. Both in the original statement and in the restatement of the idea, there appears a proposition derived from a broad theoretical framework. The statement reads as follows: When the occupant of a given position in a family system reaches a particular place in his positional career having a particular individual-psychological developmental history in a given group-interactional and societal-institutional setting, then certain normative expectations will be placed upon him to take on a given role. The proposition goes on to assert that if he does so, certain consequences will occur for the actor and for the system in terms of the current situation and in terms of future positional and familial careers. Conversely, if he does not take on a specified role, other consequences will result for the actor and for the system. This example illustrates how a theoretical point of view leads to certain statements about some relationships anticipated between elements of the system described by the theoretical point of view. Such propositions must be tested empirically, and to do so, the proposition must be operationalized (see Magrabi and Marshall, 1965, for one such effort). The proposition given above is so general as to yield a multitude of hypotheses. Any position in a given family system as defined by the societal-institutional and by the group-interactional normative structures can yield hypotheses relevent to this basic proposition. The process involves specifying some physical, some psychological, and/or some social developmental state of the occupant of the position and specifying what normative expectations are associated with his condition. Fulfilling this requirement leads to the observable behaviors anticipated as a result of a proposition derived from the theory. Then research must be done to determine whether such behaviors actually are observed.

The developmental-task proposition seems especially germane to the individual-psychological facet, where it provides an excellent possibility for bridging between issues dealing merely with individuals to those which involve the family and other societal systems. Duvall (1971:148–54) also discusses family developmental tasks, as distinguished from individual developmental tasks. It appears that similar bridging from the group-interactional facet to the individual-psychological and/or the societal-institutional aspects is opened up by researching the equivalent proposition for the family group to that of the individual actors.

Family Life Cycle Stages

A central operational problem is presented by the developmental concepts which reflect the time and the change elements in family dynamics. Role sequence, positional career, and family career all require a method of operationalization which will enable the researcher to deal with the changes occurring in these sequences and careers. What is needed is the equivalent of the seconds, minutes, hours, days, and other units created to deal with chronological time. In the developmental theory, however, the units must be able to capture differences which occur in *processual* time. The basic way that these units are distinguished arises out of some variation in the structure of the roles and positions at one point in time as compared with another point in time. The problem the researcher has taken will determine the characteristics which he will think must be highlighted for comparison. His units of time will be based on these properties. In contrast to units of chronological time, his processual units will not all have the same chronological length. By whatever definition he develops, however, they will have as nearly the same processual length as possible—that is, they will represent comparable processual units. The term typically used for these units has been *stage*. Researchers develop units of family interaction which they wish to compare for some purpose, and they label these units *stages of the family life cycle.* (I prefer the term *category* over *stage* and *career* over *life cycle* for reasons that I have detailed elsewhere [Rodgers, 1962:23–25].) For example, we read of the courtship stage, the engagement stage, the early-marriage stage, the childbearing stage, and so on. These labels represent periods in the family career which are internally homogeneous with respect to some characteristics of importance to the person who developed them and which also are differentiated from each other on these same characteristics.

For example, a researcher proposes that distinctions will exist in economic consumption patterns in families at various periods of their careers. He first must identify at least two stages for comparison. He then decides that he will make his differentiation on the basis of the developmental level of the children (and, by implication in developmental theory, on the basis of the developmental levels of the reciprocal positions of father and mother). He further decides that one of the periods will be childhood and the other will be adolescence. He *operationalizes* the childhood stage by stating the characteristics which a family must have to be categorized in this period, and he does the same for the adolescent stage. Perhaps all that he does is to specify the age limits of the children in the two categories. He then will compare families in these two stages on certain aspects of purchasing behavior. What he has said, in effect, is that purchasing role behavior of actors in families with children at a certain developmental level will differ from purchasing role behavior of families with children at another developmental level.

I want to point out some features which this example shows about operationalization. The researcher is involved in a whole set of *decisions* about his categories. These classifications are not real but imposed on the family career by the researcher in order to make comparisons which he considers important. Thus, different categories may be developed for different problems; that is, the family career may be broken up in various ways for various purposes. This decision is *operational*. Such resolutions are not simply arbitrary but are made within the limits of the hypotheses which are being tested and within the requirements of the theory the researcher is using. He tries to develop those categories which will give him the best chance to explain the behavior he observes in the light of the theory he is using.

The family career categories most frequently used in writings reflect statistically typical families moving through statistically typical careers (Duvall, 1971; Glick, 1947, 1955, 1957; Glick and Parke, 1965; Lansing and Kish, 1957). These researchers have stated their problem implicitly as follows: "Let us take as our problem the explanation of some behavior of families which move through their careers as 'most' American families are expected to do." Their family career categories, then, are constructed to allow them to deal with their problem.

Other points requiring different ways of operationalizing the family career categories can be approached developmentally. The problem may be to analyze how behavior changes when the family career involves the death of a parent or child. Or the problem may be to examine the careers of families established by the marriage of two people who have been divorced or widowed and who enter the new bond with children from their previous unions. The family career categories for these two problems probably will be somewhat different. The researcher's attempt will be to explain most effectively the behavior found in such families by deriving propositions from the developmental theory, by formulating hypotheses to test the propositions, and by devising operational definitions for the various concepts of the theory most appropriate to these kinds of family career. The family-career categories which may be developed will be based on the kinds of role cluster, role complex, positional careers, and family careers which appear in these families, rather than some previously derived set of classifications developed for some other research problem. Although part of the explanation of behavior observed may come from comparisons of the families with statistically typical ones, the analysis will not need to be limited to explanations based on such comparisons.

In creating the categories, the researcher also will want to avoid overemphasis on one position or one set of positions. Although a research problem may focus on the actor occupying a specified position in the family, carefully following the developmental theory usually will lead to the operationalization of concepts and to the derivation of propositions which involve the other positions in the system. It will be less likely to assume that a given position, such as the youngest child, oldest child, or parent, determines the behavior in the family. Rather, although the actor in a given position may be having a very dramatic effect on family dynamics in certain situations, the actors in the other positions are also initiating action as well as reacting to that actor. If the focus is on a particular position in the system, the family career categories constructed will certainly be capable of handling the changes which occur in the career of that position. They will not ignore, however, the other positions and their reciprocal relations with the focal position.

The operationalization of a theory with respect to family career categories, therefore, takes us back to the basic concepts of role sequence, role complex, positional career, and family career. The categories themselves are devices for helping the analyst to isolate and to identify the behavioral expressions of these ideas which are critical to his particular problem. Remember that any change in the normative content of a role constitutes a new role and, thus, a new period in a role sequence and in a positional career. A change also means that the role complexes of which that role is a part are modified, thus modifying the family career. In operationalizing these concepts to express this complex process, the analyst must decide which normative alterations are significant enough to constitute a new behavior situation and, thus, a new family career category. He may wish to devise several categories which are related to changes in a particular role or in a particular role complex but which cover only a relatively limited segment of the entire positional and/or family career. On the other hand, he may wish to devise categories which will provide him with the means to analyze a considerable portion or the entire career of a position or of the family system. *Family career categories, then, are simply summarizing statements of particular role sequences, role complexes, positional or family careers which are of significance to a particular analytical problem.* Family career categories are defined always in terms of some problem and have little or no meaning independent of it. When someone refers to the establishment stage of the family, he usually is referring to the role sequences and to the role complexes associated with the period in the family system which occurs immediately after marriage and which extends to some later major role change, frequently the arrival of the first child. Labelling the category itself, however, is only useful if we have some information about the research problem in which the classification will be used and about the research questions or propositions which will be examined by the analyst.

To summarize the matter, the deviation of any specific set of family career categories is primarily dependent on the kind of research problem to be investigated. As is true in the operationalization of the basic concepts to apply to a given problem, no one right set of categories exists. Although the set developed by one analyst may be used directly by another, it may be preferable to develop a new set which adequately meets the needs of the specific problem. Of course, it is always desirable to use previously developed operations, if they are appropriate, since this application contributes to the accumulation of comparable research findings. If the operations are inappropriate, however, the results of the research will be less satisfactory, and the cumulative nature of those results will have little value. It is also true that a given research problem may be formulated for the express purpose of testing the explanatory power of a given set of categories as opposed to another set (Rodgers, 1962). The purpose of such an attempt is actually to develop, of course, a set of operational definitions which are effective in research. A given operational definition may be more valid than a competing one. One way of testing the validity is to compare the explanatory power of the two operational definitions in research.

I have examined two matters related to operationalizing the developmental theory which are peculiarly associated with it. There are some other general problems related to the strategies that one might use in testing theories.

STRATEGIES FOR TESTING THEORIES

Just as no one correct way exists to operationalize the concepts of a theory for research, various strategies may be used in designing the investigation. How a researcher lays his plans for testing a theory will depend on his own particular substantive interests, the funds and facilities which he may have available, and the amount of time which he may have to devote to his interests. Although the availability of funds and research facilities may limit the scope of a given project, the ultimate quality of that project will be more contingent on the skill and the ability of the researcher, assuming he has the time to devote to the plan. Some of the best research has been carried out under very limited physical and fiscal conditions.

Some researchers set out to put an entire theoretical system to the test. The range of such an undertaking, of course, is dependent upon the extent of the behavior which the theory attempts to explain. As we have seen, the developmental theoretical system attempts to interpret behavior within a broad scope and over long time spans. Consequently, to achieve this ambition will require a major investment in time and funds. In addition, a number of unresolved theoretical and methodological issues probably should be addressed before a full-scale effort is initiated. Taking all of these factors into account, then, it seems unlikely that a strategy aimed at assessing the entire theory will be selected by anyone for some time to come.

In adopting a more limited research goal, the investigator has several possible bases for selection of a specific research problem. The most obvious, of course, is to pick an area for study in which he has personal interest. Thus, an investigator may be concerned particularly with the following: husband-wife interactions; sibling relationships; parent-child interactions; power or decision-making processes; the development of specific roles; political, religious, economic, or educational activities; families with excess or deficit structures, mental or physical disabilities; and so on. There are a host of potential propositions which may be formulated to test the developmental theory in any of these areas. The advantage of such a modest strategy is that the high interest on the part of the researcher is likely to keep him motivated enough to follow through on a continuing stream of research which may in time accumulate a substantial base of empirical support for the theory in that limited area. A disadvantage, on the other hand, may be that certain fields in need of empirical investigation and theoretical extension remain untouched.

A researcher consciously may approach his contemplated research by seeking out problems which appear to be central or salient to the viability of the theory. He may, as Dubin (1969:175–77) puts it, select "strategic propositions" for his attention. In seizing on this tactic, the investigator will be attempting to submit the theory to some critical tests as a way of improving it in the most efficient manner. For example, a researcher may set out to test a proposition that a family's ability to meet a major crisis or disaster is explained most fully by certain developmental variables as opposed to some other set of variables, such as educational level, economic position, or community support. The comparison of competing explanations is an excellent and commonly used way of proving strategic propositions.

Finally, an investigator may proceed with the objective of further specifying or expanding a particular area of the theory which is not fully developed. This goal may place him in the position of doing exploratory research or of dealing with propositions which are less rigorous than those found in more highly developed research areas in their statement of anticipated relationships. The value of such research, nevertheless, is high, since it is a necessary foundation for the exacting requirements of the explanatory investigation to follow. Since earlier discussion has indicated some of the areas in which research following this exploratory procedure may be appropriate and since we will be encountering such fields in the chapters to come, I shall not dwell any further on this subject now.

In initiating a particular research project, a researcher may have more than one of the above strategies in mind. Or, even though he may have a single objective, the payoff of his research may yield results which contribute in one or more ways. There are several possible areas where a researcher may focus his attention while he is achieving one or more of these general research objectives. He may wish to work strictly with interactional or with transactional studies. He may focus on a specific facet of family development analysis. He may undertake a problem in which he analyzes a given role or role cluster in some depth and which he follows through in a considerable portion of its career. He may place the focus on a particular developmental category, that is, on a specific role complex, which carries some special interest theoretically or behaviorally. He may select a particular behavioral phenomenon and may explore the implications for a developmental explanation. Finally, the investigator may choose a comparative approach, preferring to deal with two or more different cultural or subcultural settings, with two or more roles or positions, or with two or more developmental periods. Although a theory directs the researcher's attention to a particular kind of explanatory approach, considerable freedom remains to choose a variety of investigatory activities in pursuit of the verification of that theory.

A PREVIEW

In the chapters to follow, I shall refer to a number of research problems which have been investigated or which may be undertaken and which have the potentiality for contributing to testing and to improving developmental theory. I shall be dividing these points differently than I have before, however. I shall begin with three chapters dealing with research on families essentially normal in the sense that their structure and the functioning of the actors do not involve atypical factors. The first two chapters will deal with interactional analysis, and the third main division will focus on transactional analysis. Having established a kind of base line for comparison, I shall turn in the next two chapters to families which do not fit the norm. The first of these will analyze family systems in which either the structure or the actors within the system are atypical in some way. The succeeding chapter will deal with the implications of various kinds of stress for positional and for family careers. Since the great bulk of the theoretical and the empirical work available deals with families in American society, I shall tend to restrict the discussion along those lines. A well-developed theory is ideally applicable to a broad range of cultural settings. I shall conclude this section on testing the theory, therefore, with a discussion of the application of developmental theory to American subcultures and to non-American cultural settings. Although the empirical work available is limited, I shall attempt to show that, even in its present state, it is possible to test the theory in a variety of cultures other than in dominant middle-class white America. My anticipation is that these discussions will demonstrate both the empirical base which now exists to support the developmental approach and, at the same time, will indicate the kind of work which remains to be accomplished.

REFERENCES

CHRISTENSEN, HAROLD, ED.
  1964 *Handbook of Marriage and the Family*. Chicago: Rand McNally & Company.

DUBIN, ROBERT
  1969 *Theory Building*. New York: The Free Press.

DUVALL, EVELYN M.
  1971 *Family Development*, 4th ed. Philadelphia: J. B. Lippincott Company.

GLICK, PAUL C.
  1947 "The family cycle." *American Sociological Review* 12 (April): 164–74.

———
  1955 "The life cycle of the family." *Marriage and Family Living* 18 (February): 3–9.

———
  1957 *American Families*. New York: John Wiley & Sons, Inc.

———, AND ROBERT PARKE, JR.
  1965 "New approaches in studying the life cycle of the family." *Demography* 2: 187–202.

HAVIGHURST, ROBERT J.
  1953 *Human Development and Education*. New York: Longmans, Green and Company.

HOFFMAN, LOIS W., AND RONALD LIPPITT
  1960 "The measurement of family life variables." Chapter 22 in P. H. Mussen (ed.), *Handbook of Research Methods in Child Development*. New York: John Wiley & Sons, Inc.

LANSING, JOHN.B., AND LESLIE KISH
  1957 "Family life cycle as an independent variable." *American Sociological Review* 22 (October): 512–19.

MAGRABI, FRANCES M., AND WILLIAM H. MARSHALL
  1965 "Family developmental tasks: a research model." *Journal of Marriage and the Family* 27 (November): 454–61.

MERTON, ROBERT K.
1957   Social Theory and Social Structure, rev. ed. Glencoe, Ill.: The Free
Press.
RODGERS, ROY H.
1962   *Improvements in the Construction and Analysis of Family Life
Cycle Categories.* Kalamazoo, Mich.: School of Graduate Studies,
Western Michigan University.

5

Family Careers— Interactional Analysis:

Recruitment, Maintenance of Biological Functioning, and Socialization

In introducing the developmental conceptual framework in Chapter 3, I distinguished between explanations of family behavior which were derived from behavioral or normative patterns external to the family system and those which were derived from within the family system. The former type of explanation was called *transactive* and the latter type *interactive*. My concern in this chapter and in the following one will be with explanations which are chiefly or primarily interactive. The discussion of interactional research has been divided by using the major functions introduced in Chapter 3. This approach provides a useful way of focusing on a particular area of research analysis while, at the same time, it gives the freedom to range through the various research strategies identified in the last chapter. There will be no attempt to exhaust any particular area, either in covering every possible strategy or in reviewing all the research which may have been carried out. I want to provide enough material to show that the developmental theory is a viable one for empirical research and to provide some indication of the directions which past research has taken and which future work may take. As a consequence, I hope to stimulate the reader to extend for himself the implications which the developmental theory has for research and, perhaps, to launch some readers on an exciting intellectual pursuit.

Although I shall be using the basic functions as a way of dividing up the focus of the analysis, keep in mind that functionalism is not the *theoretical* focus. Rather, as each area is examined, keep alert to the three basic facets of analysis: societal-institutional, group-interactional, and individual-psychological. Of course, remember the basic concepts already shown to be central to the theoretical approach.

REPRODUCTION AND RECRUITMENT

Typically, reproduction is relegated to the childbearing stage and is concerned almost exclusively with biological reproduction of offspring. But reproduction is an issue which is salient to the family over a major portion of its career continuing well beyond the childbearing period. Furthermore, there are two other processes by which new members may be added to the family structure, namely, adoption and mate selection.

The case of adoption is fairly clear. Although American norms tend to emphasize adoption of children in infancy and during the relatively youthful period for parents, primarily because this span is viewed as the best time for both child and parent, adoptions do occur for children even into the teen years and by parents who are in their forties and beyond. Thus, whereas adoption of an infant child by parents in their twenties and thirties may approximate (though certainly is not identical with) the process of biological reproduction and may have similar antecedents and consequences in the family career, other types of adoption almost certainly have strikingly different implications for the role dynamics of the family. We shall take an initial look at adoption in this chapter but will return to it in the discussion of the atypical role complexes in a later chapter.

The process of mate selection as a form of recruitment is somewhat more problematic. In the nuclear family system, the process is essentially the stage before the establishment period or, perhaps a phase of it. Sometimes it is taken up in the analysis of the launching stage of the nuclear family (Duvall, 1971). In this context, the focus is generally on the impact of the departure of a member from the nuclear family and almost never on the impact on the newly established family. The consequence is that *developmental* analysis of mate selection in nuclear family systems is sparse, though a wealth of sociological work on mate selection from a nondevelopmental perspective exists. Although there is a cyclical stance toward the family, each nuclear family seems to come into existence de novo, and the analysis of the establishment stage is often carried out as if the newly married couple had no previous history as a pair before marriage. We shall give this matter more specific attention in a later portion of this chapter.

But what of the application of the developmental approach to the analysis of recruitment and of reproduction in non-nuclear systems? A theoretical method designed to explain family phenomena ought not to be limited to a particular cultural setting. The conceptual framework of developmental theory allows for various normative structures at the societal-institutional level as well as at the group-interactional level. A discussion of reproduction and of recruitment allows an initial consideration of the application of the theory to extended family systems as well as to nuclear ones. A more extensive discussion appears in the chapter on cross-cultural analyses.

Biological Reproduction

There is a certain element of irony in the fact that the quest for empirical support for the developmental theory begins with this process. Surely no area of human behavior is more closely associated with the family or has a more basic impact on family careers. There is an overwhelming body of literature concerned with population growth and biological reproduction. A review of the major modern work in this field shows that there are a few monumental studies which may be regarded as primary sources: the Indianapolis study (Kiser and Whelpton, 1943–58), the Growth of American Families study (Freedman et al., 1959; Whelpton et al., 1966), the Family Growth in Metropolitan America study (Westoff et al., 1961, 1963), a series of studies undertaken in the Caribbean area (Stycos, 1955; Hill et al., 1959; Stycos and Back, 1964), and research involving families of middle- and lower-class status in the United States (Rainwater, 1960, 1965). Seven other references round out the basic resources (Chilman and Liu, 1968; Freedman, 1961–62; Kiser, 1962; Liu, 1967; Rainwater, 1967; Hill, 1968a, 1968b).

As the titles of the references imply, there is a general recognition of the relationship between reproduction and the family. Most, though not all, contain the term *family* in their titles. Indeed, one of the sources (Westoff et al., 1961:298) contains the following statement:

> Size of family is in part determined by social relations within the family. Attitudinal and structural variables affect not only the number of children desired but also affect efficacy of fertility planning.   .
>
> No student of fertility seriously contests this premise. . . .

Such a recognition notwithstanding, there is a remarkable paucity of data which attempts to explore the processes of family interaction related to reproduction! With the exceptions to be cited, the great mass of effort has been devoted to identifying demographic characteristics of the samples studied and to utilizing these properties as the major explanatory variables. Such efforts illustrate in a classic manner the precision paradox versus the power paradox identified by Dubin which was discussed in the first chapter.

Although these variables appear to do an admirable job of predicting *outcomes*, they do very little in the way of explaining *process*. Indeed, Westoff et al. (1963:197) concluded in their follow-up study that there was little point in following up family relationships variables in attempting to explain fertility behavior. This readiness to dismiss so precipitously the impact of family variables on reproductive behavior seems particularly strange in view of the authors' own statement made in the earlier volume after discussing the lack of association found between family variables and fertility. At that time, they stated (Westoff et al., 1961:308):

> . . . families are always adjusting to new sets of circumstances, circumstances that affect not only future fertility patterns but also affect the relationships between dependent fertility variables and the independent variables. *This synthesis of past and present in the process of becoming* is best exemplified by the change in the relationship between marital adjustment and desired size of family following a fertility-planning failure. [Italics added.]

The portion of the quotation which is italicized is as an explicit recognition of the developmental character of fertility behavior.

The problem which this series of quotations highlights seems to be generally present in the work reviewed. It is to some extent a matter of the theoretical approach with which the research begins and to some extent a matter of the operationalization of that theory. Aaron V. Cicourel (1967) is particularly illuminating in some comments which he has made on the methodology of fertility studies. He begins from a social-interactionist position which leans heavily on the orientation of Garfinkel (1960, 1964). Cicourel makes two basic arguments, both of which have theoretical as well as methodological implications. First, he points to the fact that most research on population problems begins from a theoretical perspective, which he terms the *table of organization approach*. From such a stance, the emphasis is placed on the standard demographic variables and assumes some sort of rational tie between these variables and the fertility behavior of individuals. The view is a rather simplistic one: "Role taking in everyday life is a function of position in the social structure." Again, the close relationship with the developmental approach can be seen. However, Cicourel (1967:60–61) goes on to argue for a different posture which he defines as a variant of the social interaction approach, in which a new set of variables becomes significant:

> The table of organization view stresses the actor's location in the social order vis-a-vis others, e.g., his familial, occupational, educational, religious affiliation or experience, as stable properties in accounting for the actor's expected behavior. The alternate perspective proposed here

focuses upon the routine, common sense, expected background features of everyday life. . . . What is missing from conventional theories, therefore, is the familiar, common, routine, and usually unnoticed "background expectancies" as invariant features of all social interaction. The actor achieves stability in his perception and interpretation of his environment by necessarily invoking these background expectancies.

Thus, the researcher's structuring of his theory predisposes him to make certain assumptions about the process of human fertility behavior which, in consequence, causes him to miss some major explanatory variables (Cicourel, 1967:63):

> A social interaction conception of the family suggests an ambiguous relationship between the family's social organization and its articulation with problems of population growth. A source of confusion here stems from the observer's failure to separate the intended rationality of scientific theorizing and research, from actor's common sense reasoning in everyday life. The rationality of everyday life, the rationality of the "man on the street," is not to be confused with the scientific rationalities implied in the scientist's construction of a model. Everyday rationality relies upon a world of appearances and folk notions of achieving practical solutions to practical problems.

This point of view is extremely compatible with the further insights of developmental theory in emphasizing the modification in normative structures of families brought about by the everyday interactional experience of the actors and by the initiated action of individual occupants of positions.

The second argument made by Cicourel deals with the way one gathers data. Here he points out that collecting information is itself an interactional experience. Researchers cannot assume that the meaning which they have attached to the wording of their questions is the same one which the respondents will attach, given the "everyday rationality" which is derived from their interactive histories. According to Cicourel (1967:61), the typical data-gathering operation proceeds somewhat as the following extract points out:

> The source of most of the information on fertility and family planning is to be found in some variant of social or sample surveys whereby standard questions are posed and asked orally or written for persons to answer with precoded answers. This methodological strategy is particularly suited to the rationality of the theory proposed above (the "table of organization" perspective) concerning kinship, development, population growth and the survival of society over time. The individual responds to that conception of the world, with whatever alternatives that the researcher presents him, and hence the conception of himself and his way

of life that enables the researcher to decide where the individual stands in the general scheme of things that links kinship with economic development and population growth. The methodology has built into it measurement, theory and substance and the actor's interview participation remains somewhat passive and divorced from his actual day-to-day activities.

Thus, the task of the theorist-researcher is to go beyond this imposed rationality to gather the kind of behavioral data which derives from the day-to-day activities of the respondent and which in turn will provide a more powerful explanation of the phenomenon under investigation. In his article, Cicourel (1967:63–80) provides suggestions for such a method and illustrates it from his own work.

Research on fertility behavior of families which fails to gather extensive data on the interactive patterns of a household cannot possibly hope to find significant relationships between family variables and fertility behavior. *The basic design of the research precludes such findings.* And researchers must ask what the standard demographic variables so frequently utilized as explanatory variables are intended to measure. What behavior do these categories represent? It is not that social class, occupation, religious affiliation, social mobility, residence, and the like are insignificant for fertility behavior. They stand for important interactive phenomena which, along with the everyday family experience, will reveal the processes explaining reproductive behavior. In this particular situation (and I suspect in a number of others), demographic variables are what Dubin (1969:61–62) calls "summative units," by which he means "a global unit that stands for an entire complex thing." He says:

> Analytically a summative unit is one having the property that derives from the interaction among a number of other properties. Without specifying what these other properties are, or without indicating how and under what circumstances they interact, we add them all up in a summative unit. Thus, a summative unit has the characteristic of meaning a great deal, much of which is ill-defined or unspecified. . . . Such units are useless in theories and theoretical models that are designed for the purpose of testing propositions.

Some people who have used such units may feel that to say that they are useless is a bit strong. If one opts for a theoretical approach which will *explain process* and will not simply *predict outcome*, the evaluation seems apt. It is of no small significance that three of the five major studies cited at the beginning of this section do not deal in any notable way with the explanation of process. The Growth of American Families study was almost exclusively demographic in character. The Indianapolis study, certainly a pioneering work, had as one of the major criticisms directed toward it the lack of an organizing theory to guide it (Kiser, 1962:161). The Family Growth in Metropolitan America study, designed to profit from the Indianapolis study experience, originally was intended to correct this inadequacy. The attempt, however, ultimately was given up, and the major effort continued to center on essentially demographic characteristics (Kiser, 1962:161–62).

The central point is that the research does not go beyond the societal-institutional facet for explanation of reproductive behavior. The position appears to be that norms defining the roles attached to the basic demographic divisions of social class, religion, occupation, and so forth, are not modified significantly enough at the group-interactional and at the individual-psychological levels to make any difference in the overall pattern of reproductive behavior. The developmental approach, however, asserts that what happens at these levels does make a difference, and it is a significant one. The societal-institutional facet certainly provides a basic starting point, but the development of analytical categories to deal with the dynamic changes in the positional and in the familial careers within these societal-institutional categories is essential.

The two remaining research efforts reported by Hill et al. (1959) and by Rainwater (1965) provide considerably more potential for explanation from the developmental perspective. Each of these studies indicates dramatically how the basic theoretical approach taken governs the kinds of methods used and the findings which result. Both begin with the kind of sensitivity to the interactional characteristics of fertility behavior (and of the data-gathering process) suggested by Cicourel. Both devote considerable attention to an attempt to identify the key interactive process variables capable of explaining such behavior.

Fertility Behavior in Puerto Rico. In this study, Hill et al. (1959) determined early that their choice of conceptual framework was a crucial decision, since it inevitably would specify the kinds of problems which would command their attention.[1] They related that the alternatives were soon reduced to a choice between structure-function and interactive-system approaches. They selected the interactional frame of reference for the following reasons (Hill et al., 1959:29–30):

> Its key concepts form a set of analytic tools most useful in the study of the dynamics of human fertility. Some of the components of the system are: (1) status and inter-status relations, which become the bases of

[1] It is difficult to do justice to this research in this type of discussion. Since I first became acquainted with the work, it has represented to me an excellent example of how research should be planned, should be executed, and should be reported. I can only urge readers who are particularly interested in the theory-research process to read the volume and some of the other literature which resulted from this project which are listed in Hill et al. (1959:471–73).

authority patterns and initiative taking; (2) role, role conceptions, role taking, role playing, and role organization; and (3) processes of communication, consultation, conflict, compromise, and consensus.

The interactional approach provides more than tools for observation, it provides a body of generalizations about family planning and problem solving which can be drawn upon in the formulation of diagnostic study questions. They may be used as guideposts in the quest for the social psychological antecedents of success in fertility planning and control. These antecedents differ in quality from the psychological and socioeconomic correlates of fertility in previous studies. They pertain to the dynamic quality of interaction systems and are oriented to intragroup processes rather than to individual traits and characteristics.

The project was divided into three phases: (1) an exploratory phase in which field studies were carried out for the purpose of establishing hypotheses; (2) a verification phase in which these hypotheses were tested on a representative sample of families; and (3) an experimental validation phase in which field studies were executed to confirm the importance of the survey variables and to provide some base for action programs (Hill et al., 1959:26–27). Only portions of the second and third phases are directly relevant to our present concerns.

Hill et al. begin with the societal-institutional facet in two major ways: First, they analyze the overall demographic setting of their study by detailing the characteristics of Puerto Rico as a whole and then narrow down their data to an analysis of the demographic characteristics of their study population (Hill et al., 1959:7–23, 51–54). Second and beyond this procedure, they analyze a number of the basic societal-institutional characteristics which may bear on their problem. Thus, they examine the broader implications of demographic and other characteristics, such as the facts that Catholicism is the dominant religion, that the island is highly agricultural, that it has a strong Spanish cultural orientation, and a variety of other matters. Each of these truths in effect sets the societal-institutional normative stage within which the group-interactional and the individual-psychological norms develop (Hill et al., 1959:42–63). The sorting out of this process constitutes the remaining concern of the report.

Without going into detail, a thorough analysis of the size preferences of families, the facilitating mechanisms in planning fertility, and the incidence of birth control led to the development of two typologies of families. One of them was constructed on the dimensions of folk-urban qualities and the other on the dimensions of familistic—person-centered characteristics (Hill et al., 1959:191–217). Though the first of these categories begins with some of the classic demographic variables, Hill et al. use the typology to illuminate the interactive processes relevant to fertility within each of the constructed models. Thus, value orientations, family size preferences, family structure and marital relations characteristics, family action potentials, and fertility control are differentiated within each of the types developed. Similarly, the familistic—person-centered typology is used to explicate the interactive processes occurring within each type, as well as to show the relationship between the demographic background characteristics and these types.

This entire analysis leads to the development of a *preliminary analytic model* isolating key sets of variables and suggesting the initial way they are related to each other and, ultimately, to the behavior to be explained, that is, effective family planning and fertility (Hill et al., 1959:218–40). In this model, the demographic variables of residence, education, occupation, type of marital union, religious affiliation, age at marriage, and rental value of domicile are grouped together as a set of independent variables along with the influence of key reference groups. Their relationship to the dependent variables of effective family planning and fertility, however, is mediated by four sets of *intervening* variables. (Intervening variables are those factors which are found in the explanatory chain between the variable originally believed to explain a phenomenon and the phenomenon being explained. Thus, for example, knowing age alone may explain intention to marry—but knowing educational aspirations of persons of the same age will allow for a better explanation. Therefore, the variable of educational aspiration "intervenes" between age and intention to marry.) They are the following: (1) *general value system*, composed of measures of fatalism-striving, traditionalism-modernism, aspirations for self and for children, and tendencies toward general planning; (2) *informational and attitudinal attributes*, consisting of information about methods, about attitudes toward birth control, and about extent of agreement on birth control; (3) *specific family-size atitudes*, made up of attitudes toward importance of children, ideal family size (present and past), summary index dealing with size preferences of families, pressure of fertility on family resources, and interest in spacing children; and (4) *family-action possibilities*, constructed from measures of marital happiness, agreement on general issues, sexual satisfaction, communication on general issues, communication on family-size ideals and on birth control, modesty handicaps, and familistic organization types (degree of wife autonomy, degree of male dominance, extent of prohibitions exercised by husband, and family readiness for action of birth control).

Dubin's (1969:81) comment on intervening variables is significant here. He states: "To employ the concept of intervening variable usually involves an implicit admission that the starting theoretical model is inadequate and must be supplemented by addition of the intervening variable." In this particular case, it probably is more accurate to say that Hill, Stycos, and Back, having recognized the inadequate explanatory power of demographic variables for fertility behavior, explicitly set out to demonstrate by their model what these categories actually stood for in terms of interactive variables. Indeed, from the developmental perspective, their variables are not intervening ones at all. Rather, they are variables operating at the group-interactional facet and at the individual-psychological facet levels, which specify the dynamic meaning of the societal-institutional demographic variables of a static nature.

After having identified the variables in a preliminary way, the researchers performed a statistical inquiry utilizing both correlational and factor-analytical procedures. The major effect was to reduce from almost fifty to eight the number of factors that showed sufficient strength of relationship with family planning and with fertility. Of these eight, only social status (which included the elements of rental value of domicile, education of husband and wife, occupation of husband and wife) was a demographic factor. This finding provides a rather striking contrast to the other studies cited above. The remaining seven factors were communication, timing of the perception of family size as a problem, planning-striving, ideas about family size, concern about family size, fatalism, and sex and marital adjustment. These components generally correlated higher with the dependent variable of competency in the use of facilities and birth-control methods than with the dependent variable of actual fertility control. The two most highly correlated factors were communication and timing of perception of family size as a problem. That these factors correlated more highly with competency was viewed by the researchers as support for their theoretical approach, since this variable was more closely related to social behavior than to fertility control, which also included biological variations in fecundity.

Lest the impression be given that this analysis resulted in explaining a major share of the dependent variables, it must be reported that the multiple correlation coefficients for all eight variables with the two dependent variables was only 0.365 with competence and 0.261 with fertility control. These findings mean that the eight factors really explained only 13 percent of the variance in competence and 7 percent of fertility control variance. The conclusion must be drawn that some important variables were un-identified. The result does provide, however, an illustration of how a particular statistical method affects the findings of a research project. Some variables which earlier had been identified as providing important insights were lost in the factor analysis. (Two of these variables were familism and empathy.) Others, which could not be quantified adequately, could not be included in the analysis at all. Since earlier they had been shown to have an important bearing on the behavior to be explained and since this research still must be classified as exploratory, it is unwise simply to drop the variables from all further consideration. The fact that they are *theoretically* important should force the researcher to seek out other modes of analytical treatment.

Let us follow this research analysis further. Having carried out the statistical analysis to the point of identifying eight key variables, the investigators constructed a new factor analytic model. This model showed that communication was a central or "hub" (to use the authors' term) variable in explaining the two independent variables. The other most important variable was the timing of perception of family size as a problem. On the basis of this new model, then, the researchers designed an experiment to test whether or not attempts to manipulate the explanatory variables would result in changes in the dependent variables.

The experiment essentially involved various methods of education concerning birth control and the determination of whether these methods changed subsequent planning and fertility behavior of a new sample of families. Four types of respondent families were identified for exposure to the educational program. These four types and their characteristics were as follows (Hill et al., 1959:261):

Respondent Type	Attitudes Toward Family Limitation	Adequacy of Family Organization	Information on Birth Control
Ready	High	High	High
Uninformed	High	High	Low
Ineffective	High	Low	High
Opposed	Low	High	High

The three factors of favorable attitudes toward birth control, adequate family organization, and sufficient information about birth control were viewed as necessary conditions for adequate birth control usage and, thus, for fertility control. The experiment showed that, indeed, these conditions were necessary—but were not *sufficient* to completely explain how to employ birth-control methods. A new variable was identified by the experiment which the researchers called *saliency*. Saliency meant that "contraception had to be recognized as more relevant and important than any other course of action for which the family was presumably also ready" (Hill et al., 1959:327–28). Thus, a new interactive factor in the family behavior was introduced. Further analysis of the experiment showed that changes in values and in commitment to family limitation could cause the *initiation* of birth control. Educational methods could modify the relevant values held by the opposed group and could increase the saliency of the generally favorable members. It also was shown that increasing communication was important in *continuing* consistent use among those who were already employing birth-control methods. Educational techniques appeared to improve communication and, thus, to provide for increasing saliency.

In summary, four basic conditions of the family appeared to be crucial to explaining family planning and fertility behavior: adequate motivation to take action (saliency), knowledge and acceptability of birth-control means, goals related to having a small family, and efficient family organization (Hill et al., 1959:331). Although each was necessary, *all* of them had to be present if *sufficient* conditions were to exist to explain family fertility. Ultimately, therefore, the explanation for fertility behavior rests to a greater degree in the role organization of families than in their demographic characteristics. Whereas the actual statistical findings of this study are inadequate to verify the theory proposed, the essential fact remains that significant progress toward explanation of fertility behavior was made by identifying factors associated with interactional characteristics of families.

Some brief comments concerning the application of this research to the developmental approach are in order. There is ample evidence in the findings of Hill, Stycos, and Back to indicate that the key variables identified have a developmental character to them. This support is most notable in the case of the variable "timing of perception of family size as a problem." It became apparent that as the number of children increased, the impact of the new member on the family began to have an effect on the way the couple viewed the addition of more members. The concept of saliency is, in effect, a recognition of this change in view. Although a particular goal concerning family size may be present and may be recognized by the couple, though this acknowledgment was not always the case, the effect of actually moving toward this goal (and, in the Puerto Rican case, frequently beyond it) had a definite impact on the couple's desire to utilize some means of controlling fertility. Interaction was called for to produce this result. Communication, that is, discussing the desire to limit family size and/or the discussion of the means to do so, composed a necessary interactive process. Family organization, that is, the way roles were defined and were played, also entered into the achievement of the goal. From a developmental perspective, then, it would be important to have data which would show how these key variables change over the career of the family. Such data were not gathered by these researchers. A proposition derived from the developmental theoretical perspective, however, would be that the way the role organization of the family changed with respect to the achievement of the limitation of fertility over the career of the family would go far to explain the outcome of a given household size.

Rainwater's Research. The work which Rainwater (1965) carried out differs in several respects from the Puerto Rican study. Although it uses the same basic interview method, it is essentially exploratory with no attempt to follow up with either a validation or with an experimental phase. Data analysis is considerably less complex with tabulations of percentages and with some use of statistical tests of significance. The primary means of bringing out findings, however, is through the use of quoted excerpts from interviews which illustrate a general finding. Rainwater does not set down a systematic theoretical statement at the beginning but rather follows a general approach which emphasizes the importance of "conjugal role structures." The primary value of this study for our purposes, then, is its wealth of case material and the potentialities which his analysis of role structures provides for further research along this line.

Although he does not negate the value of the classic demographic studies, Rainwater is very clear in his position on their limited value. In this regard, he states (Rainwater, 1965:276–77):

> It is unfortunate that family planning research has been defined primarily as an applied branch of demography, since the concepts of primary usefulness in this field lie not so much within the typical interest and technical competence of demographers as within the range of techniques and interests of family sociologists and social psychologists. The very success of demography in specifying the independent and dependent variables . . . has perhaps tended to encourage overly ambitious standards of certainty in family planning studies . . . [and] to discourage sponsoring agencies and investigators from pursuing other lines of inquiry and to project an overly narrow pattern on the kind of research that is thought of as appropriate for this field.
>
> This study will have achieved its goal if it contributes in a small way to cracking the overly quantitative mold into which those studies seem to have cast our conceptualization of the process by which families come to prefer a particular number of children and are successful in achieving the goals they set for themselves.

Rainwater clearly subscribes to the point of view that demographic variables are only indicators of key interactional characteristics. They are predictive of outcome, but not explanatory of process. He has used two primary demographic characteristics, religion and social class, both of which provide basic societal-institutional normative structural information. The findings with respect to religion are mixed, with some differences between Catholics and non-Catholics being found, but also many similarities. With respect to social class, however, he asserts (Rainwater, 1965:277):

> Further, social class is seen as exercising its influence primarily through two characteristics of the family as a social system which vary from one

class subculture to the other: first, the conjugal role-organization, values, and practices that are characteristic of different social classes, and second, the particular role concepts and the values and practices attendant on them that are deemed appropriate for men and women in different social classes. The first category has to do particularly with the kind of separateness and connectedness, the division of labor, that is characteristic of marital relations; the second has to do with the various non-familial role behaviors that are to be expected of men and women.

As a result of the interview data from both husbands and wives (one hundred fifty-two couples along with fifty husbands and fifty-five wives who were not married to each other), Rainwater adapted a typology of conjugal role-relationships originally developed by Bott (1957) which distinguished three types: (1) joint conjugal role-relationships in which the predominant pattern involved shared or interchangeable activities and where it was expected that even when only one partner had responsibility, the other should be interested and sympathetic with respect to the activity; (2) segregated role-relationships in which the predominant pattern involved separate and different activities for husband and wife but in which they may either be organized into a functioning unit or in which there is a minimum of day-to-day articulation between husband and wife activity; (3) intermediate conjugal role-relationships in which the predominant pattern falls between these two extremes and, although there is considerable emphasis on a formal division of labor, there is also stress on relating as individuals. Thus, in this latter type, husbands and wives do not simply "go their own ways," but neither do they place a strong emphasis on "togetherness." Therefore, much parellel activity takes place in which each partner is carrying out an individual activity but in the presence of the other. The differences between the three types may be illustrated by evening activity in which a husband and wife may engage in refinishing a piece of furniture together or may play a card game (joint), as opposed to the husband going to the local bowling alley while his wife stays home to sew or to iron (segregated), as compared to the husband watching television while his wife reads in the same room (intermediate) (Rainwater, 1965:30–31).

The data show clear class differences in the distribution of these types as follows: upper-middle class, 88 percent joint and 12 percent intermediate; lower-middle class, 42 percent joint, 58 percent intermediate; upper-lower class white, 19 percent joint, 58 percent intermediate, and 23 percent segregated; upper-lower class Negro, 12 percent joint, 52 percent intermediate, and 36 percent segregated; lower-lower class white, 4 percent joint, 24 percent intermediate, and 72 percent segregated; lower-lower class Negro, 28 percent intermediate and 72 percent segregated (Rainwater, 1965:32). Thus the upper-middle class emphasizes joint relationships; the lower-middle class favors intermediate relationships slightly more than joint ones; the upper-lower class whites and Negroes have predominantly intermediate relationships, with a slightly larger minority favoring segregated ones over joint ones in the white families but three times the minority of Negroes doing so; and the lower-lower class whites and Negroes overwhelmingly emphasize segregated relationships with about a quarter of the remaining ones being intermediate. A number of findings are shown to be related to these three types.

The explanatory advantage of the role-relationship typology over social class is demonstrated quite clearly in examining satisfaction with sexual relations. While a social-class division shows a descending satisfaction moving from middle class to lower-lower class, when the data on the lower class are analyzed by role-relationship type, it is shown that more satisfaction is clearly related to the intermediate type (it will be recalled that there were few joint types in the lower class) and less satisfaction with segregated types. Furthermore, when a comparison between husband and wife concerning who derives greater or equal satisfaction is made, the intermediate types are found to be approximately twice as likely to have equal satisfaction, whereas the segregated types show three-to-four times as many husbands more satisfied than wives (Rainwater, 1965:64–70).

With respect to family-size preferences, Rainwater finds a considerable spread by class, race, and religion, which he points out is usually masked by demographic studies showing that over 90 percent of American families express an ideal family size preference of from two to four children (1965:280–81). When it is recalled that social class and conjugal role-relationships were closely related, this finding gives some indication that family size preferences also should be closely connected to role-relationship types. Rainwater apparently was unable to systematically analyze his data along these dimensions, perhaps, due to the small number of cases which would occur in such a complex breakdown. There are, however, some clues in his data and at least one specific finding according to role-relationship categories. Rainwater tested the hypothesis that wives in families which emphasize joint-role organization would not tend toward large families. He reasoned that there would be some opportunity for personal involvement with the husband, whereas wives in families with intermediate segregation might look to larger families as a way of gaining a sense of deeper interpersonal involvement through their children. The data for middle-class wives strongly supported the hypothesis. The data for middle-class husbands point in the same direction, but not as strongly (Rainwater, 1965:192–94, 286). Further data about concern with the homemaker and parent roles as opposed to roles oriented toward egocentric concerns showed the former preferred smaller families and the latter larger ones. This finding is interpreted to mean that large families provide a kind of compensation for the guilt felt over this egocentric or selfish point of view (Rainwater,

1965:194–95, 287). Finally, the data show that orientation toward outside interests of a social or intellectual kind as opposed to an orientation toward children is related to small vs. large families (Rainwater, 1965:191–92, 286–87).

Probably some of the strongest evidence for the conjugal role-relationship approach to fertility behavior is found in the analysis of the effectiveness of contraceptive practice (Rainwater, 1965:227–43, 293–96). A relatively rough classification was made by dividing the sample according to whether they were effective users (those who practice contraception regularly and consistently) or were *ineffective* users (those who either employed no method or who employed a technique inconsistently and sporadically). (See Table 5.1 for the findings by social class, religion, and race.)

TABLE 5.1 · *Effective and Ineffective Contraceptive Practices* [1]

		Effective	Ineffective
Before Birth of Last Wanted Child			
Middle-Class Protestants	(38)	92%	8%
Upper-Middle Class Catholics	(10)	60	40
Lower-Middle Class Catholics	(13)	38 *	62
Upper-Lower Class (White and Negro)	(80)	31 *	69
Lower-Lower Class (White and Negro)	(96)	3	97
After Birth of Last Wanted Child †			
Middle-Class and Upper-Lower Class Protestants	(38)	98%	2%
Middle-Class and Upper-Lower Catholics	(33)	73	27
Upper-Lower Class Negroes	(18)	50	50
Lower-Lower Class Protestants	(27)	33	67
Lower-Lower Class Catholics and Negroes	(31)	13	87

* Combined for analysis.

$X^2 = 84.31$ df $= 3$ P $< .0005$ T $= .55$

† $X^2 = 66.93$ df $= 4$ P $< .0005$ T $= .46$

[1] Reprinted from Lee Rainwater, FAMILY DESIGN (Chicago: Aldine Publishing Company, 1965); copyright © by Social Research, Inc., 1965. Reprinted by permission of the author and Aldine. Atherton, Inc.

Clearly, middle-class Protestants were most effective, with Catholics of the middle- and upper-lower classes improving after the birth of the last wanted child. Lower-class whites and Negroes, although improving somewhat after the birth of the last wanted child, remain predominantly ineffective in contraceptive use. When the role-relationship categorization is utilized to analyze the lower-class couples, Table 5.2 reveals a striking difference.

TABLE 5.2 · Conjugal Role-Organization and Effective Contraceptive Practice Among Lower-Class Couples [1]

		Effective	Ineffective
Before Last Wanted Child			
Joint Role Relationships *	(8)	50%	50%
Intermediate Segregation *	(39)	26	74
Highly Segregated	(51)	6	94
After Birth of Last Wanted Child			
Joint Role Relationship †	(6)	100%	—
Intermediate Segregation †	(30)	60	40
Highly Segregated	(39)	26	74

* Combined for analysis
$X^2 = 8.39$ P $<$ .005   T $=$ .29
† Combined for test
$X^2 = 11.19$ P $<$ .001   T $=$ .39

[1] Reprinted from Lee Rainwater, FAMILY DESIGN (Chicago: Aldine Publishing Company, 1965); copyright © by Social Research, Inc., 1965. Reprinted by permission of the author and Aldine. Atherton, Inc.

Powerful explanation of the variations in effective contraceptive use is found in the role-relationship configuration. Rainwater is unable to find the same sort of explanation for the middle-class group, primarily because among Protestants there was so little difference to begin with and among Catholics there was little change between the two periods (1965:295–96).

A relationship between effectiveness of contraceptive practice and the wife's satisfaction with sexual relationships also was found among lower-class white Protestants and Negroes. This finding is interpreted by Rainwater as follows (1965:295—the basic data are found on pages 240–41):

> A highly segregated conjugal relationship makes it difficult for couples to function in the close cooperation required both for mutually gratifying sexual relations and effective contraceptive practice. In this context, contraception tends to become a bone of contention in relation to the wife's wish to avoid anything connected with sex, and her aversion to sexual relations is reinforced by her anxiety about becoming pregnant coupled with the difficulties she experiences in doing anything effective about it.

Fertility Control—A Summary. The area of fertility control—though in-adequately researched at the group-interactional and at the individual-psychological levels—provides major promise as an arena within which to test and to improve the developmental theory. The Hill et al. (1959) and the Rainwater (1965) studies, though of necessity incompletely presented, have shown something of the level of explanation of fertility behavior which may be found by focusing more explicitly on the role rela-tionships in the family. It is interesting that in both studies a most signi-ficant change in fertility behavior was found at a point that the Hill group designated by the variable *saliency* and at a point that Rainwater found after the last wanted child. These discoveries supply clear evidence that the role structures of families have a definite developmental quality to them with respect to reproductive behavior. Changes in behavior are related directly to the changes in the family structure precipitated by addi-tion of new members. It is also apparent in both studies that fertility con-trol is not an issue confined to families in the childbearing stage, since the biological ability to bear children reaches well into the forties—and some-times beyond—for women. The role structures must deal with this matter over a considerable span of the family career. Research designed to explore propositions derived from a developmental theoretical base should produce results which will powerfully explain the reproductive behavior within families than has proven to be the result of studies following a demographic approach. Many potential propositions are contained in the two studies which we have examined.

Consequences of Biological Reproduction. There is yet another side to the matter of biological reproduction to which we must pay attention from a developmental point of view. This aspect involves the developmental characteristics with respect to the outcome of reproduction. Central to developmental theory is the basic notion that the addition of members to the system changes the system. Biological reproduction obviously adds members to the system. There are two situations which provide a useful way of dividing our discussion: The first one involves the coming of the first child where the primary effects are the changes occurring in the role rela-tionships of the husband and wife. The second one deals with the coming of a second or later birth-order child where not only the adult roles are involved, but also those of the other children in the family.

A great deal of attention has been paid to the child in studies of parent-child relationships. But, as Alice Rossi (1968) shows, far less attention has been paid to the parents. Beginning in the 1950s, some consideration has been given to the fact that the entire impact of the parent-child relation-ship does not fall on the child. Rossi reviews some of this literature and identifies several developmental characteristics associated with parenthood. She notes the following (Rossi, 1968:30–36):

1. There are strong cultural pressures similar to the ones on men to find full manhood in their occupations, for women to become parents in order to achieve full womanhood.

2. Pregnancy often is not the result of a voluntary decision; and voluntary termination of pregnancy is not positively valued, which may lead to higher levels of dissatisfaction in parenthood.

3. Because it is possible to delay pregnancy through contraceptive use and because women often continue working after marriage until the first pregnancy, the major role transition point for women is more frequently pregnancy than marriage.

4. Egalitarian role relationships have an increased possibility of developing in the marriage in which pregnancy is delayed and may have an important impact on both parent-child roles and later on husband-wife roles.

5. The phasing of parenthood is often different than it used to be, with parenthood frequently occurring before education is completed and before establishment in an occupation takes place.

6. Parenthood, in contrast to marriage and work, is essentially irrevocable, further adding to possibilities of negative reactions to parenthood roles.

7. With respect to preparation for parenthood, there is little training provided; there is little opportunity to learn during pregnancy (as compared to courtship as a learning period prior to marriage); there is little opportunity to move into the parental role gradually once birth occurs; and there are very few guidelines for successful parenthood.

In addition, Rossi (1968:36–39) notes some important factors associated with the expressive-instrumental aspects of parental roles which do not follow the strict sex differentiation asserted by Parsons (1955). Rossi's article deals rather heavily with the impact of the first child. Attention should be given, as well, to the effects of later children on family dynamics.

Some pieces of research on the topic of family size as it relates to various factors of family dynamics do exist (Bossard and Boll, 1956; Elder and Bowerman, 1963; Boocock, 1966; Nisbet, 1961; Rosen, 1961). Rossi (1968:33) notes, however, that the typical approach leaves much to be desired:

Unfortunately, the theoretical point of departure of sociologists' expectations of the effect of the family-size variables is the Durkheim-Simmel tradition of the differential effect of group size or population density upon members or inhabitants. In the case of the family, however, this overlooks the very important fact that family size is determined by the key figures *within* the group, i.e., the parents. To find that children in small families differ from children in large families is not simply due to the impact of group size upon individual members but to the very different involvement of the parent with the children and to relations between the parents themselves in small versus large families.

We already have seen that studies note the influence of the number of children on the reproductive behavior of parents. As yet, however, little research exists to show the changes which take place in the role clusters of occupants of the husband-father and wife-mother positions as a result of second- and higher-order births. In general, then, Rosen's (1961:576) observation, which Rossi quotes, still aptly sums up the situation: "Considering the sociologist's traditional and continuing concern with group size as an independent variable (from Simmel and Durkheim to the recent experimental studies of small groups), there have been surprisingly few studies of the influence of group size upon the nature of interaction in the family."

But, of course, the developmental perspective highlights more than the *size* of the group. The presence of actors to occupy positions in the system provides an entire set of issues dealing with the way roles are allocated, are played, and are adapted. A special kind of data is needed on *whole family systems*, as well as on particular role complexes within the systems. These data do not exist as yet. Research remains very much at the exploratory level in this rather significant area. Theory shows that there most certainly are important processes arising out of adding children to the family system. Some studies deal with kinds of relationships which exist among siblings, with family size and parent-child relationships, and with family size and marital satisfaction. We have bits and pieces, but relatively little data about family systems as such.

A systematic inquiry in this area will of necessity deal with all three facets of analysis. What are the societal-institutional implications of the addition of new actors in the system? Does each new actor simply fill a position designated primarily according to age and sex (e.g., infant son or daughter)? To what extent do societal-institutional norms exist for the incumbents of different ordinal positions (e.g., second child or second son)? At the group-interactional level, do similar differentiations in roles take place? The theory includes the recognition that the second child occupies a somewhat different position than the first, simply because now a sibling relationship prevails. But beyond this observation, what is the nature of the normative structure developed at the group-interactional level for higher order births? What individual-psychological aspects must be taken into account? Sibling rivalry provides a long-standing focus for speculation by psychologists. Research shows, however, that the relationships are complex, with various potential liaisons being formed for cooperative as well as for competitive purposes (Sutton-Smith, 1970). What is the character of these various combinations, and what are their underlying bases? These questions are all issues for which some empirical foundation already has been laid but which require considerably more investigation. Fascinating exploratory opportunities arise from taking the developmental perspective.

Adoption

As suggested in introducing this section on reproduction and on recruitment, only a brief discussion of adoption will occur now, with a more extensive examination reserved for the chapter on atypical family careers. Material on adoption, heavily devoted to agency practices, sees the process of adoption from a procedural and/or legal standpoint. Additional matter explores the characteristics of adoptive children and of adoptive parents, primarily from an individual-psychological point of view. Far less literature takes as its problem the analysis of the impact on the family career of the addition of children by the adoptive route (Kirk, 1964, summarizes this material). The purpose here is to indicate some of the factors which may be useful to explore in an examination of the interactive implications of adoption. One way of doing this analysis is to distinguish between adoption of a child as the first child in contrast to adoption of a child as the second or subsequent child in the family. These two basic types can be further subdivided by distinguishing between the adoption of infants as compared with the adoption of older children.

Regarding the adoption of the first child, who is an infant, one may assume that many of the same kinds of interactive processes which occur in normal biological reproduction take place. Matters having to do with providing facilities for a newborn child in the family, with reorganizing the husband-wife roles through the introduction of the parental roles, and with other such processes may be relatively similar; however, one obvious difference which has some intriguing implications is that in adoption, the experience of pregnancy and the expectant-parenthood roles are not the same. This distinction does not imply, though, that no experience of expectant parenthood occurs. Given that the legal requirements of most states and that the investigative procedures of most child-placing agencies place an extended period between the decision to adopt and the actual acquisition of the child, certainly a span exists in which the couple may develop roles as expectant parents. The process of deciding to adopt may in some ways parallel resolutions to have children by biological reproduction. The application and the qualification as adoptive parents may correspond to the pregnancy experience, including the relationship with an obstetrician during the prenatal period. Both prior to adopting the child and in the post-adoptive period, some distinctive developmental characteristics fall in each of the facets.

The adoption of a child beyond infancy as the first child provides some additional issues of interest. In such a situation, the child may also be involved in the preadoptive process. Role relationships which may have more similarity to courtship than to expectant parenthood may occur. In adoptions of older children a trial period probably occurs when the child is placed in the home, but final legal adoption is delayed until it is determined whether the child and the adoptive parents are compatible. The role characteristics of such a situation must have considerable significance, particularly if the child is old enough to be aware of the trial nature of the situation. Assuming adoption is finally realized, the process by which a child who has already learned certain roles is incorporated into an already existent family career provides additional theoretical interest. Again, the process may have some resemblance to the early adjustment of a married pair, though there probably are also some important differences.

Regarding the adoption of second or subsequent children, again some possible similarities and important differences in the family role process exist. With the adoption of an infant, the other children (or the other child) now enter into the proceeding and also, depending on their age, may participate in the expectant process. The introduction of a new member has implications for their roles but may have unique qualities when the new member is adopted. When that child is no longer an infant, it is even possible that he may be older than or of similar age to one or more of the children already present, Again, the introduction of a new member who already has a role history outside the family provides some fascinating analytical potentialities. It should be quite clear that many possibilities in the developmental theoretical approach exist for deriving some exciting research propositions.

Mate Selection

I stated that there were two basic reasons for the inclusion of this topic in the consideration of reproduction and of recruitment. First, with respect to nuclear-family systems, mate selection—typically referred to as the establishment stage—is the process by which the new family is formed. Second, in extended-family systems, the marriage of a child usually represents either the loss or the gain of a member. If a system is patrilocal, the marriage of a son means the gaining of a female member for the system, and the marriage of a daughter means the loss of a female member. If the system is matrilocal, the effect is usually the opposite, with other variations, of course. These extended family differences will not be analyzed in any detail at this point, since they are more relevant to the chapter which attempts to show the potentialities for cross-cultural applications of the developmental theory. It will suffice to mention that the basic theoretical approach can be applied to systems other than the nuclear family. In some ways, the extended family, unlike the nuclear one, is more truly cyclical. That the marriage of an offspring represents a modification in the basic role structure of the existing extended family system, rather than the establishment of an entirely new system helps to validate this contention. The normative structure of most extended family systems, however, is much more complex than this example and usually provides for a "splitting" of the system at certain prescribed points. But we are getting ahead of ourselves. Let us return to the matter of mate selection in nuclear family systems.

Since nuclear systems are typically neolocal in their residence patterns, mate selection represents a loss of membership to the family of orientation as well as the establishment of a new family of procreation. Thus, at a minimum, the implications for the role structure of the family of orientation involves vacating a position in that structure (Kirkpatrick, 1967: 229–36, deals with this point). Many more factors, however, are included. From the time the dating process begins, through to the more serious experience of courtship, various implications exist for those who occupy the parental positions and the sibling positions in both families of orientation. American folklore, as represented in novels, drama, cartoons, and comic strips, is full of the indications of the roles which should be played by the family members toward a courting couple. The striking fact is that the behavioral-science literature is not similarly rich (Burchinal, 1964; Hill and Aldous, 1969), although we do have considerable material which has attempted to explain why a given pair marries (Katz and Hill, 1958). Involved are a number of variables which relate to the family background. There are the factors of social class, area of residence, and attitudes toward parents, to name those most frequently used. Presumably, as with the case of the demographic variables in fertility research, these variables ultimately stand for interactional characteristics of families. Such data, however, are rarely gathered directly. Once again, a number of research propositions are derived from the developmental theory which could explore the impact of courtship on the family of orientation and the complementary problem of the impact of the family of orientation on the courtship.

The other type of material dealing with the premarital period focuses on the premarital interactive process of the couple and views it as a period in which marital roles are becoming increasingly manifest. A great share of this material has been aimed at predicting marital success or adjustment on the basis of the adjustment in courtship. (Burgess and Cottrell, 1939; Burgess and Wallin, 1944; Burgess and Locke, 1951; Kirkpatrick, 1963). A strong emphasis in this research is on psychological characteristics of the individuals, but some variables emphasize aspects which may be tied to the interactional dynamics of the pair.

The article by Rhona Rapoport (1964) provides a unique example of an attempt to apply developmental theory to the courtship period. Utilizing the two basic concepts of developmental task and critical role transition, Rapoport sets forth the basic proposition that the accomplishment of certain "phase-specific tasks" in engagement will lead to a more effective handling of the critical role transition of marriage and, thus, to a better marital adjustment. The research is admittedly exploratory, and the article reports work on a small number of cases with little information on either the interactional character of courtship or on the long-term outcome. These facts notwithstanding, the work is an excellent illustration of how developmental theorists may approach this first period of the family career.

Summary

Three basic factors have been reviewed in this section: First biological reproduction was analyzed, both with respect to the developmental implications for fertility behavior and to the role transition to parenthood that is precipitated by having children. Then some of the issues associated with the atypical form of reproduction represented in the adoption process were reviewed. Finally, the issue of mate selection was examined with a brief consideration of extended family systems but a lengthy look at the impact of mate selection on both the family of orientation and the family of procreation. There is room for much empirical work in this area before a major base of evidence to support the developmental theory will exist. Probably such work will result in a number of modifications of the theory which will improve its explanatory power.

MAINTENANCE OF BIOLOGICAL FUNCTIONING

The discussion dealing with the maintenance of biological functioning and of family interactions may be divided into four main areas: (1) nutrition; (2) health and medical care; (3) sanitation; and (4) shelter. To a great extent, the whole general area of maintenance of biological functioning has been ignored by family and other sociologists. The major exception to this generalization, perhaps, lies in the area of health and medical care—but here the concern has been more with *illness* than with *health* and more with the social organization of medical-care groups than with the processes of providing medical treatment to individuals and to groups in the society. Furthermore, little has been done with *family* roles in health and in medical care, whereas a great deal has been done with non-family roles.

Nutrition

Home economists, of course, have for many years made nutrition a major concern of theirs. Their material tends toward—though it is not exclusively limited to—concerns with food preparation as well as with the planning of "balanced diets" and, thus, places major focus on the mechanics of achieving a nutritious outcome. Some work in child development and cultural anthropology has concerned itself with feeding and weaning patterns of the young, and, in particular, material with a psychoanalytic bent has dealt with the psychological consequences of various patterns. Family sociologists have dealt with food preparation as a part of the analysis of the division of labor and of the provision of food ("breadwinning") as part of the examination of the distribution of goods and services. Each of these elements provides a perfectly legitimate way to deal with the matter of food intake, not to mention the analyses of rituals surrounding the intake of food. Yet in many ways, concern with nutritional behavior seems analogous to the analysis of fertility behavior which we have just finished. There is nothing any more basic to family life, certainly, than insuring adequate nutritional intake for each member. In many countries today, from an applied point of view, dealing with the problem of helping families to gain an adequate intake is as major an issue as aiding them in controlling their fertility. Probably a great many demographic analyses have been done to show which groups have a given level of nutrition, the methods used for achieving this level, and who has the responsibility for the method. Yet, little or nothing is known about the role relationships which probably more directly account for these outcomes. In many countries, inducing people to change a particular dietary practice is a problem very similar to persuading them to change a particular fertility-control practice. Nevertheless, we probably have even less data concerning the family patterns of interaction surrounding nutrition than surrounding fertility control. To my knowledge, no parallel exists to the Hill et al. or to the Rainwater studies on fertility control in the area of nutritional patterns. This lack provides some intriguing possibilities. The fact remains, however, that we have little empirical work to follow. Therefore, any consideration of roles associated with nutrition will be left to the section on division of labor.

Health and Medical Care

As mentioned at the outset of this section, the major concern in sociology with respect to health and to medical care has either been with illness or with the social organization of various types of medical groups (hospitals, surgical teams, nursing teams, and so on). Furthermore, the focus seems to be more on mental than on physical illness. There are at least two other fields under which this general topic of health and medical care may fall from a developmental perspective: transactional behavior, in which the analysis will focus on the relationships between the family system and the medical system (Silver, 1963), and family career stresses, in which the analysis will focus on the impact of various types of illness on the family system. In addition, the closely-related area of disability arising out of a medical cause will be analyzed under atypical family careers. Since there is no major body of data on normal role patterns with respect to health and medical care, and there is no developmental anlysis of changing role patterns, the major discussion is reserved for the section dealing with the stressful impact of illness and with the impact of illness on the ability to play roles.

Sanitation

Whenever analyses of the reduction in morbidity and mortality are carried out, one of the prime areas cited as responsible for the trend in Western cultures and in the "developing" nations is the improvement in sanitation practices. A major concern in the growth of American urban and suburban regions during the 1950s and the 1960s was the pressure placed on sewage and garbage disposal facilities. There was a high stress, particularly during the latter part of the decade of the sixties and of the early seventies, on environmental pollution. Heavy emphasis was placed on water pollution resulting from inadequately treated industrial and residential wastes being discharged into rivers and lakes. Increasing concern also was seen dealing with the disposal of solid wastes from industrial and from domestic sources.

In spite of the fact that sanitation is hardly taken for granted in general, the analysis of any family activity in this area is essentially absent, probably quite simply because there is relatively nothing to examine. Certainly Americans generally are not conscious of the process of waste disposal, except when a garbage strike occurs or the sewer closes up. The typical middle-class home built at the beginning of the second half of the decade included two bathrooms, a garbage disposal unit, and an automatic dishwasher as standard installations, all closely tied to sanitation but facilitating a lack of consciousness on the part of the family concerning this necessary activity. The closest that most family researchers appear to approach the subject of sanitation is seen in questions concerning the division of labor in which typical areas of inquiry include the responsibility for washing dishes and for taking out the garbage or trash. A continuing increase in adoptions of automatic dishwashers and of food-waste disposers and a trend toward more in-home incinerators are taking place, and development is under way of some new devices designed to handle most of the solid waste not now processed by the disposers or by burning. Questions about division of labor in this area may soon yield a high "not applicable" response rate indicative of an increasing lack of necessity for concern with such matters. The whole area of sanitation, however, will continue to preoccupy governments at all levels. It may well be that the best way to deal with the family-related aspects of sanitation even now is within the area of transactions between the family system and the governmental system.

Shelter

The discussion of shelter will be restricted to a consideration of housing, though it may be argued that other types of "shelter" such as clothing are also essential to the maintenance of biological functioning. The limitation here seems justified on the basis that the matters which have been treated in this section deal with activities or with generalized facilities which tend to involve all family members somewhat simultaneously. Clothing, on the other hand, is a much more individualized matter. A family probably has only one house, one general approach to sanitation, medical and health matters, and nutrition. The fact does not imply that differing individual needs or desires are not at least partially met by this general system. The provision of clothing represents, however, a much more individualized kind of activity than the other practices. The provision of clothing, then, is included under the general category of distribution of goods and services.

Some minimal attention has been paid to housing from a developmental point of view; but, unfortunately, no great body of research exists. Two rather early treatments by Agan (1950) and by Gutheim (1948) were both basically descriptive. At about the same time, Bossard (1951) developed an index designed to determine the amount of space necessary for family interaction which was based on family size and, thus, could be applied developmentally. Later, Abu-Lughod and Foley (1960) presented an analysis of housing according to a developmental approach. Their analysis showed, besides the type of dwelling unit and size of dwelling unit, the typical tenure status, the location preference, and the amount of mobility in each of several family life cycle categories. Beyer (1965) paid considerable attention to family characteristics with respect to housing and some attention to the family life cycle, but he failed to bring explicit research data to bear on his discussion. In 1969, Smith et al. reported on an observational experiment of family interaction in a demonstration housing unit constructed in a home economics laboratory in which the family life cycle category was a major analytical variable. There were significant differences between life cycle categories for wives concerning amount of house privacy (the wife was alone in the house), entertaining of guests with no other family members present, and interaction with at least one other family member. For husbands, significant differences by life cycle were found in amount of time spent in the house, house privacy, and location privacy (being alone in a part of the house when other family members were present in the house). There also were some data on privacy vs. interaction experiences of children. The study is limited, however, both by the small sample (only twenty families with five members each, five from each of four life cycle categories) and by the fact that the families were not living in their own homes but in an experimental setting. Such research is difficult to carry out under any circumstances. It is also true that placing all families in the same spacial situation held constant the effect of differing housing facilities on interaction patterns.On the other hand, there is always the issue of how real or natural or normal or representative behavior observed in such an experimental laboratory situation may be. Smith et al. recognized these and other limitations to their work. More data are needed on the way in which families interact with respect to shelter and as a result of the kind of shelter which they have. Until we have such information, little can be done beyond speculation concerning the developmental characteristics of the family in relation to its shelter.

In general, then, the developmental analysis of the area of maintenance of biological functioning represents a relatively unexplored domain. The matters discussed in this section have been analyzed typically with an emphasis on the social organization in the broader society rather than on family organization, thus more transactional data tends to be available. In view of this fact, it may be possible to assemble rather quickly adequate data from the societal-institutional facet. It is clear, however, that major work remains to be accomplished for the other two facets.

SOCIALIZATION

In turning attention to the area of socialization, we see some fascinating paradoxes. Because of the almost literal explosion of research on child development after World War Two, an overwhelming body of material on socialization of children exists but relatively little material about socialization of adults, despite the general recognition that the process continues throughout life. In the midst of the great body of material dealing with the socialization of children, there is a general recognition of the major role the family takes in the process, but the bulk of the matter tends not to deal with family organization and interaction as a major variable for analysis. We can find some major exceptions to these two generalizations, of course (Cf., for example, Aberle, 1961; Borgatta and Lambert, 1968; Brim, 1966 and 1968; Clausen, 1966 and 1968; Dager, 1964; Hill and Aldous, 1969; Miller and Swanson, 1958; Parsons, 1955; Sears et al., 1957; Sewell, 1963; Whiting and Child, 1953; Winch, 1962; Zigler and Child 1969). The implications of such key limitations in the material are serious for the family development theorist. In a very significant sense, the process of socialization is central to the developmental approach. Focusing as the theory does on the role structure of the family and on processes which bring about change in this structure, the process of learning and of incorporating roles by an actor-occupant of a familial position becomes of central importance.

I noted in Chapter 3 that the concept of developmental task, as redefined by the ideas of the developmental theory, essentially was concerned with the process of socialization as defined by Broom and Selznick (1968: 86–87) to include (1) concern with the basic physical and emotional disciplines, (2) imparting culturally accepted aspirations, (3) acquiring necessary cultural skills, and (4) learning appropriate social roles. Furthermore, in Chapter 4, I took the position that the developmental task was in essence a major proposition which could yield a large mass of hypotheses for testing and for improving the developmental theoretical framework. The developmental theory consistently demands attention to the fact that such roles arise out of the contributions from the three facets which were explored in some detail. Thus, the concern with socialization as exhibited by family development theory attempts to avoid the extremes often exhibited in the work in this area.

Zigler and Child (1969:473–74) have provided an excellent review of the various approaches to socialization, and they conclude with a statement which appears to be in close harmony with what family development theory calls for:

> In this section, we have attempted to convey some sense of the conflicting viewpoints which currently characterize thought about socialization. . . . For the purpose of this chapter the essential question is not whether man is basically an active or passive agent or inherently good or bad, but rather whether all possibilities must be considered in arriving at a comprehensive view of socialization. We advocate the broad approach. We need not choose between the active and passive views of man; we need to use them both. The active, mediational cognitive characteristics of the child are important in the socialization process at every stage of development; on the other hand, they do not determine every aspect of the socialized behavior which emerges. . . . That we need not choose between the positive and negative should also be evident. A child possesses biological appetites and behavioral propensities, continuous expression

of which would make any social order impossible. There *is* an aspect of man that is primitive and gluttonous. This fact directs the student of socialization to concern with the problem of impulse control and to the particular practices employed by the society in blocking or rechanneling individual characteristics which pose a threat for the social order. On the other hand, to say that socialization is nothing more than this is also an error. Observations of the child's desire to become an increasingly effective social being do not seem likely to be illusory. There appear to be inherent forces in the child which align themselves on the side of socializing agents, thus making the child an active and cooperative figure in his own socialization.

Citing the fact that Child's earlier version of the chapter carried a definition of socialization which had been criticized as overly oriented toward conformity to cultural norms and asserting their desire to avoid such an emphasis, Zigler and Child (1969:474) offer the following definition of socialization: "Socialization is a broad term for the whole process by which an individual develops, through transaction with other people, his specific patterns of socially relevant behavior and experience." This definition, it would appear, calls for the kind of analysis of "transaction with other people" in the family setting which is set forth in the developmental approach. We shall refer to this process, of course, as *interaction* and shall reserve the term *transaction* for the relationships occurring outside the family setting.

For the purposes of this discussion, it seems more profitable to indicate the sorts of research problems relevant to a developmental theorist's investigation, rather than to attempt a review of the existing material. A careful perusal of the references cited, coupled with the discussion to follow should yield more than a lifetime's worth of fascinating research propositions and hypotheses.

From the standpoint of practicability there appear to be two basic strategies for approaching a developmental analysis of the family context of socialization. On the one hand, a researcher may select a particular role associated with a specified familial position and may attempt to analyze the socialization process with respect to that role. My (Rodgers:1966) article on occupational socialization is an example of such a strategy. Deutscher's (1962) work on postparental couples and Komarovsky's (1962) analysis of working-class couples represent an alternative strategy, in which the focus is placed on a given role complex, and analysis of the socialization process in preparation for ordering the complex is attempted. The distinction between the two types of research problems is analogous to the distinction between longitudinal and cross-sectional research. In the former, the socialization process is traced over a major portion or over all of the specified role career. In the latter, a slice of the familial career is abstracted, and the analysis proceeds by an intensive investigation of as much of the socialization interaction as possible with respect to as many of the roles in the selected role complex as deemed appropriate. To put this difference in another light, one approach provides considerable *depth* of analysis, and the other provides greater *scope*. Neither, quite apparently, is a simple task. (For more on these strategies and others, cf., Hill, 1964.)

In choosing the first type of problem, the analyst attempts to isolate one particular role and to identify the factors involved in moving that role from a latent to a manifest state in the position occupied by a familial actor. Depending on the role chosen, such an examination may carry the researcher into a study of a major portion of the career of the actor in the family of orientation and over into the family of procreation. Thus, for example, an analysis of the development of the occupational role may well follow the socialization process from childhood through retirement. Such a study may show not only the dynamics of the socialization experience of a male actor in the period before marriage and/or his first job but also may examine the familial socialization about work which takes place in the family of procreation with respect to the husband-father position.

Similarly, some important work may be accomplished about female family members, which may bring to light significant factors in the socialization process contributing to the feelings of conflict or the lack of such feelings that some working mothers have in their families of procreation. Such an analysis will bridge the gap between the kinds of examinations carried out by Komarovsky (1946) with respect to the family of orientation and those of Nye and Hoffman (1963) with respect to the family of procreation. Parallel studies of marital, parental, political, religious, economic, and other roles may be designed. It may be postulated, as a matter of fact, that the most effective method for the control of fertility behavior may be found by an analysis of the socialization process with respect to reproductive behavior which occurs in the family of orientation, as opposed to factors in the family of procreation's interactive experience. From a developmental perspective, such a proposition is quite appropriate.

A somewhat different type of research yield comes from the analysis of a selected role complex. Although the analysis of a given role career provides an extensive body of data about the socialization experience of a particular occupant of a familial position, the intensive examination of a portion of the familial career with respect to socialization provides data on the complex cross-pressures which may occur where each position may be experiencing socialization with respect to one or more roles in its role cluster. One need only imagine the study of a familial role complex where three child positions are occupied, with male actors aged seven and three and with a female actor aged five, and where the husband-father position is occupied by an actor approaching the first major advancement in his occupational role and where the wife-mother occupant is contemplating taking on additional transactional roles in the community or in the occupational sphere.

In the recognition that each actor is both an agent *and* recipient of socialization, the groundwork is laid for a challenging research enterprise. Laying out the analytical plan to account for factors in all three facets and with respect to a variety of role areas so as to reveal the many potential interrelationships that may be present simultaneously is an exacting task. The full potentiality for developmental theory of such an approach, however, can be realized only by the accumulation of comparative data for a number of similar role complexes with differing structures in terms of age, sex, spacing, and plurality combinations. Such an ultimate goal may appear to be an impossible undertaking at this point in the history of the developmental approach. When it is recognized, however, that the great bulk of research which now exists about socialization, about personality or about almost any other area of behavioral research has been accumulated in the past thirty-to-forty years, the suggestion seems less formidable. It should also be pointed out that, although some new data-gathering and data-analysis techniques will need to be developed, the research proposed has the advantage of the solid foundation of research methodology already created in the behavioral sciences. The primary obstacle, therefore, appears to be gaining the commitment of a sufficient number of theorist-researchers to the potential gains in understanding of family behavior which can be achieved through the developmental approach. In summary, then, I see the area of socialization as a most significant one for analysis in its own right. Beyond this assertion, the socialization process is a central element to the entire developmental theoretical perspective, because the major basis for developmental explanation of family behavior is found in understanding the changing roles of the various positions in the family over its career.

REFERENCES

ABERLE, DAVID F.
  1961 "Culture and socialization." Pp. 381–99 in F. L. K. Hsu (ed.), *Psychological Anthropology: Approaches to Culture and Personality*. Homewood, Ill.: Dorsey Press.

ABU-LUGHOD, JANET, AND MARY M. FOLEY
  1960 "Consumer strategies." Pp. 97–118 in Nelson Foote et al. (eds.), *Housing Choices and Housing Constraints*. New York: McGraw-Hill Book Company.

AGAN, TESSIE
1950   "Housing and the family life cycle." *Journal of Home Economics* 42 (May): 351–54.
BEYER, G. H.
1965   *Housing and Society*. New York: The Macmillan Company.
BOOCOCK, SARANE S.
1966   "Toward a sociology of learning: a selective review of existing research." *Sociology of Education* 39 (Winter): 1–45.
BORGATTA, EDGAR F., AND WILLIAM W. LAMBERT, EDS.
1968   Handbook of Personality Theory and Research. Chicago: Rand McNally & Company.
BOSSARD, JAMES
1951   "A spatial index for family interaction." *American Sociological Review* 16 (April): 243–46.

1953   *Parent and Child*. Philadelphia: University of Pennsylvania Press.

————, AND ELEANOR BOLL
1956   *The Large Family System*. Philadelphia: University of Pennsylvania Press.
BOTT, ELIZABETH
1957   *Family and Social Network*. London: Tavistock Publishers, Ltd.
BRIM, ORVILLE
1966   "Socialization through the life cycle." Pp. 1–49 in Orville G. Brim and Stanton Wheeler (eds.), *Socialization After Childhood: Two Essays*. New York: John Wiley & Sons, Inc.
1968   "Adult socialization." Pp. 182–226 in John A. Clausen (ed.), *Socialization and Society*. Boston: Little, Brown & Company.
BROOM, LEONARD, AND PHILIP SELZNICK
1968   *Sociology*, 4th ed. New York: Harper & Row, Publishers.
BURCHINAL, LEE G.
1964   "The premarital dyad and love involvement." Pp. 623–74 in Harold Christensen (ed.), *Handbook of Marriage and the Family*. Chicago: Rand McNally & Company.
BURGESS, E. W., AND L. S. COTTRELL
1939   *Predicting Success or Failure in Marriage*. New York: Prentice-Hall, Inc.
————, AND HARVEY J. LOCKE
1951   Predicting Adjustment in Marriage. New York: Henry Holt and Company.
————, AND PAUL WALLIN
1944   "Predicting adjustment in marriage from adjustment in engagement." *American Journal of Sociology* 49 (January): 324–30.

CHILMAN, CATHERINE S., AND WILLIAM T. LIU, EDS.
1968   "Family planning and fertility control." Special issue of *Journal of Marriage and the Family* 30 (May).

CICOUREL, AARON V.
1967   "Fertility, family planning and the social organization of family life: some methodological issues." *Journal of Social Issues* 32 (October): 57–81.

CLAUSEN, JOHN A.
1966   "Family structure, socialization, and personality." Pp. 1–53 in L. W. Hoffman and M. L. Hoffman (eds.), *Review of Child Development Research*, Vol. 2. New York: Russell Sage Foundation.

————
1968   "Perspectives on childhood socialization." Pp. 130–81 in John A. Clausen (ed.), *Socialization and Society*. Boston: Little, Brown & Company.

DAGER, EDWARD Z.
1964   "Socialization and personality development." Pp. 740–81 in Harold Christensen (ed.), *Handbook of Marriage and the Family*. Chicago: Rand McNally & Company.

DEUTSCHER, IRWIN
1962   "Socialization for postparental life." Pp. 506–25 in Arnold M. Rose (ed.), *Human Behavior and Social Processes*. Boston: Houghton Mifflin Company.

DUBIN, ROBERT
1969   *Theory Building*. New York: The Free Press.

DUVALL, EVELYN M.
1971   *Family Development*, 4th ed. Philadelphia: J. B. Lippincott Company.

ELDER, GLEN, AND CHARLES BOWERMAN
1963   "Family structure and child rearing patterns: the effect of family size and sex composition on child-rearing practices." *American Sociological Review* 28 (December): 891–905.

FREEDMAN, RONALD
1961–62 "The sociology of human fertility; a trend report and bibliography." *Current Sociology* 10/11.

————, ET AL.
1959   *Family Planning, Sterility, and Population Growth*. New York: The McGraw-Hill Book Company.

GARFINKEL, HAROLD
1960   "The rational properties of scientific and common sense activities." *Behavioral Science* 5 (January): 72–83.

————
1964   "The routine grounds of everyday activities." *Social Problems* 11 (Winter): 225–50.

Goslin, David A., ed.
1969   Handbook of Socialization Theory and Research. Chicago: Rand McNally & Company.
Gutheim, Frederick, ed.
1948   Houses for Family Living. New York: The Woman's Foundation.
Hill, Reuben
1964   "Methodological issues in family development research." Family Process 3 (March): 186–206.

────   1968a   "Research on human fertility." International Social Science Journal 20 (June): 226–62.

────   1968b   "A classified international bibliography of family planning research, 1955–68." Demography 5 (1968): 973–1001.
────, and Joan Aldous
1969   "Socialization for marriage and parenthood." Pp. 885–950 in David A. Goslin (ed.), Handbook of Socialization Theory and Research. Chicago: Rand McNally & Company.
────, et al.
1959   The Family and Population Control. Chapel Hill, N. C.: University of North Carolina Press.
Jacoby, Arthur P.
1969   "Transition to parenthood: a reassessment." Journal of Marriage and the Family 31 (November): 720–27.
Katz, Alvin, and Reuben Hill
1958   "Residential propinquity and marital selection. A review of theory, method, and fact." Marriage and Family Living 20 (February): 27–35.
Kirk, David
1964   Shared Fate. Glencoe, Ill.: The Free Press.
Kirkpatrick, Clifford
1963   The Family: As Process and Institution, 2nd ed. New York: The Ronald Press Company.

────   1967   "Familial development, selective needs, and predictive theory." Journal of Marriage and the Family 29 (May): 229–36.
Kiser, Clyde V., ed.
1962   Research in Family Planning. Princeton, N.J.: Princeton University Press.
────, and Pascal K. Whelpton, eds.
1943–58   Social and Psychological Factors Affecting Fertility. Vols. 1–5. New York: Milbank Memorial Fund.
Komarovsky, Mirra
1946   "Cultural contradictions and sex roles." American Journal of Sociology 52 (November): 184–89.

1962 *Blue Collar Marriage.* New York: Random House, Inc.

LIU, WILLIAM T., ED.
1967 *Family and Fertility.* Notre Dame, Indiana: University of Notre Dame Press.

MILLER, DANIEL, AND GUY E. SWANSON
1958 *The Changing American Parent.* New York: John Wiley & Sons, Inc.

NISBET, JOHN
1961 "Family environment and intelligence." Pp. 273–87 in A. H. Halsey et al. (eds.), *Education, Economy and Society.* New York: The Free Press.

PARSONS TALCOTT
1955 "Family structure and the socialization of the child." Pp. 35–131 in Talcott Parsons and Robert F. Bales (eds.), *Family, Socialization, and Interaction Process,* Glencoe, Ill.: The Free Press.

QUEEN, STUART, AND JOHN B. ADAMS
1952 *The Family in Various Cultures.* Chicago: J. B. Lippincott Company.

RAINWATER, LEE
1960 *And the Poor Get Children.* Chicago: Quandrangle Books.

1965 *Family Design: Marital Sexuality, Family Size, and Contraception.* Chicago: Aldine Press.

1967 "Family planning in cross-national perspective." Special issue of *Journal of Marriage and the Family* 32 (October).

RAPOPORT, RHONA
1964 "The transition from engagement to marriage." *Acta Sociologica* 8: 36–55.

RODGERS, ROY H.
1966 "The occupational role of the child: a research frontier in the developmental conceptual framework." *Social Forces* 45 (December): 217–24.

ROSEN, BERNARD C.
1961 "Family structure and achievement motivation." *American Sociological Review* 26 (August): 574–85.

ROSSI, ALICE S.
1968 "Transition to parenthood." *Journal of Marriage and the Family* 30 (February): 26–39.

SEARS, ROBERT R., ET AL.
1957 *Patterns of Child Rearing.* Evanston, Ill.: Row, Peterson, and Company.

SEWELL, WILLIAM H.
1963 "Some recent developments in socialization theory and research."
      The Annals of the American Academy of Political and Social
      Science 349 (September): 163–81.

SILVER, GEORGE A.
1963 Family Medical Care: a Report on the Family Health Maintenance
      Demonstration. Cambridge: Harvard University Press.

SMITH, RUTH H., ET AL.
1969 "Privacy and interaction within the family as related to dwelling
      space." Journal of Marriage and the Family 31 (August): 559–66.

STYCOS, J. MAYONE
1955 Family and Fertility in Puerto Rico: A Study of the Lower Income
      Group. New York: Columbia University Press.

———, AND KURT BACK
1964 The Control of Fertility in Jamaica. Ithaca, N.Y.: Cornell Univer-
      sity Press.

SUTTON-SMITH, BRIAN, AND B. ROSENBERG
1970 The Sibling. New York: Holt, Rinehart & Winston, Inc.

WESTOFF, CHARLES F., ET AL.
1961 Family Growth in Metropolitan America. Princeton, N.J.: Prince-
      ton University Press.

———
1963 The Third Child: A Study in the Prediction of Fertility. Prince-
      ton, N.J.: Princeton University Press.

WHELPTON, PASCAL K., ET AL.
1966 Fertility and Family Planning in the United States. Princeton,
      N.J.: Princeton University Press.

WHITING, JOHN, AND IRWIN L. CHILD
1953 Child Training and Personality: a Cross-Cultural Study. New
      Haven: Yale University Press.

WINCH, ROBERT F.
1962 Identification and Its Familial Determinants. Indianapolis: The
      Bobbs-Merrill Company, Inc.

ZIGLER, EDWARD, AND IRWIN L. CHILD
1969 "Socialization." Pp. 450–589 in Gardner Lindzey and Elliott
      Aronson (eds.), The Handbook of Social Psychology, 2nd ed.,
      Vol. 3. Reading, Mass.: Addison-Wesley Publishing Company,
      Inc.

Family Careers— Interactional Analysis:

Division of Labor,
Maintenance of Order, and
Maintenance of Meaning

In every organization, some attention must be given to insuring that members of the system are recipients of goods and services which are either needed or considered desirable in daily life. There are two interrelated aspects to this activity. On the one hand is the matter of designating who are the appropriate recipients of the various goods and services. On the other hand is the issue of who should be responsible for providing the goods and services to the recipients. In essence, a necessity arises to organize in such a way as to designate both the privileges and responsibilities of membership in the organization. Intertwined in the whole process is another matter having to do with the ability to give or to withhold goods and services and, thus, to control to some extent the behavior of another actor in the system. This latter area may be seen generally as associated with power and with authority relationships in the system. These three areas, then, seem to be associated with three basic questions: (1) Who should *receive* various goods and services? (2) Who should *provide* various goods and services? and (3) Who should *decide* how goods and services are distributed and who distributes them?

There does not appear to have been any great concern in family study with the designation of the recipients of the various goods and services. Although probably clear limitations to the availability of all types of goods and services exist, an assumption seems to prevail. According to it, within these limitations no particularly systematic distinctions are made as to who is to receive the goods and the services in terms of familial positions occupied. For example, the amount of food may be limited, but the assumption appears to be that no normative structure of consequence exists which will designate the distribution of food in a discriminatory manner according to positions held in the family. Whether such a general supposition is warranted may be open to some question, of course. This assumption may be only an indication of the ethnocentric orientation of American family research. In traditional Japanese family structure, for example, there is evidence that food was served according to age—first to the male members of the family, second to the female members, and last to widowed wives of sons (who were termed *cold-rice* relatives) (Queen and Adams, 1952: 90–91). Such a procedure was clearly associated with the position which the actor occupied in the family system. Similar evidence exists in other societies. These facts notwithstanding, there is no body of research which concerns itself directly with this issue and, assuming no real scarcity exists, casual observation of most modern industrialized (perhaps Western) societies seems to indicate that goods and services are distributed in the family more on the basis of need than on the basis of position occupied.

In contrast, there prevail a long-standing concern and a considerable accumulation of research data on the designation of responsibility for providing goods and services. This division of labor research can provide many potentialities for developmental analysis. Consideration of the third area —the one having to do with the power and the authority to determine the method of distribution—will take place when the more general topic of order is discussed. Also included in this latter area will be decision-making even though it is sometimes difficult to distinguish between the assignment of decision-making activity as simply a matter of division of labor or as a matter of power and authority.

Studies of Role Complex Patterns

A pattern in the division of labor material exists which has appeared in some of the matter discussed earlier. There are studies which analyze the patterns in a given role complex, such as division of labor in early marriage, in the child-rearing period, in the postparental period, or in retirement, and studies which examine the division of labor comparatively in several different role-complex settings. Often this research attempts to determine the kinds of patterns examined by Rainwater (1965) in his typology of conjugal role-relationships; that is, a basic focus is on the degree to which the roles are segregated or are specialized as opposed to a good deal of sharing of common tasks on the part of the actors. Although most studies deal primarily with only the roles of husbands and wives, some also have included child roles in their work. A rather typical approach is represented by the work of P. G. Herbst (1952 and 1954), who developed an instrument which asked the respondent to report on who typically carried out certain household tasks. Murray Straus (1963*a*; 1963*b*) has further refined Herbst's approach. It is possible to develop scores from Straus's instruments which will determine whether for various tasks and decisions there is husband dominance, wife dominance, autonomic division of labor or power (each actor has specific spheres which are exclusively theirs), or syncratic division of labor or power (actors share certain areas). It is also possible to discover the degree to which the child actors participate in these spheres of activity. Other work (Rodgers, 1967; Jacobsen, 1968) utilized the Straus instrument in research on the occupational socialization of ninth grade boys in an effort to determine if such factors had any relationship to the work socialization process. At the time this book is being written, specific data related to the various role complexes at differing family career points are still being analyzed.

In other similar research, all of which focuses on the husband and wife positions only, Goodrich et al. (1968) found by studying newlyweds in their fourth month of marriage that considerable variation existed in marital role orientations. The investigators were able to tie these various orientations to several other social and psychological factors. Their conclusions, from a developmental point of view, are of some interest (Goodrich et al., 1968:389):

> An extensive factor-analytic treatment of these data has produced eight patterns of marriage. An interpretation of these has suggested that, during the initial stage of marriage, there are different developmental presses as regards adaptation to inner conflict for the male and for the female. The data also suggest that residual problems of autonomy and dependence in these young couples may correspond to styles of relating to relatives and of husband-wife communication. Implicit in these interpretations is the notion that, at each life stage, there is an interaction between intrapsychic and psychosocial elements which together influence the couple's pattern of adaptation.

This study is particularly significant for the developmental approach because it explicitly began with the goal of gaining the sort of data on couples in their early marriage experience over an extended period of time which is called for in the basic theoretical formulation including all three facet levels.

Two studies of role patterns in the middle years of marriage both found evidence of equalitarianism as well as role specialization in the same families (Burchinal and Bauder, 1965; Wilkening and Bharadwaj, 1967). In a study of over 1,000 unbroken white families of high school sophomores, Johannis (1957*a*, 1957*b*, 1958) reported on the family division of labor with respect to economic activity, child-care activity, and household tasks. Again the findings show a considerable range both in shared pursuits and in the proportion of actors in a given position who reported being involved in a particular practice.

Komarovsky's (1962:49–81) excellent study of working-class families in the childrearing years reports on the division of labor particularly with respect to the husband's participation in domestic activities traditionally viewed as the responsibility of the wife. Komarovsky found that cooking, laundry, and cleaning were rejected by a large majority of wives as activities for husbands and that doing the dishes was an activity in which nearly two-thirds of the husbands rarely participated. There was substantially more participation in grocery shopping and in infant care, in which there was almost equal division of husbands into categories of never or hardly ever, occasionally, and frequently or regularly. Much higher participation from husbands was found in planning for Christmas gifts, buying home furnishings, and caring for older children. Although these data show a rather traditional division of labor, an expectation prevails that help from the husband will be forthcoming if there are circumstances which require it.

Taking a somewhat different tack, Bott (1957) intensively studied twenty London families with children under ten years of age who had been married from four to eleven years. She attempted to relate conjugal role relationships to the family's larger social network. Bott developed three basic conjugal relationship types: complementary (activities different and separated but fitted together to form a whole), independent (activities carried out separately without reference to each other), and joint (activities carried out together or by either partner at different times). She typed families by which kind of oganization predominated, since each household exhibited some arrangements of each kind. Bott used the term *social network* to refer to the fact that the external relationships which the various families participated in were such that not all acquaintances knew each other. Thus they did not form a true social group. Rather, there were varying degrees of "connectedness" with respect to these outside acquaintances. Bott labeled a *close-knit* network one in which many of the family's acquaintances knew each other independently of the focal family, and she called a *loose-knit* network one in which few contacts existed between the family's acquaintances other than those in which the focal family was involved. Bott's (1957:59–60) classic hypothesis was as follows: "The degree of segregation in the role-relationship of husband and wife varies directly with the connectedness of the family's social network." Her reasoning was that where there was little connection between the family's acquaintances, the husband and wife would have to look to each other for more emotional satisfaction and for more help with familial tasks. Where there was considerable connectedness, she expected this practice to be less the case.

Her basic findings were as follows (Bott, 1957:62): One family had high conjugal segregation combined with a close-knit network; five families had a joint conjugal pattern with a loose-knit network; nine families had intermediate conjugal segregation and were intermediate also in the connectedness of their social network; the five remaining families were in a state of transition with respect to both variables. Bott carries through a number of interesting analyses which are basically qualitative rather than quantitative because of the small number of cases and the extensive interview data which she possessed. Her approach is especially stimulating from a developmental perspective, since it raises the possibility that the transactional aspect of family roles has a basic significance even for roles which heretofore have been viewed as essentially interactive in nature.

The work of Udry and Hall (1965) raises some cautions which indicate that considerably more research needs to be done. In an attempt at a partial replication of Bott's basic hypothesis, these researchers could find no such relationship between social network and marital role segregation in an American sample of middle-class, middle-aged couples. Instead, Udry and Hall found that low role segregation was most likely to occur in couples with higher education and in which the wife was employed outside the home. As a result, they suggested that Bott's hypothesis may be appropriate for only certain portions of the family career and possibly only for certain social-class levels.

At least some partial support for Udry and Hall's suggestion that role segregation may be related to certain portions of the family career is found in a study by Ballweg (1967) of families with the husband over the age of sixty-five. The data of this study indicate that retired husbands are much more likely to participate in household tasks than are husbands who are still working, with a concomitant decrease in household task performance of the wives.

In a study of three-generation families, Hill (1970:49–50) used six items to assess role specialization. He found that all three generations in the sample followed a medium to high specialization by sex. Contrary to Ballweg's findings, however, the oldest generation was most specialized, the middle generation somewhat less specialized, and the youngest generation less specialized yet. Two studies, then, show differences in role structure by period of the family career but have somewhat contradictory findings.

Deutscher's (1959:109–20) study of postparental (but preretirement) family life contains a specific analysis of the relationship between role complementarity and a positive evaluation of the postparental situation. Although he did not cover some of the particular household tasks which some of the other studies did, he has gathered data on whether a number of activities are done together or apart. Activities associated with house and yard, weekend recreation, culture, and travel are more likely to be joint activities. Work and involvement in the husband's occupation, still being a parent, hobbies, informal gatherings, being a grandparent, clubs and organizations, and being sick are more likely to be individual activities. Church and religion, relaxing and loafing, and care of parents are more equally divided between joint and individual participation categories. Deutscher finds, however, that joint vs. separate activity does not show any statistically significant difference in the positive or in the negative evaluation of the postparental period. His interview data, nevertheless, give evidence that a very important relationship exists between complementarity of roles and a positive view of this period. Possession of data of the sort gathered in some of the other studies would be most interesting in the light of this relationship.

The basic difficulty with the kind of research which we have been discussing is that it is hard to determine the extent to which the division of labor findings are explained by the role-complex structure and to what extent they may be explained by other variables. In some cases, the sample was composed of families with a more-or-less similar role-complex structure as a matter of convenience rather than as an attempt to provide an analysis of the relationship between role complexes and the division of labor. We do not have the kinds of comparable data necessary for a rigorous test through comparisons of samples which differ only in role complex makeup. Needed are studies which either provide cross-sectional data on division of labor for several different role-complex structures or longitudinal studies of division of labor. I know of no examples of the latter, though Hill (1970) provides some cross-sectional information.

Two other studies have had samples which made it possible to analyze data cross-sectionally by the family career category. The work by Harold Feldman (1964) emphasized marital communication and marital adjustment, an issue treated in the section on maintenance of meaning and motivation later in this chapter. In the other study, Blood and Wolfe (1960: 49–53, 68–72) made a specific analysis of the division of labor of husbands and wives in the Detroit area; and, furthermore, one phase of that analysis is by stage in the family life cycle. The items that Blood and Wolfe used are based on the Herbst ones. Basically they found that making home repairs, mowing the lawn, and shoveling snow (an item which cannot be used in many parts of the United States but which fits nicely in Detroit!) are male roles. Getting the husband's breakfast, straightening the living-room for company, and doing the evening dishes are female roles. Keeping track of money and bills and doing the grocery shopping are accomplished jointly. Thus, there tends to be high role specialization in Detroit couples. The changes in task performance for each effort are not analyzed by stage of family life cycle. The data do show, however, that role specialization increases in an approximately linear manner from the beginning to the end of the family career and that there is a similar linear increase in the share of household tasks performed by the wife with some fall off in the post-parental and the retired periods.

Increased sharing between husband and wife was also found by Hill (1970:49) in the United States and by Silverman and Hill (1967:358) in Belgium. The Silverman and Hill analysis is of particular interest because it is an excellent example of the manner in which the developmental theory provides a better explanation of a phenomenon than a competing theory. Blood and Wolfe (1960) had explained the changes in task allocation in terms of a theory of "availability." That is, during certain periods of the family career one spouse takes on certain tasks simply because he is the more "available" one. At other periods the other spouse may carry out that task or it may be one that is shared. However, Silverman and Hill in analyzing both their data from Belgium and the Detroit data conclude (1967:359): The best theory for explaining both Detroit and Louvain variations in task allocation is family development theory which puts availability theory in time perspective over the couple's life cycle. Task performance, adherence to sex definitions of task assignments, and task specialization are shown to vary in both social settings with changes in the size and composition of the family over its life cycle.

Tracing One Role Career

Before completing our discussion of the division of labor, we should direct our attention to one other possible manner of researching this area developmentally. It would be interesting to do something similar to what was suggested for the socialization process—one role may be traced over its entire career. I have discovered only one study which has attempted this approach. Helena Lopata (1966) carried out in-depth interviews with one thousand Chicago housewives, and from this data comes a description of the various stages in the social role of housewife. The stages which she establishes have a striking similarity to those developed in the early years of the developmental approach in which the family career was often divided into the establishment, expanding, stable, contracting, and stable periods (Hill and Rodgers, 1964:173). Lopata sees the housewife role as divided into becoming a housewife, the expanding circle, the peak stage, the "full-house" plateau, the shrinking circle, and the minimal plateau stages. Her article shows the potentialities of this approach, even though this particular report emphasizes qualitative description rather than quantitative analysis. Hopefully the study represents a stimulus for further research of this kind.

Analysis of the division of labor over the career of the family has high potential for producing propositions based on developmental theory and for providing hypotheses for testing and for improving the theory. Since so much family interaction may be seen as related to the division of labor, it is to be expected that much more work will appear in this area.

THE MAINTENANCE OF ORDER

Three distinct, but interrelated, matters fall under the general heading of the maintenance of order: First, there is the matter of power and authority, which includes the process of decision-making as well as other issues. Second, there is the area of family disorganization, which includes the topics of organization and reorganization as well. Third, there is the topic of conflict resolution. Some of the issues already discussed are related closely to the general problem of maintaining order in the family system. For example, socialization has as one of its consequences and, thus, as one of its functions to maintain a level of order by instilling into actors the norms by which they are expected to govern their behavior. Similarly, the division of labor establishes an orderly manner for carrying out the important task of providing goods and services to the members of the group.

Looking ahead, we can anticipate that an outcome of the maintenance of meaning is to provide for some basic value and goal agreement which provides an orderly foundation for group relationships. There are, however, some qualitative differences which result in including only the three areas listed above in this section. For example, family disorganization and conflict resolution are included in this section, but the one on maintenance of meaning and motivation deals with marital and family adjustment. The reason for this somewhat arbitrary division is that family disorganization and conflict resolution are closely related to role relationships and to the way they are structured.

On the other hand, research in marital adjustment has tended to emphasize the matters of emotional compatibility, love relationships, value and goal consensus, and other elements which appear to be closer to the general area of meaning and motivation for participating in a group. This line of reasoning can be carried a bit further by indicating that there appear to be two logical explanations for the dissolution of a marital relationship which may occur singly or in combination: The first explanation is based on the inability of the partners to develop a set of reciprocal roles which allowed for the kinds of achievement of goals upon which they might be assumed to agree. This factor is illustrated by classic case of the couple who are "madly in love" but who simply cannot get along in their daily lives with one another. The second possible basis for dissolving a marriage is the inability to agree on the key values and goals and/or the failure to find the kind of emotional rewards which one expects from the marital relationship. This kind of reason is not nearly so related to the inability to work out adequate reciprocity in role relationships as it is to failure to find common basic meanings in the relationship itself. I do not argue that the two areas are mutually exclusive, but I do argue that they are analytically distinct and are related to two different functional areas in the family system. Conflict resolution must deal with discords about role organization and with dissensions about values. (Sprey [1966] makes some similar points in a most helpful conceptual article on family disorganization.)

Power and Authority

Blood and Wolfe (1960:11) distinguish between power and authority as follows:

> Power may be defined as the potential ability of one partner to influence the other's behavior. Power is manifested in the ability to make decisions affecting the life of the family.
> Authority is closely related to power. Authority is legitimate power, i.e., power held by one partner because both partners feel it is proper for him to do so.

In the terms used in developmental theory, then, authority refers to *roles* and power refers to *role behaviors,* since authority is a quality defined as appropriate, whereas power is shown in how people actually behave. Thus, although an ideal may prevail at the societal-institutional level—or even at the group-interactional level—that decisions ought to be made on a democratic or equalitarian basis (authority), the actual pattern of behavior may show that a more patriarchal or matriarchal structure (power) exists. Few studies have gathered data on comparisons of what ought to be vs. what is. Most studies purportedly deal with power, rather than with authority, since they contain information on how things are done—or, at least, perceived to be done—in families. The problem is more complex than this focus allows, however, since there is some evidence that people's perceptions of how things are done are not very accurate when compared with how things actually are done (Olsen, 1969). Furthermore, power and decision-making frequently are intermingled in research in such a way that it is not always possible to separate them.

Studies of Power. In my (1967) study of occupational socialization of ninth-grade boys, I have data from the boy and from both his parents about who decides in certain areas of behavior. Since these facts are in reports from each respondent, rather than observations of family behavior, they are actually perceptions of power and decision-making, of course. Following Straus's (1963) approach, I also gathered data on *ultimate power* as measured by who has the last word with respect to a set of decisions. The findings concerning decision-making indicate rather high agreement on perceptions among the three respondents of each family. All agree that mother has the highest decision-making responsibility in most areas, except in the financial areas where father has a slightly higher influence. There is also general agreement that sons have a good deal of responsibility in selecting their own clothing and their friends. One interesting difference in perception occurs concerning the control of the son's recreational activity. Sons feel they control this area more than parents report. In the area of the last word, there is also high agreement. Fathers have more power with respect to automobile and insurance purchases, mothers more in household operation and food budgets, with joint power prevailing in the other areas. Sons are viewed as participating somewhat in the areas of auto purchases, vacations, housing choice, household operation, and in parents' and children's social activities. The general picture, however, is one of very low power for the son. Analyses of differences in power at varying points in the family career are not yet completed.

Blood and Wolfe (1960:41–44) do have such family career analyses. Although their basic findings are quite similar to mine in regard to the general distribution of decision-making participation, their findings on the change in power by stage in the family life cycle show an interesting pattern. In a system in which a score of 4.00 indicates equal power and scores above this figure show more power for the husband, the scores are as follows: honeymoon—5.35; preschool—5.71; preadolescent—5.41; adolescent—5.06; unlaunched—4.68; postparental—4.79; retired—4.44. The pattern for childless couples (corresponding in age to the preschool, preadolescent, and adolescent parents) is 5.30, 4.72, and 4.20. Thus, although husbands in childless couples continue to have reducing power until the latter portion of the career, couples who have children show an increase in power for the husband with a falling off as the children get older, a minor rise in the postparental period, and then a lowering of power in retirement. (For more on this subject, see also Wolfe [1959].) In interpreting their data, Blood and Wolfe (1960:44–45) come to the following conclusions:

> In summary, the power to make decisions stems primarily from the resources which the individual can provide to meet the needs of his marriage partner and to upgrade his decision-making skill. . . . power in

American marriages is not a matter of brute coercion and unwilling defeat so much as a mutual recognition of individual skills in particular areas of competence and of the partners' dual stake in areas of joint concern.

In her study of working-class marriages, Komarovsky (1962:220–35) found some support for the Blood and Wolfe interpretation in her analysis of "personal leadership or competence" as a source of marital power. But she also found that such factors as ideology, physical coercion, social rank, and the relative stake in the relationship carried important implications for the power structure. Komarovsky (1962:234–35) concludes her analysis, therefore, with this statement:

> More intensive comparative studies, we believe, will confirm the lesson of Glenton that the power structure of marriage in a given class is the net result of a great variety of social factors, reinforcing and occasionally off-setting one another. Patriarchal or equalitarian mores; patterns of mate selection; the relative bargaining position of each sex in a given social milieu; the relative personal, educational and economic attainments of men and women; and the roles men and women play in the community —all together give the conjugal power structure of a socioeconomic class its peculiar character.

Since Komarovsky's examination included no attempt at developmental analysis, we shall have to add that these factors may quite likely vary by the period in the family career with which one is concerned. In effect, the kinds of elements which both the Komarovsky and the Blood and Wolfe research have identified fall nicely into the facets of analysis with which developmental theory concerns itself. Blood and Wolfe's data show that these factors vary, at least in their consequences for family power, through the family career. Indeed, attempts to replicate the Blood and Wolfe findings have been made in several European countries (Buric and Zecevic, 1967; Michel, 1967; Safilios-Rothschild, 1967; Silverman and Hill, 1967). These studies showed power exercised differently in different periods of the family career, and these patterns for different countries did not all coincide with Blood and Wolfe's American data. Rodman (1967) attempts some explanations for why this distinction appeared between countries which relate both to the group-interactional and to the societal-institutional facets of the family. Rodman (1967:322) states: "The balance of marital power is influenced by the interaction of (1) the comparative resources of husband and wife and (2) the cultural and subcultural expectations about the distribution of marital power."

There are many other studies that may be cited. Perhaps, it will be best to indicate only a selected few which in one way or another are particularly relevant to the developmental approach. Bowerman and Elder (1964) sensitize the researcher to a fact clearly recognized in developmental theory —that the power dimension operates in several different types of role complexes. Thus, the researchers specifically separate out the "conjugal power structure" as referring to the husband-wife role complex, the "parental power structure" as referring to the father-mother role complex, the "child-rearing power structure" as referring to the parent-child role complex, and the "family structural patterns" as referring to power relations which involve all three of the previously identified role complexes. Although their empirical work deals only with adolescence, there is no reason to assume that the basic theoretical approach cannot be extended to the other periods in the family career.

Similarly, Papanek (1969) identifies the effect that certain authority patterns have on various role complexes in the family with adolescents. She (Papanek, 1969:88) finds, for example, that, "if the authority roles of husband and wife are highly differentiated, the boy and girl roles and (with respect to open expression of affection and 'democracy') the adult and child roles, are more sharply differentiated. The father-daughter relationship is especially affected."

Smith (1970) provides a modification of the French and Raven (1959) power model, which he applies to parent-adolescent power relationships. He identifies four types of parental power related to the basis from which the power derives: outcome-control (ability to reward or punish), referent (general disposition of the child to turn to parent for guidance), legitimate (right to control out of obligation or norms accepted by the child), and expert resource (parent possesses supposedly useful knowledge). Smith further recognized Secord and Backman's (1964:273–93) insight that power was exercised according to the degree to which the influenced person was dependent on the powerful person and to the degree that the influenced person had alternative resources available to him. Smith (1970:869–70) found that the bases of power were far more important in explaining power relationships than were the conditions of dependency or available alternatives. This study provides some interesting developmental questions. First, do the bases for parental control vary in differing periods of the family career? Second, do the conditions of dependency and available alternatives also vary over the career?

Decision-Making and Consumer Behavior. More directly associated with decision-making is a whole body of material about consumer behavior. Over the years, some of this work has been particularly concerned with various aspects of the family career and its relationship to decisions with respect to consumption. Thus, an early volume in the *Consumer Behavior* series (Clark:1955) concerned itself especially with the life cycle. Then Lansing and Kish (1957) utilized the family life cycle as an explanation for a set of consumer purchases. A later volume in the *Consumer Behavior* series (Foote, 1961:57–80, 140–64, 239–65, 276–97) contained analyses by Reuben Hill, William F. Kenkel, Howard S. Becker, Mirra Komarovsky, and Bernard Farber all of which have specific family and/or developmental concerns. Later, Hill (1965) reported on some specific findings from a study of three generation families and their decision-making patterns in which a conscious developmental approach was taken. Finally, Evans and Smith (1969) carried out an analysis of decision-making patterns which utilized social-class and family life cycle categories.

We can summarize this section by stating that the developmental approach anticipates changes both in roles and in role behavior at all three facet levels along the power and authority dimensions over the family career. The data, though limited, appears to support those expectations. Considerable work remains, however, which will more fully explicate the kinds of changes which take place, the variables which appear to precipitate these changes, and the consequences of these changes for family dynamics. Developmental analysis of family power structure also may contribute to the further understanding of power relationships in general. Perhaps in the process, many of the existing shortcomings in conceptualization and in research methodology may be alleviated (Olsen, 1969; Safilios-Rothschild, 1970).

Family Disorganization

Some years ago, L. L. Geismar (1960) and his associates (1959, 1963) carried out some work designed to provide a method for analyzing family disorganization by utilizing other kinds of data than those found in reports of divorce, desertion, crime, child neglect, and the like. The basis of this method was the measurement of role performance of family members in several categories representing both interactional and transactional arenas. The motivation for developing such a measure arose out of reaction to a somewhat questionable orientation which still appears in family study; that is, families are assumed to be organized until they come to the attention of official agencies through some crisis or through some disruptive event. (See, for example, Goode, 1966.) Families function at various levels along an organized-disorganized dimension, even though they do not come to the attention of any public agency and do not become part of the official statistics.

Some theorist-researchers working in the area of family stress have shown that the level of functioning before a crisis or stress event is a major explanatory variable in determining the impact of the event on the family. A developmental point of view will anticipate that certain role-complex patterns are more vulnerable to disorganizing influences than others, even though they do not necessarily result in behavioral manifestations which are severe enough to come to official attention. Casual acquaintance with families at various points in their careers indicates that certain role-complex patterns seem to be more subject to problems and that some periods appear hectic, whereas others are relatively calm. Developmental theorists expect that such periods will be characterized by major changes occurring in roles in several positions, if not simultaneously, at least in close proximity to one another. Maintaining order in such high change periods represents the expenditure of considerable effort on the part of the actors in the system.

A further implication of such a view is that, at the very time when individual actors are attempting to incorporate new roles into their role cluster as well as to deal with the resultant reciprocal role consequences of such changes, attention also must be paid to the continuing problem of the general maintenance of order in the system as a whole. Put another way, when little change is occurring, positional occupants are able to handle matters of system order with little difficulty, since they are not heavily involved in resolving role changes in their own role clusters or in those of reciprocal roles. In periods of high role change, however, actors must not only deal with these issues, but with general system order as well.

Most research which deals with family disorganization tends to begin by identifying a more or less public event as an indicator of disorganization. But there is a place for research about what may be termed *normal families,* that is, families that have no such indicators to bring them to public attention. Such research will be aimed at identifying periods in the familial career when the maintenance of system order is either more or less demanding. From an applied standpoint, such research may be viewed as leading to "preventive medicine." It will be useful to the helping professions in determining when family problems may be most likely to be most disruptive and in developing programs of aid to families during such periods (see Aldous and Hill, 1969, for an example.) There are, therefore, both pure theoretical and applied reasons for urging a concerted research program aimed at identifying the ebb and the flow of order-maintenance dynamics over the family career. Discussion of the various aspects of official disorganization appears in the subsequent chapters covering atypical role complexes and family stress.

Conflict Resolution

Open clashes between actors in the family system of a verbal and/or physical sort are probably inevitable, regardless of the general level of adjustment and organization of the family. The family, then, must develop modes of resolving such conflicts in order to maintain order. The degree of success achieved in developing these means is probably related to the degree of satisfaction and to the level of organization which one finds present in the family. The process of conflict resolution is analytically distinct from levels of adjustment and of organization.

The tendency in family research is to focus on particular role complexes, more usually dyads such as the husband-wife or parent-child combinations, rather than on the entire system at one point in time or over a period of its career. In this area, the tendency has been to deal more with husband-wife marital adjustment and with parent-child interaction primarily from the point of view of childrearing practices. Some work has been done with observations of husbands and wives resolving conflicts in laboratory situations (Strodtbeck, 1951; Kenkel, 1963; Goodrich and Boomer, 1963). Such studies, of course, are subject to all the criticisms associated with laboratory experiments which revolve around the question of whether such artificial situations actually provide an accurate representation of the day-to-day interactive patterns of subjects. Proponents of the methods usually argue that subjects tend to use those patterns of behavior which they normally employ, even though the experimental situation may be contrived. To a certain extent, this argument appears to be a valid one, though it fails to deal with the issue of the process by which conflicts may normally be precipitated in the family's "natural" setting. This latter issue, of course, is of central significance to the developmental theoretical approach. In fairness, it must be pointed out that the typical social survey research method which utilizes the questionnaire or interview method for gathering data does not appear to hold any superiority in this respect.

Blood's and Spiegel's Approach: Emphasis on Consensus-Equilibrium. Two theoretical articles, one of which is based on an empirical study, seem relevant to this issue. Blood (1960) has dealt with conflict resolution in the family both from the standpoint of the basic sources of conflict and with respect to the modes for resolution of conflict. The sources which he cites arise out of the basic characteristics of the family system as being nonvoluntary, intimate, small in size, and subject to almost continual change. This latter point, particularly, identifies the basic developmental character of the family system as one in which the roles and actors are constantly in the process of adjusting to new situations. Blood identifies two types of mechanisms for dealing with conflict: normative and instrumental. In the first category, he places avoidance, allocation of rights and duties to particular roles, and equality of treatment. In the second category, he includes increasing the facilities for family living, utilization of priority systems, enlarging areas of autonomy, and the development of safety valves for tension reduction. Finally, he identifies four processes for conflict resolution: discussion, mediation, accommodation, and separation. Thus, Blood emphasizes heavily the basic structural characteristics of the family along with certain facilitating mechanisms as both the sources of conflict and the resources for resolving them.

Spiegel (1957) has presented an approach to conflict resolution which arises out of his work with families of emotionally disturbed children as compared with families in which no manifest disturbance could be identified. Although he is a psychoanalyst by profession, his approach is characterized by insights which range over the three facets of concern to developmental theory. Like Blood, Spiegel identifies the fact that there are certain built-in potentialities for conflict in the family system. Basing his approach on a conceptual schema revolving around the complementarity of roles, he cites five reasons which he believes to be important sources for the inevitable failure of complementarity to always prevail. These are the following: cognitive discrepancy, in which there is a failure to have familiarity with the required roles; discrepancy of goals; allocative discrepancy, which arises out of questioning the actor's right to a role he wishes to occupy; instrumental discrepancy, in which what we have called *facilitating mechanisms* of various types are lacking; and discrepancy in cultural value orientations.

In attempting to restore the lost complementarity, Spiegel posits two basic kinds of processes: The first major type of resolution is *role induction*. Through it, the discrepancy is resolved by one or another actor unilaterally giving in and taking on the role expected of him. This goal may be accomplished by coercing; by coaxing; by evaluating (in which positive and negative sanctions are used in a more general manner than in coercing or coaxing) by masking, in which information is withheld or incorrect information is given in order to settle the conflict; or by postponing in the hope that one of the parties to the conflict will change his behavior, given a bit of time.

The second major type of resolution is *role modification*, which involves bilateral (or, perhaps, multilateral—though Spiegel does not deal with this specifically) change in role expectations. Such alteration may be achieved by joking, by referral to an outside party, by exploration of alternatives, by compromise, or by consolidation. Another type, which Spiegel posits as being transitional between the two major kinds, is role reversal. In this situation, an attempt at empathic insight is made. The consequence of such a process, he says, may be either to move to role induction or to role modification.

Spiegel treats each of his two major types of conflict resolution as having a temporal order, in which one strategy may lead to the next. Thus, failure to achieve behavioral modification through coercion may lead to coaxing, and so on. Spiegel does not claim to have firm empirical basis for this order, however, and makes it clear that there is need for additional research to explore these ideas.

Neither Blood nor Spiegel carry their analyses to the issue of whether the modes of conflict resolution which they postulate may vary according to the period in the family career when the conflict may arise. One basic question from the developmental perspective is whether or not families tend to utilize one mode more extensively than another depending on the kind of role-complex structure which exists. It would appear logical, for example, that the mode of resolution of conflict between parent and child might differ considerably if the child were of preschool age as opposed to being in his teens. Similarly, it may be anticipated that husbands and wives in early marriage will use differing modes than those in the postparental or retirement period. The extent to which conflict involves only a dyad or is more widespread in involving several actors in the system certainly appears to have some bearing on the process as well. In addition, it may be that certain factors tied to basic role expectations of given positions lead to different modes of conflict resolution used by actors in those positions. The research of Cutler and Dyer (1965) appear to give some hint of this possibility in the case of young married couples. The investigators found that husbands more frequently adopted a wait-and-see approach, whereas wives tended to select open discussion and sharing of the issue. In Spiegel's terms, husbands seemed to use postponement, whereas wives sought alternatives.

Sprey's Perspective: Stress on the Normality of Conflict. Finally, in a most seminal article, Jetse Sprey (1969) takes an entirely different tack to the matter of familial conflict. He suggests a conceptual point of view which, rather than emphasizing consensus-equilibrium in the family, emphasizes conflict as a natural and continuing state. The issue for theoretical explanation then becomes "how is orderly cooperation between family members possible?" rather than "why conflict?" (Sprey, 1969:703) as in the Blood or the Spiegel approach. Sprey argues further that a major analytical problem is explaining the management of conflict. Indeed, he would not accept the title of this subsection, "Conflict Resolution," as appropriate except as it might deal with the *elimination* of one of the parties to the conflict (Sprey, 1969:704–706). This exclusion, of course, would mean separation and/or divorce, since we could assume along with Sprey that "less conventional techniques such as doing away with one's spouse" might be a bit extreme.

The point of view expressed by Sprey and the focus which derives from the developmental approach do not appear to be incompatible. It is true that some of the roots of developmental theory are found in theoretical approaches which tend to emphasize equilibrium, role complementarity, and adjustment mechanisms and, therefore, which tend to view conflict as abnormal. Hill (1971:19–23), however, has pointed out that the developmental theory also recognizes growth and change as a normal family process which raises questions about the equilibrium-seeking nature of the family system. Hill suggests that the resolution of the problem lies in the idea of *feedback* processes of social systems.

A developmental perspective recognizes the normality of conflict and conflict resolution as a *continuing* process. Thus, perhaps, Sprey's term *conflict management* is more appropriate, since it tends to emphasize the ongoing nature of dealing with differences in the family career and does not have the implication that there is a state of the family in which conflict is totally absent. Sprey's article sensitizes the family analyst to take a perspective highlighting some analytical problems which may tend to be ignored.

Once again, we are left in the realm of speculation concerning the relationship between the family career and the conflict management modes. There appears to be more guidance from the developmental theory as presently formulated in identifying the sources of conflict and the development of propositions to be explored, than there is in suggesting the processes by which conflict is managed (for one nondevelopmental treatment, see Turner, 1970:135–63). In this latter area, an extension of Sprey's approach may make the greater contribution. What has been accomplished is the identification of yet another rich field which remains to be explored from a developmental perspective.

THE MAINTENANCE OF MEANING AND MOTIVATION

Two general matters, closely related to the facets of analysis, fall into area concerning maintenance of meaning and motivation. The first consideration is at the group-interactional and individual-psychological level and involves the issue of finding meaning in the existing relationships within the family system; that is, it may be postulated that the continuance of the family system is tied to the necessity for individual actors to find significant reasons for maintaining membership in the system. The second matter, located at the societal-institutional and at the group-interactional levels, is the more general one of values or philosophy of life. Once again the issues are certainly not separable in the day-to-day familial dynamics, but good reason exists for making the analytical distinction.

At the outset of the discussion on the maintenance of order, I stated that one of the basic reasons for dissolving a marital relationship may be the failure to find the kind of meaning in that relationship which one or both partners have sought. I asserted that most of the material about marital adjustment in one way or another reduced itself to this issue. Regardless of the specific area of concern which may be identified as being the source of marital difficulty—sexual relationships, economic relationships,

social relationships, personality characteristics, and so on—what is ultimately being analyzed is the extent to which one or more actors finds the
kinds of meaning in the relationship which he considers satisfactory. I do
not confine this examination to the marital relationship alone but extend
it to all the relationships which may exist in the family system. I am not
discussing again the matter of dealing with conflicts which may arise. I am
identifying the issue of whether the *roles themselves*, both those associated
with the actor's position and those in the reciprocal positions, are meaningful.

To put the point simply, a woman may play the role of homemaker in
such a manner that there are no serious conflicts of sources of disorganization. This participation does not necessarily imply, however, that the role
itself provides the kind of meaning for her which will motivate her to
continue in that role. Or, to extend the illustration, simply because the
woman plays the homemaker role in the manner prescribed does not mean
that actors in reciprocal roles will find their relationship with her meaningful enough to motivate *them* to continue in the reciprocal roles, even
though she may find the role most meaningful. Perhaps the husband would
find much more meaning in the relationship if the wife emphasized her
role as companion or lover, even if this shift meant less adequate performance in her homemaker role. Perhaps actors in the child positions
would find much more meaning in the relationship if the mother emphasized her role as their emotional supporter. Thus, although no overt conflict
may arise, the matter of stressing a given role in the cluster over its other
roles may lead to a loss of meaning for continued participation in the
system.

Marital Adjustment

The material on marital adjustment is far too voluminous to review in
detail here, nor will there be any great merit in doing so (three reviews may
be found in Kirkpatrick, 1963:375–407, 665–78; Bowerman, 1964; Bernard,
1964). The great share of the material deals with marital adjustment in a
manner similar to the demographic approach observed in fertility study.
As a consequence, not much can be gained from it with respect to the
interactive patterns which are of central concern. In addition, there is very
little material dealing with *family* adjustment in the way the developmental
approach requires. Therefore, a few studies have been selected which are
suggestive of a developmental analysis of the maintenance of meaning in
the family system.

Komarovsky's Study. Komarovsky's (1962:82–219, 259–79) analysis
based on interviews with working-class couples, most of whom were under
forty years of age and all of whom had children in the home, provides a

number of insights bearing on the maintenance of meaning in marriage. In exploring a wide range of topics—sexual relations, marital communication, interpersonal competence, and in-law relationships—the case studies she presents frequently point to an underlying concern with the meaning which the various roles have to the husband and wife. The relationships appear to hold the marriage bond together in many cases in spite of what may be evaluated as major maladjustments. For example, Komarovsky (1962:85) quotes one wife as follows with respect to sexual relations: "There is more to sex than just sex. There's being together and knowing you love each other. It doesn't always have to be hot." Further data from couples who are sexually adjusted, but generally unhappy with their marriages, and from couples who are sexually maladjusted, but happy, appear to provide support for the view which underlies this quotation. There is a broader meaning to the sexual relationship than the narrow physical experience. The data on marital communication and on self-disclosure to the partner provide similar implications. Although it is a common middle-class assumption that marital partners must share with one another for marital happiness, in many of these working-class marriages Komarovsky (1962:126–32) found that "marriage is not for friendship." Fully a third of the sample do not share their innermost thoughts with their spouses; however, the extent of sharing of such intimate areas of one's self is not correlated directly with marital happiness.

Thus, Komarovsky (1962:133–47) finds couples who are happy though sharing very little, others who are unhappy though fully disclosing themselves, as well as those who share fully and are happy and those who do little sharing and are unhappy. For each *deviant* type there appear to be other meanings in the relationship which serve to provide either a positive or negative evaluation. For example, Komarovsky (1962:121–22) found that qualities associated with the major institutional roles of provider, homemaker, parent, and in-law were first in importance for the evaluation of what makes a good husband or wife, whereas general human qualities of kindness, loyalty, honesty, or not nagging were second most important. I conclude from Komarovsky's data that an explanation of the adjustment level of the marriage must go beyond the simple tabulating of certain types of behaviors to an exploration of the underlying meaning of those behaviors in the perception of the actors. There was no analysis of Komarovsky's data which compared families in differing role-complex structures, however, so that it is not possible to determine whether these meanings may vary according to this basic developmental variable.

Blood's and Wolfe's Analysis. Blood and Wolfe (1960:115–267) also have reported extensively on areas of husband and wife relationships which fall within the field of maintenance of meaning. In a number of cases, their analyses include family life cycle breakdowns. In discussing the place of children in marriage, wives in the Detroit area listed having children as second in importance only to companionship with the husband. Twenty-six percent of the wives listed children as most important and 28 percent listed them as second in importance (Blood and Wolfe, 1960:117).

Blood and Wolfe asked these wives for both positive and negative factors associated with having children. The pleasure and the emotional satisfaction derived from offspring was most frequently mentioned by wives at all stages of the life cycle, though interesting variations occurred (see Table 6.1).

TABLE 6.1 · Good Things about Having Children, by Stage in Family-life Cycle

GOOD THINGS ABOUT HAVING CHILDREN	STAGE IN FAMILY-LIFE CYCLE				
	Age of Oldest Child				Postparental
	Under 6	6–12	13–18	19+	
1. Pleasure	44%	46%	57%	43%	53%
2. Companionship	15	16	18	22	18
3. Purpose	17	17	13	17	16
4. Strengthens family	13	15	9	11	7
5. Strengthens marriage	10	4	3	—	1
6. Security	1	2	—	5	5
7. Nothing	—	—	—	2	—
Total	100	100	100	100	100
Number of families	126	137	101	63	83

Reprinted with permission of the Macmillan Company from *Husbands and Wives* by Robert O. Blood, Jr. and Donald M. Wolfe, Table 62, p. 140. © by the Free Press, a Corporation, 1960.

On the negative side, there are also some interesting data (see Table 6.2). It is clear that the more experience the wives had with children, the less likely the women were to see them as problems, though Blood and Wolfe interpret the postparental responses as nostalgic. It is relatively easy to explain the reasons for life-cycle variations where problems are mentioned. Younger children restrict the freedom of the couple more than older children; and, in addition, couples who have had experience with children for some years are probably less likely to be as conscious of losing freedom as those who have only relatively recently lost it. Aside from the interest inherent in these data, they tend to support my interpretation that there are underlying meanings to certain phenomena which are associated clearly to the motivation (or to the lack of it) for maintaining one's association with the familial system. The positive reasons all seem to be tied to such an interpretation, with at least some of the negative ones also having this implication.

TABLE 6.2 · *Problems Children Present, by Stage in Family-life Cycle*

PBOBLEMS CHILDREN PRESENT	STAGE IN FAMILY-LIFE CYCLE				
	Age of Oldest Child				Postparental
	Under 6	6–12	13–18	19+	
1. None	21%	22%	36%	39%	54%
2. Financial	14	19	10	17	10
3. Illness	15	19	12	9	10
4. Burdens	21	13	16	20	9
5. Worries	10	11	17	8	12
6. Restrictions	19	15	9	5	5
7. Conflict	—	1	—	2	—
Total	100	100	100	100	100
Number of families	127	137	101	64	79

Reprinted with permission of the Macmillan Company from *Husbands and Wives* by Robert O. Blood, Jr. and Donald M. Wolfe, Table 64, p. 143. © by the Free Press, a Corporation, 1960.

From the Blood and Wolfe data on companionship, it is possible to infer underlying meanings which apparently differ over the career of the family. The four types of companionship and the percentage of wives reporting each type were as follows: organizational companionship, in which the husband and wife participate together in various organized groups—37 percent; informative companionship, in which there is communication about events having happened while the couple was separated —40 percent report this interaction occurring daily and an additional 37 percent report at least weekly experience; colleague companionship, in which couples get together with the husband's work colleagues—41 percent report never having this interaction happen, and another 30 percent report it only occasionally; and friendship companionship, in which the couple get together with mutual friends—20 percent report that they know all of their husband's friends quite well and another 28 percent report that they know most of their husband's friends (Blood and Wolfe, 1960:151–55). The interpretation which I apply to these data is that the general idea of companionship is related most closely to meanings that are family system related. This explanation is enhanced by data which show the highest satisfaction with companionship is most closely related to informative companionship, the next highest with friendship companionship, with colleague and organizational types following at a considerably lower level (Blood and Wolfe, 1960:168, Table 79).

Family-life cycle variations in satisfaction with companionship are of some interest. Overall satisfaction with companionship takes the form of a U-shaped curve (Blood and Wolfe, 1960:156, Table 70). Satisfaction is the highest in the honeymoon period before children come and drops off steadily through the preschool, preadolescent, adolescent, and unlaunched stages. It rises again in the postparental and retired stages, though it never again regains the levels reported at the stages before adolescence. Interestingly couples who remain childless throughout marriage have wives who report the highest satisfaction at all comparable periods, and there is a somewhat less drastic reduction in satisfaction as the marriage persists. It is apparent, then, that the presence of children in the family role complex has a definite negative impact on the companionship experience of the husband and wife. This finding complements the one above that for the wife, the meaning of their children's companionship rises in each successive stage of the life cycle (Blood and Wolfe, 1960:140, Table 62).

Further evidence for the relationship between the maintenance of meaning and changes in the family career is found in the analyses of the variables of understanding and of love. Understanding, which presumably contributes to emotional well-being, is reported by the Detroit area wives as being the third most important value in marriage (Blood and Wolfe, 1960:181). It even is listed as more important than affection, though it is considerably less important than companionship and having children. Nevertheless, 15 percent of the wives ranked understanding first in importance, whereas an additional 20 percent ranked it second. Also of significance, however, is that when wives were asked what they did "to get it out of your system" when they had a bad day, only 5 percent of the urban wives and 3 percent of the farm wives spontaneously mentioned positive interaction with the husband, whereas another 3 percent of the urban wives mentioned negative interaction with the husband (Blood and Wolfe, 1960:185, Table 84). When asked directly whether they discussed their bad days with their husbands, 45 percent of the urban and 54 percent of the rural wives said that they always or usually did, whereas an additional 27 percent of the urban and 21 percent of the rural wives said they did about half the time (Blood and Wolfe, 1960:190, Table 88).

Analyzing the responses over the family career (Blood and Wolfe, 1960:188, Table 87), the researchers found that 5 percent of the honeymoon wives spontaneously report positive interaction, followed by 9.4 percent of the preschool wives, 4.3 percent of the preadolescent, 2 percent of the adolescent, 1.6 percent of the unlaunched, 3.5 percent of the postparental, and none of the retired wives. Thus, mothers of preschool children seem to gain the most positive support from their husbands with a falling off during the remainder of the childrearing period and with a slight increase again in the postparental period. On the negative side, 25 percent of the honeymoon wives report negative interaction after a bad day, but only 2.4 percent of the preschool and 5.7 percent of the preadolescent wives report similarly. The only other group reporting negative interaction is the postparental one with 2.3 percent. The mean frequency of telling troubles to the husband (the researchers used a scoring system ranging from 0 = never to 4 = always) by life-cycle category was as follows (Blood and Wolfe, 1960:192, Table 90): honeymoon—2.65; preschool—2.58; pre-adolescent—2.43; adolescent—2.43; unlaunched—1.78; postparental—2.31; and retired—2.22. Thus, once again we see the dropping off of communication with the husband over troubles during the childrearing period and a slight rise again during the postparental and the retired periods.

Finally, the satisfaction with understanding over the life cycle shows a similar pattern, with a rise from the honeymoon period to the preschool period but then a drop back to a level below that of the honeymoon period and a continuing drop until the postparental period, at which time satisfaction with understanding rises to its highest level and drops back to a level for retired wives which is the second lowest of all (Blood and Wolfe, 1960:217, Table 106). It must be said, however, that this variation takes place in the general range between the category of "all right—can't complain" and the one of "quite satisfied." Therefore, it appears that while there is a reduction in turning to the husband as the family career progresses and although there is some reduction in the satisfaction with his understanding, there is still an overall level of positive meaning in the relationship when troubles occur. Of course, families in which there may not have been a general positive satisfaction were probably no longer together and, thus, did not appear in the study sample.

To complete the picture from the Blood and Wolfe data, we need only report that the life cycle pattern of satisfaction with love is an essential duplicate of what we have seen for understanding (Blood and Wolfe, 1960:232, Table 117). Qualitatively, wives in the first four life cycle categories tend to fall in the "quite satisfied—I'm lucky the way it is" response category. The unlaunched, postparental, and retired wives fall in the somewhat less enthusiastic "it's all right, I guess—I can't complain" category with the unlaunched the least satisfied, the postparental the most satisfied, and the retired falling between the two.

Considerable attention has been devoted to the Blood and Wolfe data primarily because it is almost unique in its attention to analysis of findings across the family career. The four areas of companionship—having children, understanding, and love—all show considerable association with the more general topic under consideration, the maintenance of meaning in the family system. Furthermore, the data have shown that a considerable difference exists across the family career in these variables. All this information suggests two points: First, studies which would delve more deeply into the underlying meanings for commitment to the family system, or lack of it, appear to be indicated by the findings of Blood and Wolfe. Second, studies which would serve to provide cumulative data confirming, disconfirming, and extending the findings of this study would be desirable, particularly if they were more consciously based on the developmental theoretical framework.

Feldman's Work. Another study provides some cumulative data comparable to the Blood and Wolfe analysis. Feldman's (1964:119–26) research on the husband-and-wife relationship, based on the analysis of questionnaire data, provides pertinent information about communication patterns, about marital satisfaction, and about marital values. The information is particularly relevant since the basic design of the study involved analysis of data by family role complexes over the family career. We need only summarize the major findings which relate to the family career and to the maintenance of meaning in order to determine to what degree the Feldman data confirm or fail to support those of Blood and Wolfe.

The major variable in this study was frequency of marital discussions. Overall, Feldman found that there was a statistically significant linear reduction in the frequency of discussion over the family career but with an interesting upturn in frequency in the postparental period. Thus, the Feldman result parallels the findings of Blood and Wolfe. There are several breakdowns of Feldman's general finding as it relates to other variables of further interest. Feldman discovered that discussion of conventional and objective topics (home repairs, religion, news, culture, sports) tended to increase over the career, whereas discussion of more personal topics and ones more closely related to familial matters (sex, husband's hobbies, children, parents of the couple) tended to decrease. By differentiating the subjects of discussion, Feldman has added new information.

The meanings attached to these discussions, which are of central interest to us, as well as other behavior from which meanings may be inferred, also are somewhat more differentiated. For example, the further along in the family career they are, the more likely the couple are to feel closer together after discussing the impersonal topics, rather than the more intimate ones. To further support this finding, whereas the general category of "marital values" tended to increase in value during the career, the subarea of affective values (sex, having children, feeling needed, and being in love) decreased in importance. Added to these data is the finding that couples tend to have fewer "gay times" outside the home as the career progresses. There is also a less punitive response to marital conflict, with more calm talk about differences in the later periods of the family career. Expressiveness toward the spouse also declines. The overall trend, therefore, appears to be one of increasing objectivity in the marital relationship over time.

In contrast to these findings, however, are some U-shaped curves with respect to various aspects of marital satisfaction. Thus, similar to the Blood and Wolfe findings, Feldman finds that stated marital satisfaction, satisfaction with the life cycle stages in general, satisfaction with independent

children, satisfaction with the early years of marriage, and marital stress all
tended to show high levels at the beginning and at the end of the career
with lower levels in the middle periods. The honeymoon group had the
highest satisfaction of all, with the elderly having the next highest. Also
high were couples in the launching period and those with young adults as
oldest children. Those low in satisfaction were the families whose youngest
children had just entered school, parents of teenagers, those whose eldest
child had just entered school, and those with all school age children. In
dealing with marital conflict, couples in the postparental period, in the
launching period, in the beginning period, and in the period with young
adults in the home tend to use a "suppressive mode," that is, not thinking
about their conflict and forgetting it. On the other hand, couples in the
middle childrearing periods tend to use this mode very little. These are the
same couples who are lowest in marital satisfaction. Complementing this
finding is the additional information that couples who have high positive
feelings after value discussions with the spouse are the elderly ones, the
postparental ones, the just-married ones, and the ones with young adults in
the home. Again the low categories are the couples with school-age children,
those with the oldest child in school and the youngest one preschool, those
with the oldest child just having entered school, and the couples in the
launching period. Thus, Feldman (1964:126) concludes:

> As the marriage progresses it is characterized by a lower frequency of
> verbal communication, more objectivity, less spontaneity, less affectivity,
> more wife authority although less sex frequency activity, and more calm-
> ness and impunitiveness. Satisfaction with marriage tends to be higher at
> the beginning and ending periods of marriage, as is suppression of con-
> flict and affectivity after values discussions. One explanation for these
> findings is that at the beginning of marriage reactivity, sexual relations
> and enchantment with knowing the other increases affectivity toward the
> other. The stress periods, near the middle of marriage, have a continuing
> high enchantment level but there is the beginning of disillusionment with
> the other as filling the romanticized ideal. Near the end of marriage the
> couples come to grips with marriage and begin to accept the other more
> realistically. Companionship as a value begins to supersede the affective
> romantic orientation and satisfaction increases.

Rollins and Feldman's Study. Later analysis of the Feldman data
(Rollins and Feldman, 1970), shows that the careers of the husband-father
and the wife-mother positions differ in the satisfaction experience. The four
charts reproduced (see Figures 6.1–6.4) provide interesting pictorial representation of these variations. Rollins and Feldman (1970:27) interpret
their findings as follows:

These data suggest that marriage has very different meanings for husbands than for wives and that very different events within or outside the marriage and/or family influence the developmental pattern of marital satisfaction in men and women. This might help explain the fact that some studies have found family life cycle differences for both men and women and some for women only. It seems that men are influenced more by events both before and after there are children in families while women are influenced more by the presence of children.

Some Concluding Comments. These findings of Feldman and of Blood and Wolfe are reminiscent of the work of Pineo (1961), who carried out a comparative analysis of data gathered by Burgess and Wallin (1953) in a study of early marriages and of the same couples twenty years later. Pineo found that there was a general drop in marital satisfaction and in adjustment, a loss of intimacy as measured by confiding, kissing, and reciprocal resolution of conflicts, whereas at the same time personal adjustment and evaluations of the mate's personality remained relatively unchanged. Since the term *disenchantment* assigned by Pineo to this process carries a negative connotation which does not seem to be justified by the overall findings of the Blood and Wolfe and the Feldman studies nor necessarily by his own analysis, I interpret these data as indicating *changes* in the basic meaning content which couples attach to their relationships. Some of these meanings may have negative connotations, and some may be more positive in nature. What is needed is research which will sort out the way these various meanings are related to one another within the dynamic interactive experience of families through their careers. Though none of these investigations gathered data on the experience of the occupants of the child positions, it is apparent that children are inextricably involved in the entire process. This fact is in direct agreement with the developmental orientation, but lack of systematic data prevents making any definitive statements about the precise relationships which may exist.

One caution is in order concerning the Blood and Wolfe and the Feldman research. Since the analyses are based on cross-sectional, rather than on longitudinal data, we cannot be certain that the respondents in any family role-complex cohort will follow the pattern which the data show on a cross-sectional basis. Hill (1964) has raised such cautions in his discussion of the methodological problems in developmental research. It is possible that factors associated with historical conditions at the time of marriage, that factors prevailing when the data were gathered, or the like may be partially explanatory of the findings. In all candor, I do not expect that historical conditions are so strong as to account for the major proportion of the variance observed, but the possibility must be recognized. The methodological difficulties associated with testing a theory which ultimately

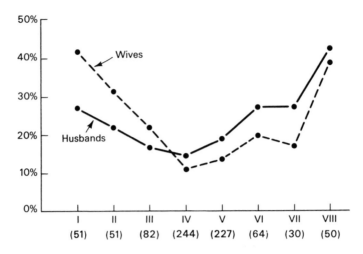

FIGURE 6.1 · Percentage of individuals at each stage of the family life cycle (from Stage I, "beginning marriage," to Stage VIII, "retirement") reporting their marriage was going well "all the time." (Figures in parentheses indicate the number of husbands and also the number of wives in each stage. There was a total of 1598 cases.) [From: Boyd C. Rollins and Harold Feldman, "Marital satisfaction over the family life cycle," Journal of Marriage and the Family, 32 (February, 1970), 25.]

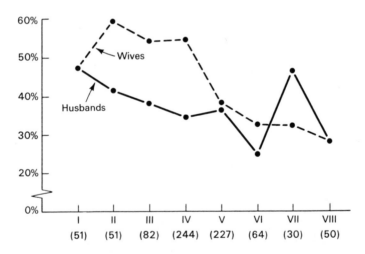

FIGURE 6.2 · Percentage of individuals at each stage of the family life cycle (from Stage I, "beginning marriage," to Stage VIII, "retirement") reporting negative feelings "once or twice a month" or more often from interaction with their spouse. (Figures in parentheses indicate the number of husbands and also the number of wives in each stage. There was a total of 1598 cases.) Note—In this case, a decline in the curve indicates greater marital satisfaction. [From: Boyd C. Rollins and Harold Feldman, "Marital satisfaction over the family life cycle," Journal of Marriage and the Family, 32 (February, 1970), 25.]

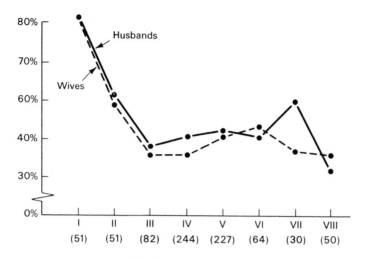

FIGURE 6.3 · *Percentage of individuals at each stage of the family life cycle (from Stage I, "beginning marriage," to Stage VIII, "retirement") reporting "positive companionship experiences with their spouse at least "once a day" or more often. (Figures in parentheses indicate the number of husbands and also the the number of wives in each stage. There was a total 1598 cases. [From: Boyd C. Rollins and Harold Feldman, "Marital satisfaction over the family life cycle," Journal of Marriage and the Family, 32 (February, 1970), 26.]*

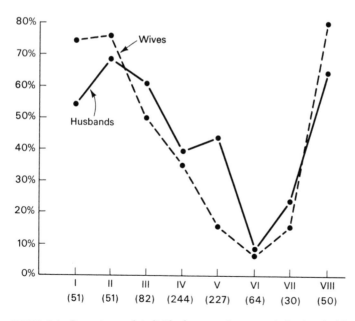

FIGURE 6.4 · *Percentage of individuals at each stage of the family life cycle (from Stage I, "beginning marriage," to Stage VIII, "retirement") reporting that their present stage of the family life cycle is very satisfying. (Figures in parentheses indicate the number of husbands and also the number of wives in each stage. There was a total of 1598 cases.) [From: Boyd C. Rollins and Harold Feldman, "Marital satisfaction over the family life cycle," Journal of Marriage and the Family, 32 (February, 1970), 26.]*

calls for a longitudinal research design will be discussed in the last chapter on the unresolved issues in developmental theory. For the present, these two studies by Blood and Wolfe and by Feldman provide a number of potentially fruitful propositions inviting further investigation.

Studies which focus on a particular role-complex structure may yield important data on the process of maintenance of meaning in the family. Some of the work already cited on mate selection, on early marriage, and on the transition to parenthood has this potential. The change reported by Blood and Wolfe (1960) and by Feldman (1964) in the postparental and the retirement periods, as well as work by Deutscher (1959, 1962, 1964), by Cumming et al. (1960, 1961), by Cavan (1962), by Phillips (1957), by Townsend (1957), Shanas (1961), Shanas and Streib (1965), Streib (1958), Streib and Thompson (1960), Thompson and Streib (1961), and Troll (1971)—all this work shows the value of the strategy of exploring intensively a particular period of the family career. The article by Rollins and Feldman (1970) indicates, as well, the propositions which may be derived from a review of this material as well as of the more conventional marital adjustment studies.

To summarize, the analysis of the maintenance of meaning within the family system from a developmental perspective will delve beyond the variables typically discussed in the studies of marital and family adjustment. Such investigations attempt to tease out the intricate changes in the saliency of meanings which are suggested by the work I have cited. In my judgment, such an approach ultimately should provide a much more significant understanding and explanation of the general level of functioning which occurs in the family than has been thus far gained from the extensive work which has been carried out.

Values and Philosophy of Life

In concluding this section on the maintenance of meaning, the matter of a general philosophy of life or general value orientations must be treated. This area seems related to the societal-institutional and to the group-interactional facet levels, since the general process is one of the family selecting from the general value structure of the society and from its own familial experience in the present and previous generations a value orientation which will provide basic meaning in life for the household. Such orientations certainly will involve economic, political, and other similar perspectives, as well as the obvious religious and more generally philosophical points of view which we ordinarily associate with such a topic. It is possible to do little more than to direct attention to the area, since no research can be located which has systematically investigated the matter from a developmental point of view. There are, of course, numerous studies of the area of child socialization which have values as a central focus (Rosen, 1964; Piaget, 1948; see also references in section on socialization, Chapter 5). This work is subject to the limitations from a family development theoretical point of view which were cited earlier in the discussion of socialization. The study of Bossard and Boll (1950) with respect to rituals in family life also has some interesting implications for the maintenance of meaning. Unfortunately, there has been no major attempt to follow up on this interesting aspect of family life, though there appears to be little question that such rituals represent a major mode of expressing central meanings which are of value to family members. Finally, of course, there are the studies of mate-selection values and the values in marital adjustment which may also be somewhat relevant.

As in the treatment of marital adjustment and the maintenance of meaning, research is needed which takes a considerably different focus than that previously attempted. Up to now, studying value orientations has been a means of studying some other area, for example, the socialization process, marital adjustment, mate selection, occupational choice, economic behavior, and so on. Value orientations *themselves* should be studied from the perspective of the way they are expressed in the interactional experience of the family system and, particularly, the way they change over the career of the family system. It may be anticipated that the saliency of certain kinds of value orientations vary during the family career. There is room for endless speculation here as to what those patterns may be. What is needed is empirical evidence gathered by researchers who have begun from a developmental theoretical perspective.

INTERACTIONAL ANALYSIS—A GENERAL SUMMARY

In the preceding two chapters, I have attempted to show how the developmental theoretical approach may be applied to the interactional dynamics of the family. Through the device of dividing the interactions according to functional areas, I have endeavored to cover a wide range of internal family dynamics, admittedly with varying levels of success. Even though the focus was on interactional phenomena, societal-institutional and individual-psychological aspects entered the picture from time to time. Rather than demonstrating rigorous tests, given the state of development of the theoretical approach and of the accumulated research findings, I have indicated the *potentiality* for rigorous testing of the developmental theory. We turn now from the dynamics of family *interaction* to the dynamics of family *transaction*.

REFERENCES

ADAMS, BERT, N.
1970 "Isolation, function and beyond: American kinship in the 1960's." *Journal of Marriage and the Family* 32 (November): 575–97.

ALDOUS, JOAN, AND REUBEN HILL
1969 "Breaking the poverty cycle: strategic points for intervention." *Social Work* 14 (July): 3–12.

BALLWEG, JOHN A.
1967 "Resolutions of conjugal role adjustment after retirement." *Journal of Marriage and the Family* 29 (May): 277–81.

BERNARD, JESSIE
1964 "The adjustments of married mates." Pp. 675–739 in Harold C. Christensen (ed.), *Handbook of Marriage and the Family*. Chicago: Rand McNally & Company.

BLOOD, ROBERT O., JR.
1960 "Resolving family conflicts." *Conflict Resolution* 4 (June): 209–19.

———, AND DONALD M. WOLFE
1960 *Husbands and Wives*. Glencoe, Ill.: The Free Press.

BOSSARD, JAMES H., AND ELEANOR S. BOLL
1950 *Ritual in Family Living*. Philadelphia: University of Pennsylvania Press.

BOTT, ELIZABETH
1957 *Family and Social Network*. London: Tavistock Publications Ltd.

BOWERMAN, CHARLES E.
1964 "Prediction studies." Pp. 215–46 in Harold C. Christensen (ed.), *Handbook of Marriage and the Family*. Chicago: Rand McNally & Company.

———, AND GLEN H. ELDER, JR.
1964 "Variations in adolescent perception of family power structure." *American Sociological Review* 29 (August): 551–67.

BURCHINAL, LEE G., AND WARD W. BAUDER
1965 "Decision-making and role patterns among Iowa farm and non-farm families." *Journal of Marriage and the Family* 27 (November): 525–30.

BURGESS, ERNEST W., AND PAUL WALLIN
1953 *Engagement and Marriage*. Philadelphia: J. B. Lippincott Company.

BURIC, OLIVERA, AND ANDJELKA ZECEVIC
1967 "Family authority, marital satisfaction, and the social network in

Yugoslavia." *Journal of Marriage and the Family* 29 (May): 325–36.

CAVAN, RUTH S.
1962 "Self and role adjustment during old age." Pp. 526–36 in Arnold M. Rose (ed.), *Human Behavior and Social Processes*. Boston: Houghton Mifflin Company.

CLARK, LINCOLN H., ED.
1955 *Consumer Behavior*, Vol. 2. *The Life Cycle and Consumer Behavior*. New York: New York University Press.

CUMMING, ELAINE, ET AL.
1960 "Disengagement: a tentative theory of aging." *Sociometry* 23 (March): 23–35.

———, AND WILLIAM HENRY
1961 *Growing Old: The Process of Disengagement*. New York: Basic Books, Inc., Publishers.

CUTLER, BEVERLY R., AND WILLIAM G. DYER
1965 "Initial adjustment processes in young married couples." *Social Forces* 44 (December): 195–201.

DEUTSCHER, IRWIN
1959 *Married Life in the Middle Years: A Study of the Middle Class Urban Postparental Couple*. Kansas City, Mo.: Community Studies, Incorporated.

1962 "Socialization for postparental life." Pp. 506–25 in Arnold M. Rose (ed.), *Human Behavior and Social Processes*. Boston: Houghton Mifflin Company.

1964 "The quality of postparental life: definitions of the situation." *Journal of Marriage and the Family* 26 (February): 52–59.

EVANS, RICHARD H., AND NORMAN R. SMITH
1969 "A selected paradigm of family behavior." *Journal of Marriage and the Family* 31 (August): 512–17.

FELDMAN, HAROLD
1964 *The Development of the Husband-Wife Relationship*. Ithaca, N.Y.: Department of Child Development and Family Relations, Cornell University.

FOOTE, NELSON, ED.
1961 *Household Decision-Making*. New York: New York University Press.

FRENCH, JOHN R. P., JR., AND BERTRUM RAVEN
1959 "The bases of social power." Pp. 150–65 in Dorwin Cartwright (ed.), *Studies in Social Power*. Ann Arbor, Mich.: Research Center for Group Dynamics, Institute for Social Research, University of Michigan.

GEISMAR, L. L.
1960   Measuring Family Functioning. A Manual on a Method for Evalu-
        ating the Social Functioning of Disorganized Families. St. Paul,
        Minn.: Family Centered Project.

————, AND BEVERLY AYRES
1959   "A method for evaluating the social functioning of families under
        treatment." Social Work 4 (January): 102–8.

————, ET AL.
1963   "Measuring family disorganization." Marriage and Family Living
        25 (November): 479–81.

GOODE, WILLIAM J.
1966   "Family disorganization." Pp. 479–552 in Robert K. Merton and
        Robert A. Nisbet (eds.), Contemporary Social Problems, 2nd ed.
        New York: Harcourt, Brace, and World, Inc.

GOODRICH, D. WELLS, ET AL.
1968   "Patterns of newlywed marriage." Journal of Marriage and the
        Family 30 (August): 383–91.

————, AND DONALD S..BOOMER
1963   "Experimental assessment of modes of conflict resolution." Family
        Process 2 (March): 15–24.

HERBST, P. G.
1952   "The measurement of family relationships." Human Relations 5
        (February): 3–35.

————
1954   "Family relationships questionnaire." Pp. 316–21 in O. A. Oeser
        and S. B. Hammond (eds.), Social Structure and Personality in a
        City. London: Routledge and Kegan Paul., Ltd.

HILL, REUBEN
1964   "Methodological issues in family development research." Family
        Process 3 (March): 186–206.

————
1965   "Decision making and the family life cycle." Pp. 113–39 in Ethel
        Shanas and Gordon F. Streib (eds.), Social Structure and the
        Family: Generational Relations. Englewood Cliffs, N.J.: Prentice-
        Hall, Inc.

————
1970   Family Development in Three Generations. Cambridge, Mass.:
        Schenkman Publishing Company, Inc.

————
1971   "Modern systems theory and the family: a confrontation." Social
        Science Information 10 (October): 7–26.

————, AND ROY H. RODGERS
1964   "The developmental approach." Pp. 171–211 in Harold C.
        Christensen (ed.), Handbook of Marriage and the Family. Chi-
        cago: Rand McNally & Company.

JACOBSEN, R. BROOKE
1968 "Intrafamily modes of socialization: theoretical development and test." Unpublished doctoral dissertation, Department of Sociology, University of Oregon, Eugene, Ore.

JOHANNIS, THEODORE B., JR.
1957a "Participation by fathers, mothers and teenage sons and daughters in selected family economic activity." *The Coordinator* 6 (September): 15–16.

——— 1957b "Participation by fathers, mothers and teenage sons and daughters in selected child care and control activity." *The Coordinator* 6 (December): 31–32.

——— 1958 "Participation by fathers, mothers and teenage sons and daughters in selected household tasks." *The Coordinator* 6 (June): 61–62.

KENKEL, WILLIAM
1963 "Observational studies of husband-wife interaction in family decision-making." Pp. 144–56 in Marvin B. Sussman (ed.), *Sourcebook in Marriage and the Family*, 2nd ed. Boston: Houghton Mifflin Company.

KIRKPATRICK, CLIFFORD
1963 *The Family as Process and Institution*, 2nd ed. New York: The Ronald Press Company.

KOMAROVSKY, MIRRA
1962 Blue-Collar Marriage. New York: Random House, Inc.

LANSING, JOHN B., AND LESLIE KISH
1957 "Family life cycle as an independent variable." *American Sociological Review* 22 (October): 512–19.

LOPATA, HELENA ZNANIECKI
1966 "The life cycle of the social role of the housewife." *Sociology and Social Research* 51 (October): 5–22.

MICHEL, ANDRÉE
1967 "Comparative data concerning the interaction in French and American families." *Journal of Marriage and the Family* 29 (May): 337–44.

OLSON, DAVID H.
1969 "The measurement of family power by self-report and behavioral methods." *Journal of Marriage and the Family* 31 (August): 545–50.

PAPANEK, MIRIAM L.
1969 "Authority and sex roles in the family." *Journal of Marriage and the Family* 31 (February): 88–96.

PHILLIPS, BERNARD S.
1957 "A role theory approach to adjustment in old age." *American Sociological Review* 22 (April): 212–17.

PIAGET, JEAN
1948   *The Moral Judgment of the Child.* Glencole, Ill.: The Free Press.
PINEO, PETER C.
1961   "Disenchantment in the later years of marriage." *Marriage and Family Living* 23 (February): 3–11.
QUEEN, STUART A., AND JOHN B. ADAMS
1952   *The Family in Various Cultures.* Chicago: J. B. Lippincott Co.
RAINWATER, LEE
1965   *Family Design: Marital Sexuality, Family Size, and Contraception.* Chicago: Aldine Press.
RODMAN, HYMAN
1967   "Marital power in France, Greece, Yugoslavia, and the United States: a cross-national discussion." *Journal of Marriage and the Family* 29 (May): 320–24.
RODGERS, ROY H.
1967   "Planned and unplanned aspects of occupational choices in youth: family and occupational choice." *Report to the Office of Education, U.S. Department of Health, Education, and Welfare.* Contract OE-85-026. Eugene, Ore.: University of Oregon, Department of Sociology.
ROLLINS, BOYD C., AND HAROLD FELDMAN
1970   "Marital satisfaction over the family life cycle." *Journal of Marriage and the Family* 32 (February): 20–28.
ROSEN, BERNARD C.
1964   "Family structure and value transmission." *Merrill-Palmer Quarterly* 10 (January): 59–76.
SAFILIOS-ROTHSCHILD, CONSTANTINA
1967   "A comparison of power structure and marital satisfaction in urban Greek and French families." *Journal of Marriage and the Family* 29 (May): 345–52.

———
1970   "The study of family power structure: a review 1960–69." *Journal of Marriage and the Family* 32 (November): 539–52.
SECORD, PAUL F., AND CARL W. BACKMAN
1964   *Social Psychology.* New York: McGraw-Hill Book Company.
SHANAS, ETHEL
1961   *Family Relationships of Older People.* New York: Health Information Foundation.
———, AND GORDON F. STREIB, EDS.
1965   *Social Structure and the Family: Generational Relations.* Englewood Cliffs, N.J.: Prentice-Hall, Inc.
SILVERMAN, WILLIAM, AND REUBEN HILL
1967   "Task allocation in marriage in the United States and Belgium." *Journal of Marriage and the Family* 29 (May): 353–59.

SMITH, THOMAS E.
1970   "Foundations of parental influence upon adolescents: an application of social power theory." *American Sociological Review* 35 (October): 860–73.

SPIEGEL, JOHN P.
1957   "The resolution of role conflict within the family." Pp. 545–64 in Milton Greenblatt et al. (eds.), *The Patient and the Mental Hospital.* New York: The Free Press.

SPREY, JETSE
1966   "Family disorganization: toward a conceptual clarification." *Journal of Marriage and the Family* 28 (November): 398–406.

————   1969   "The family as a system in conflict." *Journal of Marriage and the Family* 31 (November): 699–706.

STRAUS, MURRAY A.
1963a   "The Family Interaction Schedule." Minneapolis, Minn.: Minnesota Family Study Center, University of Minnesota.

————   1963b   "The Family Patterns Profile." Minneapolis, Minn.: Minnesota Family Study Center, University of Minnesota.

STREIB, GORDON F.
1958   "Older people and their families." *Journal of Social Issues* 14 (July): 46–60.

————, AND WAYNE E. THOMPSON
1960   "The older person in a family context." Pp. 447–75 in Clark Tibbitts (ed.), *Handbook of Social Gerontology.* Chicago: University of Chicago Press.

STRODTBECK, FRED
1951   "Husband and wife interaction over revealed differences." *American Sociological Review* 16 (August): 468–73.

THOMPSON, WAYNE E., AND GORDON F. STREIB
1961   "Meaningful activity in a family context." Pp. 177–211 in Robert W. Kleemeier (ed.), *Aging and Leisure: A Research Perspective into the Meaningful Use of Time.* New York: Oxford University Press.

TOWNSEND, PETER
1957   *The Family Life of Old People.* London: Routledge and Kegan Paul, Ltd.

TROLL, LILLIAN E.
1971   "The family of later life: a decade review." *Journal of Marriage and the Family* 33 (May): 263–90.

TURNER, RALPH H.
1970   *Family Interaction.* New York: John Wiley & Sons, Inc.

UDRY, J. RICHARD, AND MARY HALL
  1965   "Marital role segregation and social networks in middle-class mid-
         dle-aged couples." *Journal of Marriage and the Family* 27 (Au-
         gust): 392–95.
WILKENING, EUGENE A., AND LAKSHMI K. BHARADWAJ
  1967   "Dimensions of aspirations, work roles, and decision-making of
         farm husbands and wives in Wisconsin." *Journal of Marriage and
         and the Family* 29 (November): 703–11.
WOLFE, DONALD M.
  1959   "Power and authority in the family." Pp. 99–117 in Dorwin Cart-
         wright (ed.), *Studies in Social Power*. Ann Arbor, Mich.: The
         Institute for Social Research.

Family Careers—
Transactional Analysis

I want to begin by developing the scope and focus of the developmental theoretical concern with transactional behavior. From the conceptualization that families are semiclosed systems is derived the view that occupants of familial positions have roles which they are expected to play in other societal systems in response to societal and to familial norms. Although the basic normative content of these extrafamilial roles may be defined by the nature of the other system, there is, nevertheless, normative support from the family system. These roles have an impact upon the family by virtue of the fact that occupants of household positions play them. Therefore, they must be taken into account within the family system. Bates (1960) has analyzed this aspect of social structure and has shown that these types of roles in effect provide the bridges between the various systems of the society and result in the very interrelatedness which constitutes a community and society. He has called roles played by the same actor, but which are parts of different systems of action, *conjunctive roles*. He illustrates the concept as follows (Bates, 1960:64):

> In every society roles occur in such a relationship. For example, in our society the father-husband's provider role occurs in conjunction with occupational roles which he plays in a group outside the family. In playing the occupational roles, the father-husband occupies a position and plays roles toward members of a work group distinct from the family. In this work group the occupational roles are directed toward the performance of

functions or the accomplishment of goals distinct from family functions and goals.

If a researcher wanted to make a broad general analysis of a community or of a society, he would need to direct his attention to the way these conjunctive roles affected the functioning of the two or more systems to which they are related. In focusing on the family, however, the concern is only with analyzing the way transactional relations make an impact on the family system. There is no question here of one system being more important than the other or of one being basic and the other being secondary to the structure of society. This issue just involves limiting the scope of the analysis to a manageable one.

Transactional analysis at a microscopic level is relatively uncommon. There are a number of studies, based primarily on an institutional theoretical framework, which have explored the interrelationships between family and other societal systems at a macroscopic level. With the increasing interest in the explanation of family interactive patterns, some work at a microscopic level has occurred. I have selected for discussion some of the major transactive relationships as representative of the kinds of insights which the developmental approach may produce. In the remainder of the chapter, I shall deal with transactive behavior with the economic system, with governmental and political systems, with educational systems, with religious systems, and with the extended family system. This selection assumes a societal organization in which the nuclear family is distinct and in which the others are organizationally distinct also. Societies of a communal type and many "primitive" societies present special problems of analysis with which I shall not be concerned, though I believe that the developmental approach may be used to study such societies. I shall attempt to indicate some of the ways this method may be accomplished in the chapter titled "Cross Cultural and Subcultural Applications."

TRANSACTIONS WITH THE ECONOMIC SYSTEM

Productive Roles

One of the major historical phenomena contributing to a fundamental reorganization of the family system in Western society is the emergence of an economic system which no longer depends on the family as a basic unit of production but rather looks to the family as a source for individual workers and as a key unit of consumption. Whereas in earlier times, societal-institutional and group-interactional norms would have included productive roles as basic in each position of the family system, a contemporary American structure would include a productive role as manifest, dominant, and obligatory only in the adult male position. The adult female position could include such a manifest role, but it would tend to be recessive and discretionary.[1] In the child positions, the productive role would be latent, recessive, and discretionary. As was observed in the discussion of socialization, there would be interactive behavior designed to develop in the child positions certain kinds of latent roles in anticipation of adult productive activity. The dominant normative structure typically would not include any expectation that such roles would become manifest, dominant, and obligatory while the child performing them remained in the family of orientation. In any case, regardless of which positions such productive roles might constitute a part, they would be most unlikely to be reciprocal with roles in other positions of the family system but rather would be conjunctive with positions in the family and reciprocal to positions in a system outside the family.

This kind of structural arrangement is important to family dynamics. For example, it is usual for the occupant of one of the key positions of the family system to devote considerable time and attention to roles played in a system about which the remaining positional occupants are almost totally ignorant. Unless the occupational role of the actor is in an essentially public system, and surprisingly few occupations are public, the other family members may have so little knowledge of the structure of that system and of the position occupied by that actor as to be unable to define for themselves appropriate behavior in relationship to this conjunctive role. This lack of understanding establishes a classic anomic situation. Or, if the system is somewhat public, the family members may still have only a partial knowledge and on the basis of it may behave inappropriately, again producing a type of anomie. Since it is usually impossible for the other actors in the family system to participate in the occupational organization with employed actors, they cannot behave reciprocally and, at best, may only participate vicariously to the degree that experiences are communicated to them or that they learn about them in some other way. The employed actor, on the other hand, may encounter severe cross-pressures from the normative expectations of the two systems. Each demands a high level of loyalty and commitment and, indeed, the behavior in the occupational role is associated directly with the level of adequacy with which the employed actor may be seen as performing as an economic contributor to the family. Yet, adequate

---

[1] I am aware that, as a result of further social change in American society, this situation is becoming less common. The impact of changing family-size goals, increased professional and other occupational training for women, and the like, are part of this trend. I contend that the dominant American norms still reflect the pattern I have described, however. The essential point, nevertheless, is related to the fact that now productive roles are transactive roles, more than interactive ones.

performance in the job may mean that the employed actor is unable to meet the expectations associated with one or more familial roles. Perhaps this discussion is enough to set the stage for a discussion of the developmental analysis of the transactions with the occupational system. This situation is not entirely negative, of course. There are positive experiences in which occupational and family systems join to support one another as well.

Initially, the developmental approach seeks to examine the changes which may occur in the transactions between family and occupational systems. Since the term *career* is more commonly associated with occupational activity than it is with familial behavior, attention is drawn to the fascinating possibilities for analysis of the joint familial and occupational careers. The conjunctive occupational role, at least for the husband-father in American society, may be viewed as *mutually contingent* in its career with the role sequences of the family career. Robert and Rhona Rapoport (1965) have done an excellent job of setting forth some of the theoretical background and have analyzed some of the possibilities in the early portion of the family and occupational careers. They cite four theoretical points (Rapoport and Rapoport, 1965:382): the increasing differentiation of family and work; the variation in relative salience of family and work roles in the lives of those who play them; the modes of interaction in work and family, which tend to be isomorphic (i.e., they tend to be similar in their patterns); and the point at which the life cycle affects the relations between work and family life. The Rapoports studied a sample of professional engineers who were graduating from college and were marrying at the same time. The researchers then identified a number of patterns in both the family and the occupational sphere which necessitated some degree of mutual accommodation. They conclude the following from their analysis (Rapoport and Rapoport, 1965:393):

> While inter-system influence is probably maximal when individuals are undergoing transitions in both simultaneously, all points of status transition necessarily involve a process of readjustment, potentially affecting not only specific behavioral spheres, but others linked to it. When transitions occur simultaneously in two spheres, conflicts and stresses are not necessarily multiplied. The concurrence of the challenges presented by the two sets of tasks may, under some circumstances, have mutually beneficial consequences, and coping with one set of challenges does not necessarily detract from performance of others.

Although the Rapoports placed their emphasis on transition points in family and occupational careers, analysis of the transactions between the two at other periods also would be of interest. In some cases, a husband-father's occupational role may carry with it corollary role expectations for his wife, not with respect to a separate occupation which she holds but associated with his occupation. Thus, Hochschild (1969) showed that the wife of an ambassador tends to share in his job by communicating political and social messages in a variety of indirect ways. Whyte (1956) also demonstrated that wives of junior executives played a significant part in their husband's career mobility. There may well be variations in these expectations according to the portion of the familial career analyzed, as well as with respect to the portion of the occupational career and to the type of occupation.

In a review of some of the material on family and occupation, Aldous (1969b) found a number of occupational factors, including salience and synchronization, which were associated with the role performance of the adult male in the family. She also identified the variable of isomorphism discussed by the Rapoports. Scanzoni (1965a and 1965b) analyzed some of the ways in which clergymen resolve conflicts between occupational and conjugal roles. Presumably some of these same processes may be observed in other occupational settings. Scanzoni had no data on whether these varied over the family and occupational careers; so, this issue remains an open empirical question. Wilensky (1961) contributed to the issue of productive roles and the family by providing some insights into the way in which the occupational career, family career, and some other transactional careers may be interrelated. His analysis suggests that there are clear connections between levels of participation in the several kinds of activities in differing periods of the family and occupational careers (Wilensky, 1961: 227–31).

In relation to the wife-mother's participation in the occupational system, a major source is the volume by Nye and Hoffman (1963). The comprehensive treatment which they have given provides an excellent source of potential areas for developmental analysis. These include the effects of the working woman on children, on the husband-wife relationships, and on the wife herself. Some of their work is based partially on the developmental perspective and provides excellent leads to further investigation along developmental lines. Other more recent material includes articles by Katelman and Barnett (1968), by Tropman (1968), and by Aldous (1969a). Each is illustrative of an alternative strategy which may be used in investigating the area. One investigator focuses on the occupational orientations of the wife; another analyzes the impact of the wife's working on the husband; and the third investigates a particular occupational category. None of the studies, however, is explicitly developmental in approach.

It is of some interest that, although extensive attention has been paid to the effect of the employment of the wife-mother on children, very little analysis has been done concerning the effect of father's employment on children. Much of the material on children and occupations is associated with the socialization process. In my (Rodgers, 1966, 1967) research about the occupational socialization of ninth-grade boys, I obtained data which indicated that some visiting of the father's place of employment by family members took place, and the father's occupational experience was utilized somewhat as a way of socializing children with respect to occupations. I did not gather the kind of data, however, which would allow me to explore the more general question of the various ways in which the occupational role of the father may affect the children in the family. An examination of the sixty-eight items listed in a bibliography compiled in conjunction with this research reveals very little work of this type (Jacobsen et al., 1966).

Little information exists about the effects on family dynamics of children taking on occupational roles while they are still in the family of orientation. Although data from my study of ninth-grade boys indicates that this phenomenon is not as prevalent as it may have been at one time, 43 percent of the subjects held a part-time job at the time of the study and about 80 percent had held a part-time job at some time. Personal experience and informal discussions with parents indicates that frequently significant changes occur in familial behavior arising from such a conjunctive role occupancy.

In summary, the analysis of transactions with the occupational system and their impact on the family provides yet another rich area for testing the developmental theory. Although there have been some rather extensive investigations of certain portions of this subject, there are areas which are almost totally untouched. Research which begins with a developmental base is relatively rare.

Consumer Roles

In the earlier discussion of interactions involving decision-making and power relationships in the family, a sizable amount of material dealing with consumer behavior was cited. In general, research dealing with the family and consumption focuses on the interactional process of decision-making. Otherwise consumers are treated essentially from an individual-psychological perspective which emphasizes such matters as motivation, personal preference or taste, needs, desires, and the like. Analyses of the consumer role in the market place which deal with the buyer-seller role relationships, especially with the conjunctive nature of the consumer role as it influences family behavior, do not predominate. I suggest several reasons for this situation: The marketing system tends not to involve the individual consumer as an occupant of a specific position in the system. The consumer as a class or as a category tends to be viewed more as an object to be manipulated by the actors in the marketing system, rather than a participant in it.

One type of stance emphasizes meeting consumer demands, which implies a certain type of interactive process. Another approach results in seeing the marketing system place stress on *creating* demands for the products which are marketed. Thus, the role expectations for the merchandiser tend to place more significance in a stimulus-response relationship between seller and buyer. From the consumer side, the emphasis is placed on evaluating the goods available in the market, the value received for expenditures, and the like, far more than the stress is focused on role relationships with the seller which might influence the kinds of goods to be offered and the price placed upon them. Finally, the family and, more often, the household, tends to be used as a unit of analysis with more static than dynamic characteristics.

Thus, studies which analyze consumer behavior taking the family career into account tend to repeat the pattern of family planning research by handling it demographically. The classic article by Lansing and Kish (1957) is representative of this approach. In this study, the age of the household head, as one type of explanatory demographic category, is compared with stage of family life cycle. The construction of the life cycle category is accomplished by combining the age of the household head with the presence or the absence of children below or above age six in the case of married household heads. As in the case of fertility research, it becomes apparent that the basic concern is not so much with what may be the role characteristics of these household units as with a method of refining the easily identifiable demographic characteristics which may lead to more efficient explanation of consumer behavior in the statistical sense.

Perhaps, the basic reason for this approach is associated with the nature of the marketing system itself. It may be that consumers do not actually occupy positions in the system but stand outside it. If this explanation is the case, then there really is no conjunctive role played by family members as consumers. If these speculations are correct, a phenomenon of the latter part of the decade of the sixties, which appears to be destined to continue into the seventies, may change this situation. Increasing concern with consumer rights and with consumer protection became evident. Some rather aggressive actions were being taken to influence the production and marketing of goods and services which ultimately could include the consumer in the system as a new positional occupant.

Although it is clear from marketing research data that consumption patterns differ over the family career, it appears for the present that analysis of transactional behavior as focused on a conjunctive role of consumer is not possible. Since this alternative research approach requires that there be a clearly defined role played in the related system and since we have hypothesized that no such consumer role exists in the marketing system, then developmental analysis is impossible. It may well be that the only developmental analysis of consumer behavior appropriate is interactional, dealing with the way the family members in the decision-making process work out the means for purchasing goods and services. Once in the market-place, they follow the role definitions developed in that family interactional process, and, therefore, their behavior has little reference to the marketing system *qua* system; that is, they behave as consumers—not in roles defined by the marketing system, but by the family system.

This point of view, resulting from an attempt to apply the develop-mental theory to a particular area of behavior, has some fascinating implica-tions for research: Does the perspective provide an accurate definition of the manner in which the two systems are related? If so, is the only basic tie between them found in the interaction between a family representative as buyer and a marketing representative as seller in a relationship which is essentially outside either system? Bates (1957:106) has pointed to such an arrangement in his analysis of group structure and assigns to the group formed the term *interstitial group*. In his view, such a gathering is created primarily for the purpose of coordinating the activities of two groups from which the respective representatives come. Presumably, although some minimal normative structure may develop which is unique to the inter-stitial group, the primary definitions for roles derives from the expectations of the originating groups and are based on the achievement of goals de-veloped in the separate systems which ultimately can only be reached by relating to the other system. If all of this speculation should prove fruitful, then the basic remaining question appears to be whether there is any developmental characteristic to the relationship other than the one which can be accounted for by the interactional analysis of decision-making with respect to consumption behavior.

In this section on family transactions with the economic system, two strikingly contrasting phenomena have appeared. In the area of productive roles, there has already been a good deal of research which clearly demon-strates the active participation of family members in another system. Although some research has been cited which may provide developmental data, there is still a great deal to be learned about how the participation of family members in the occupational system affects the family system over its career. In addition, there is much to be learned about how family roles may influence the manner in which a particular positional occupant ap-proaches his occupational role. On the other hand, as a result of the same attempt to apply the developmental theory to the consumer area, the possi-bility has arisen that no transactional behavior exists as developmentally defined. It may be that consumer behavior does not involve direct participa-tion in the marketing system. Rather, the two systems of family and market may only be related by virtue of an interstitial group formed through the interactions of representatives from each system but outside either one.

Perhaps the most significant point to make is that once again the attempt to apply systematically a theoretical formulation to a set of social phenomena leads to a potential restructuring of the theory, to a potential improvement of the theory's explanatory power, and to the identification of additional needed empirical knowledge.

TRANSACTIONS WITH THE GOVERNMENTAL
AND POLITICAL SYSTEMS

In thinking about the transactional relationships between the family system and the systems of government and politics, a situation similar to the one encountered in the relationship between the family and the marketing system may exist. There is no question of the great impact which government has on the family organization, as a special issue of the *Journal of Marriage and the Family* (Sussman, 1967) attests. But a reading of the articles in that special issue also affirms that family members are not so much *participants* in government as they are *objects* of its programs.

Furthermore, although the family unit may be identified explicitly as a target of governmental concern, this practice is not always so nor has it been so in the past. Thus, Vincent (1967) found no mention of the family either explicitly or by the nature of the subject matter in fifty-nine laws enacted in 1965 by Congress related to the mental-health field. He found only sixteen references out of 825 headings and subheadings in the index to a 393-page summary of "government programs to help individuals and communities meet their own goals for economic and social development," published by the Office of Economic Opportunity in 1965. Schottland (1967) points out that the first explicit family policy expressed in federal law occurred in 1956 with the amendment of the Social Security Act which brought into being the Aid to Families with Dependent Children with the expressed goal "to help maintain and strengthen family life." It appears, then, that government programs and policies are either oriented toward a *family unit* which qualifies as a consumer of a given service by virtue of certain objective and usually demographic criteria (age, marital status, dependency status, size of family, and income) or to *individuals*, often with little reference to the impact which such services may have on the family of the individual. For example, an older form of the Aid to Dependent Children program was found frequently to have the effect of breaking up family units rather than strengthening them. Similar unanticipated or undesired consequences may be observed from other programs and policies in health, economic, housing, and legal areas.

In contrast to the model proposed to analyze the consumer-marketer system, which included an interstitial group composed of representatives of each system interacting in order to meet the reciprocal goals of the two orders, it is even more difficult to see such a model as applicable to many of the family-governmental relationships. Although the construct may be appropriate in certain situations related to some welfare programs, to some health care programs, to supervision of probationers and parolees, and in some types of services to the unemployed, it seems less so in some other major areas. Social Security beneficiaries rarely have more than casual contact with governmental representatives except by completing certain required forms to establish eligibility. Most taxing policies, although having a major influence on the family of both a positive and negative nature, rarely involve family representatives in interaction with governmental personnel. Even such programs as the Abundant Foods, available to low income families, result in the bare minimum of interaction associated with qualifying and the periodic receipt of the supplies at the distribution center. Although the examples cited are related for the most part to the federal government, though frequently administered at the state, county, or local level, there appears to be little difference in programs and policies originated at these lower levels of government.

An analysis of the relationship between governmental and family systems which begins from a developmental perspective, then, reveals both theoretical and applied matters of considerable importance. From a theoretical standpoint, an analysis of interest involves a comparison of the differing effects over the family career of relationships with government which were of a clear transactional nature, that is, which actually involved roles played in the governmental system by occupants of positions in the family, as opposed to relationships with government which did not involve such transactive roles. It should be clear to those in the helping professions that such analyses might provide some additional insights for designing programs and policies which more effectively achieved the goals originally intended for them. Such comparative analyses are increasingly feasible, because in the late 1960s there were movements toward direct involvement of citizen recipients of various governmental services in policy-making and administrative roles, similar to the trends observed in consumer-marketing relations. This trend was especially true regarding a number of the community action programs associated with the Office of Economic Opportunity in which representation on the governing boards was provided for people who were beneficiaries of the programs. Several kinds of studies are suggested by the special issue of the *Journal of Marriage and the Family* (Sussman, 1967) cited.

Concerning the family's relationship to the political system, a somewhat different set of circumstances prevail. If the political system is viewed broadly as the formally organized political parties and other formally and informally organized structures designed to influence governments through lobbying and through other types of activities, then there are a potentially wide range of transactive roles which family members may play. There may be, however, a major distinction between the *incidence* of political activity and the *prevalence* of it. Thus, although a fairly high proportion of families may exhibit voting behavior of a regular or irregular nature (a measure of incidence), it is more difficult to determine the degree to which a broad range of political activity may be a regular part of the roles of some family members (a possible measure of prevalence). Certainly considerable difference exists in the salience of political behavior affecting the family in which the members may identify themselves with a political party by conversation and periodic voting, as opposed to those who also may be actively involved in local or state party organizations, in other activities such as the League of Women Voters, or in political pressure groups. A major question derived from developmental theory asks whether such changes in saliency may be associated with varying periods of the family career. One may speculate that young childless couples may be more active politically than couples with preschool and school-aged children, based on a rationale of the amount of time which may be available for such "outside" activity. An equally plausible hypothesis, however, may predict quite the opposite pattern on the basis that young marrieds are more concerned with establishing their internal roles, whereas parents of young children may feel they have more of a stake in the political activity occurring in the community. The further developmental issue is the way political activity affects the general dynamics of the family at various periods of the career.

Analyses of the kind suggested do not appear in published form. A few years ago Stephen Wasby (1966) reviewed over sixty references dealing with the family and politics which had been published chiefly between 1950 and 1963. His review, although focusing on the influence of the family on politics, nevertheless is a good indication of the range of material available in this area. Wasby's (1966:3) discussion is divided into the following areas: "The family within polity; the family as a polity; the transmission of voting preference; the effect of relations within the family; the transmission of orientations and attitudes; political recruitment; and personality and politics." It is safe to say that the major orientation of the material reviewed is in one way or another related to political socialization. The concerns lie with such issues as the degree to which children follow the political beliefs of their parents, the conflicts arising between children and their parents over political issues, the political party preferences of children compared with parents, and the preparation of children for various kinds of political roles by parents. Even the material dealing with husband-wife interaction relating to politics is strongly oriented toward socialization by dealing chiefly with the influence of the husband on the wife's behavior (which is apparently the predominant direction of influence investigated in the matter). Items published since Wasby's review do not exhibit any great change in this central orientation (Middleton and Putney, 1963; Hess and Toney, 1967; Eckhardt and Shriner, 1969).

Although not denying the importance of these kinds of analyses, systematically developed data or theoretical attempts which dealt with family and political systems from a career perspective were not found. Again speculating on some possible patterns which may be explored, one may expect that although the issue of political socialization will have a high saliency during the childrearing years of the family, there may well be other kinds of issues which also will be of importance during this period. Furthermore the changing situations of the family through its career may well involve modifications in the kinds of transactive roles played and in the kinds of issues to which they may be directed. Thus, parallels to the types of shifts in consumption patterns observed over the family career may be found also in political roles and issues.

In summary, there does appear to be a place for some systematic analysis of the transactions of the family with the governmental and political systems which explores in detail the group-interactional and the individual-psychological facets of behavior. Although the societal-institutional analysis of the broad and pervasive impact of law and the more general governmental functions may be so macroscopic as to yield little that is new, moving to these microscopic kinds of concerns may reveal some new, significant findings in the explanation of family behavior.

TRANSACTIONS WITH THE EDUCATIONAL SYSTEM

By now, the pattern of transactional analysis suggested by the developmental theory should have become clear. Reduced to its simplest form, the pattern involves an examination of the way roles played by family members in positions in nonfamilial systems have an influence on and are influenced by the roles played in the familial system over the family career. The degree to which such analyses have been attempted varies considerably, but in general the approach has not received a heavy concentration of attention. Turning to the educational system, some change in this situation may be expected since, as Shostak (1967:139) has pointed out, "Historically, there has been a symbiotic relationship between the school and the family." Certainly all the elements are present, at least in American family life. There is the general societal expectation that a child family member who has reached a certain chronological age will enter school and will remain there until a particular age. In most states, this expectation has the support of formal law. There is the additional trend toward an extension of formal schooling with expectations that many students will continue on to a college or to a university or, failing this, at least will spend a period of time in a community college or in a vocational-technical school. Wilbur J. Cohen (1966:9), former Undersecretary of Health, Education, and Welfare, predicted that by 1975 free public education would be extended from twelve to fifteen years, with kindergartens universally present and two-year junior colleges available in every sizable community.

Not only do the child positional occupants have such dominant, obligatory, and manifest transactional roles, but parents also occupy roles in relation to the school, though they are somewhat less dominant, more discretionary, and sometimes less manifest in nature (Litwak and Meyer, 1967). Parents may be members of the local Parent-Teachers' Association, may be homeroom mothers, may sit on a parents' advisory committee with the school administrative staff, or—an increasingly frequent role—may become teacher's aides of one sort or another within the school (perhaps with pay, but frequently on a volunteer basis). The Supreme Court decision of 1954 with respect to school segregation along with subsequent legislative, administrative, and judicial actions have served to underline the longstanding close association between the family and the school. The conflicts that have arisen out of plans for bussing students to achieve racial balance, out of freedom-of-choice plans to circumvent integration, out of redrawing school district boundaries, and out of a number of other such developments, all focus in one way or another on the traditional neighborhoodschool concept and its close relationship to the families of the neighborhood.

These facts notwithstanding, no body of significant material exists which analyzes the transactional roles utilizing the kind of conceptual framework mentioned in developmental theory. This fact does not imply that there is any lack of material which in one way or another relates familial and educational variables. The Aldous-Hill (1967) bibliography, for example, lists nearly two hundred items under the subject heading "Family Transactions with Groups and Organizations—Educational." A scanning of titles reveals that the listing does not begin to encompass all the research about the relationship of certain familial characteristics to such commonly researched matters as academic performance, intellectual ability, social adjustment in school, and emotional adjustment. At the risk of oversimplifying such a large body of literature, we may say that 'the major analytic emphases seem to be based on three kinds of orientations to family variables: ones arising out of the demographic approach, ones based on intersystem relations stressing functional interdependence, and ones related to the socialization process. Studies with a demographic emphasis tend to utilize family characteristics such as socioeconomic status, parental educational attainment, marital status of parents, family size, ordinal position, and so on as independent variables to explain a dependent variable of concern. There is rarely any analysis of family role dynamics which these demographic variables may be assumed to operationalize. The intersystem analyses tend to deal with the various ways that the functions of the family and those of the school complement or conflict with each other, again without reference to role interactional matters. Finally, studies which emphasize socialization tend to deal rather narrowly with certain qualities of the family setting—cultural poverty or richness of the home, kinds of childrearing approaches, emotional characteristics of the home—in relation to a rather limited set of educational role behaviors usually involving academic achievement, general adjustment, or specific kinds of mental, emotional, or social behavior.

Such research is not insignificant or unimportant but is useful for mapping the phenomena concerning the family and the school. Another possible analytical stance exists, however, which has the potentiality for yielding other kinds of explanations and understandings of behavior in both systems. The commitment of the children, often a majority of the family actors, to this major transactional role—the academic role—over the majority of their career in the family of orientation must have profound and pervasive effects on the dynamics of the family. (These effects should be no less than the ones arising from the commitment of the adult male to the occupational role.) Some examples include the changes which occur in the role relationships between the mother and the younger children who remain at home when other children enter school, the dramatic change which must occur when the mother is left alone in the home after the youngest child begins school, and the effects of new values and expectations placed on children in the school setting which may cause a redefinition of their familial roles in a manner not always consonant with familial expectations. Developmental analysis of familial transactions with the educational system will shift the direction of attention from treating the child as a product of the family acting individually in the school setting to analyzing the effect of the child's school roles on the child and adult familial roles.

In summary, a great share of research dealing with the family and the school has been in pursuit of explanations of academic behavior. This fact is undoubtedly due in part to the ready availability of the kind of familial data typically used and to the easy access to the school as a locale for research. Transactional research which explains behavior of the family, even though the data may be more difficult to obtain, is also needed.

TRANSACTIONS WITH THE RELIGIOUS SYSTEM

The degree to which formal religious practice remains a part of life, or at least a significant aspect, is a source of considerable current debate. In 1957, a Gallup Poll showed that 69 percent of the respondents felt that religion was increasing in influence, whereas in 1968 a similar poll found 67 percent believing that religious influence was diminishing. In the decade of the sixties, there appeared to be considerable evidence that increasingly visible high-school and college-age youth were turning away from organized religion. But there was also much proof of a newly awakened religious concern on the part of youth related to moral and ethical issues arising out of the following: the war in Vietnam, race relations, concern for the poor, population growth, and pollution of the environment. In addition, there did not appear to be any major change in the long-standing belief among adults that going to church was important, at least for children. Membership figures, although admittedly a poor measure of religious practice and commitment, showed that about two-thirds of the American population were affiliated with some formal religious group, though the religious revival of the fifties seemed definitely on the wane. The true meaning of religious affiliation in the post–World War Two and post–Korean War years is difficult to assess. Herberg's (1955) interpretation of the close relationship with religion as a kind of general process of Americanization with a concomitant deemphasis on more narrow theological and other sectarian concerns seems to carry considerable veracity (see, also, Glock and Stark [1965]).

What does all this information mean for the transactional roles which may be played by family members in religious organizational systems? Little exists in the way of research material to guide us here. There are numerous studies that pertain to religious affiliation or to beliefs and their relationships to such variables as marital adjustment, mate selection, and the like. In addition, there are a number of religious treatises of varying qualitative levels which attempt to analyze the church and the family, but they are generally short on systematic data.

One source does seem to have some pertinence. Late in 1958 and continuing into 1959, Roy W. Fairchild and J. C. Wynn (1961) conducted a survey under the auspices of the United Presbyterian Church in the United States of America. The researchers gathered the data through tape recorded group interviews with parents from sixty-three Presbyterian churches throughout the United States. A total of 845 family representatives, about equally divided between fathers and mothers from mostly intact families in every phase of childrearing, participated in these two-hour group discussions. They also completed relatively brief questionnaires at the conclusion of the sessions. The churches sampled were of varying sizes from one with less than 100 members to twelve with over 1,200 members and were located in rural, small town, city, urban, and suburban areas. The respondents were, as could be expected from this particular denomination, basically middle class. The group interviews were open-ended and were conducted by trained interviewers who followed a detailed guide which centered around three key areas: problems of concern to parents, definitions and satisfactions of "good family life," and types of solutions which help families in overcoming their difficulties. Of course, both the orientation of the interviews and the setting in which they were held placed the focus on the family-church involvement. The questionnaire included three open-ended questions at the end concerning the child's experience in the church, the kinds of things parents hoped their children would remember about their family life when the youngsters were grown, and changes the parents would like to see in the church's program to increase helpfulness to families. These latter questions have particular transactional relevance. Unfortunately, the major publication which emerged from this research never gained wide recognition in family-research circles. Perhaps this result was due to the fact that the primary audience for the book was, in the authors' own words (Fairchild and Wynn, 1961:xii), "clergymen, directors of religious education, church parents, and seminarians." The research was not extensively and systematically reported in journals usually seen by behavioral scientists. There were a number of reports produced, but they were limited in circulation, primarily to church agencies.

Nevertheless, this nationwide study by Fairchild and Wynn generated many insights into the kinds of impacts which dual memberships in church and family seem to produce (the findings which follow may be found in Fairchild and Wynn, 1961:167–200). First, there is evidence that a great many families view religious participation as similar to participation in other community groups. This information is the more remarkable because these were families who were probably among the most highly committed to the church. Thus, religious faith and participation seemed to have no unique qualities to distinguish it from many other family activities of a recreational sort or from activity associated with clubs, scout groups, or school organizations. In parents' comments, there was a strong theme of general sociability and of viewing the church as a source of personal friendships. The kind of general Americanism cited by Herberg (1955) was very evident in the interpretations parents gave to their religious roles, coupled with evidence of low commitment to denominational identification. Presence in a particular church was more a result of families finding compatible associations and convenient location, rather than any particular theological orientation. Significantly, the more specifically committed to a particular role in the church, such as teaching in the church school, the more likely parents were to define their roles and their identification in theological terms as opposed to general social participation terms.

The second major finding, somewhat disquieting to the central leadership of the church, was that parents viewed the church as disrupting and as splitting up their families, rather than as bringing them together. High frequency of complaints about the church's expectations that members participate in a wide range of activities as individuals, rather than as family groups suggested that parents viewed the religious transactional obligations as a major source of family disorganization.

The third discovery emphasized the perception of members as consumers of certain services provided by the church. Thus, the church was a source of support for good mental health, for providing children with training in moral principles (often when parents admitted little participation for themselves), a source of counseling service from pastors, a source of inspiration through sermons and through worship, a source of help in child-rearing problems, a youth center with a pastor who was a leader of young people, and a source of support for parental control and authority.

There was little evidence of religious roles carrying over into the home. Family worship, though heavily emphasized in a number of ways by the church, was rarely practiced beyond a minimum of prayer at family meals. Bible reading, use of religious material distributed by the church, discussions of religious topics, all seemed to be almost nonexistent. The general theme appeared to be that parents did not have any clear idea of how to play such religious roles in the family. In view of the heavy investment which the Presbyterian and other churches had made in literature specifically intended for use in the home, this finding was most discomforting. Indeed, it ultimately resulted in a major shift in strategy for the Presbyterian Church with respect to educational literature.

Other miscellaneous findings of some interest included the revelation that little association existed between religious matters and the husband's vocation. The two realms seemed to be totally separate. Women held more active religious roles than men. There was little evidence of religious roles being tied in with husband-and-wife interaction in discussions between spouses, with joint participation in religious activities, or with reading of religious literature. Fathers were not viewed as religous teachers in the home or as major cooperators with the church school.

These findings from one nationwide study seem to indicate that the roles for transaction between family and church have a chiefly disruptive impact on the family career. This result is particularly interesting, since in the Protestant Church there has been a renewed emphasis over the past decade or two on the involvement of the laity or, in the traditional term of the Reformation, of *the priesthood of the believer* (see, for example, Mudge, 1970). A similar emphasis has also been evident in the Roman Catholic Church, primarily as a result of the consultations of Vatican II under Pope John XXIII. Judaism traditionally has been strongly centered on the family, where the religious role of the father was a major element. Thus, there is a need for a great deal more research on the transactional roles relating the family and the religious organizations before we can determine whether the kinds of results reported by Fairchild and Wynn are generally representative.

Developmental theorists will be especially interested in whether transactional religious roles change in their salience and the pervasiveness of impact at various periods of the familial career. Some research indicates that newly married couples tend to participate in church at a relatively low level but that they increase participation with the coming of children and through the childrearing years. Older age groups also seem to be more active in churches. Whether this is a function of the family career or a phenomenon of a particular period in history can be determined by careful research based on a developmental framework. A word of caution is in order, perhaps, arising out of the Fairchild-Wynn experience. Statistics show that about two-thirds of the population claim some religious affiliation, or perhaps more accurately, religious groups claim some two-thirds of the population in their membership. Fairchild and Wynn's rather startling findings from respondents who were among the most active in church participation may foreshadow even less evidence of salient transactive roles with the religious system in more random samples of the population. Such findings, however, will be of equal scientific significance to findings of high religious activity. This area is worthy of research attention.

TRANSACTIONS WITH THE EXTENDED FAMILY SYSTEM

The inclusion of a section on transactions with the extended family system places us squarely in the midst of a theoretical controversy which emerged approximately at the turn of the half-century. Apparently first in 1943 and then in several subsequent publications, Talcott Parsons (1943, 1949, 1953; Parsons and Bales, 1955) put forth the idea that the American family system is characterized by the isolated nuclear family. Parsons maintained that such a system is functional for a modern industrial society, since it allows for a kind of occupational and geographical mobility necessary in such a system; that is, in such a system, the nuclear family is not restricted in its spatial mobility by requirements of the extended family for it to remain in the same locality and to be subject to the authority of the larger family system. Neither is it bound in terms of social mobility to the ascribed status in the stratification system held by the extended family. Rather, its ties to the extended family are so loose as to result in characterizing it as relatively isolated from the larger system.

The challenge to Parsons' orientation has been carried on chiefly by two theorist-researchers, Marvin Sussman and Eugene Litwak, though others have been stimulated by their work. (For a more extensive discussion of this topic, see Adams, 1970). First, Marvin Sussman (1951, 1953a, 1953b, 1954, 1955, 1959, 1960; Sussman and White 1959; Sussman and Burchinal, 1962a, and 1962b; Sussman and Slater, 1962) took up the gauntlet in his doctoral dissertation and carried it through in a series of subsequent works. He was followed shortly by Eugene Litwak's (1958, 1959, 1960a, 1960b; Litwak and Szelenyi, 1969) doctoral study and a similar series of succeeding investigations. The challenge begins from a very simple premise: Although the two ideal types—isolated nuclear and extended families—may be a very logical way to set hypothetical extremes in a conceptual scheme, the empirical data do not appear to support these categories as being either dichotomous or mutually exclusive. Starting from such an empirical base, both Sussman and Litwak proceed to develop theoretical schema which argue that it is more plausible to view the nuclear family as intricately involved with the extended family and that such relationships actually serve to support the nuclear family in the modern industrial society in various ways. Whether one uses Sussman's concept of *kin family network* or Litwak's idea of *modified extended family*, the outcome is the same—in viewing contemporary family systems found in most industrialized areas, one inevitably must take into account relationships with other close relatives located in other nuclear families (Townsend, 1957; Young and Willmott, 1957; Bott; 1957; Sweetser, 1968; Hill, 1970).

This approach ties in well with developmental theorists' attempts to establish a bridge between the nuclear family and other systems of the society through the idea of transactional role relationships. For example, one important variable in the occupational socialization process may be whether the family is of a nuclear, modified extended, or extended variety (Rodgers, 1966:221). Litwak (in personal communication) has mentioned that he has considered the possibility that families may shift from one type to another over the span of their career. This research proposition is certainly an intriguing one with some important implications.

The research material abounds with evidence for the prevasiveness of transactional relationships between the nuclear family and the extended family (in addition to the ones cited above see Komarovsky, 1962:23–48, 205–19, 236–79; Duvall, 1954; Aldous, 1965; Scanzoni, 1965a; Nelson, 1966; Streib, 1965; Winch et al., 1967; Troll 1971). This proof should not be at all surprising, since family sociologists may be expected to direct their attention first and most extensively to extended family relationships. The question can be raised, "What remains to be done?" The Sussman and Litwak focus. has been oriented more toward the impact of transactional relationships for integration into the larger social structure. Neither sociologist has tended to analyze systematically the impact of kinsmen at all phases of family careers. Some of the research on intergenerational relations has dealt with the internal consequences for the nuclear family, especially among young marrieds and postparental couples, but the theoretical formulations tend not to have this topic as their primary explanatory goal. Thus, further integration of the developmental approach with the modified extended family approach is indicated. In approaching this integration, Irwin Deutscher's theoretical work (1962, 1964), as well as Farber's (1961) theoretical development of the family as a set of mutually contingent careers, has provided some of the basic concepts of the developmental approach. What begins to appear from such a joining together of these various theoretical approaches is a more general theory of familial behavior with respect to both the nuclear family and the extended family. The potentiality exists, for example, to begin to explain more adequately some of the transactions between the nuclear-family system and the economic system in the occupational area and some of the transactions between the nuclear family system and the extended family system, as well as the division of labor transactions of the nuclear family.

Kerckhoff's (1965) analysis of nuclear and extended family relationships offers an excellent model since he joins together the Litwak "nuclear —modified extended—extended family" typology with Bott's "segregated and joint conjugal role-relationship" typology. Kerckhoff finds a high association between joint conjugal role-relationship norms and nuclear intergenerational family norms. At the other extreme, he finds a similar association between segregated conjugal role-relationship norms and extended intergenerational family norms. Families of the modified extended intergenerational normative type lie in an intermediate position between joint and segregated on the conjugal role-relationship normative scale. On the other hand, Kerckhoff did not find such direct relationships between the typologies and the families' *behavior*. Although the husband and wife respondents in his study subscribed to *normative* definitions which were in direct relationship along the two dimensions; that is, they defined their *roles* in a congruent manner, their *role behavior* was quite deviant. Only 57 percent of the wives and 55 percent of the husbands behaved in task sharing in accord with the norms they espoused with respect to conjugal role-relationships. Kerckhoff's (1965:110–12) attempt to explain this discrepancy lies within the "situational constraints or breadth of life space." He suggests that occupational and financial considerations restrict the degree to which task sharing and intergenerational aid may be carried out. Thus, Kerckhoff thinks those families which held extended intergenerational family norms would have provided more help then they did, had they not been constrained by the occupational or economic situation in which they found themselves.

There is an alternative explanation for which Kerckhoff apparently had no data available. With regard to Litwak's suggestion that families may shift from one type to the other through their careers, it may be that an analysis including as one explanatory variable the portion of the family career in which extended family behavior is found will reduce some of the deviations; that is, families in some family career periods may be more able to engage in modified extended family relationships than at other times, since the impact of transactional relationships with the extended family *and* with the occupational and economic system may covary in some systematic manner yet to be discovered. Putting the explanation another way, the demands of transactive and interactive roles at certain periods of the family career may be such that the saliency of interactive roles precludes meeting transactive role expectations, whereas at other times transactive role saliency may take precedence. For example, a family with preschool and elementary-school-aged children in which the husband is in the early portion of his occupational career may find that the demands in these two areas prohibit any high rate of transactional relationships with the parents of either the husband or the wife, even though the norms they hold call for such relationships. It may be that, since it will be likely that the parents of husband and wife are still in a preretirement period of their own family career, the saliency of such transactional relationships with extended kin will not be high enough to demand heavy involvement. By the same token, at a somewhat later point in the family career of the two generations, the physical and economic situation of the older generation, as well as the changed familial and occupational situation of the younger generation, may raise the saliency of such norms to the degree that increased transactional behavior will reach the level of being obligatory, rather than being discretionary. Some evidence for these speculations was found in the study of three generation families reported by Hill (1970:59–80). In analyzing the help received and given by each of the generations to the others, some clear differences emerge. The parent generation gave more to both the married-child and to the grandparent generation. The married-child generation was most frequently the recipient of help; however, the grandparent generation was also a heavy recipient of help. But of special interest is the way the kinds of help are differentiated. Hill (1970:67–68) reports:

Examining the exchanges . . . by area of need highlights the functions which the modified extended family network fulfills for its constituent nuclear families about which there has been much speculative debate. By area of need grandparents required heavy help with the problems of illness (61%), household management (52%) and emotional gratification (42%) for which it would have been difficult to secure aid from non-kin sources. These are precisely the areas in which the married child generation responded by giving heavily. The married child generation in turn required help especially in the problem areas of child care (78%) and of economic assistance (49%) in which the parent generation gave heavily. The ingenuity of the modified extended family linking three generations into one network is that there is defense in depth through the middle generation to help the very vulnerable married child generation get started . . . while helping the grandparent generation at its level of need.

Thus, bringing together the family career settings of the generations provides the potentiality for increased explanatory power. Pertinent analyses require data which provides information on the impact of transactional roles on the interactional career of the nuclear family.

Developmental analysis of transactional roles with the extended family, then, proceeds from a point of view which takes into account the role-complex structures of each of the nuclear families to be studied. The examination may take into account, as well, transactional roles associated with other systems which either will enhance or will tend to reduce such transactions. Similar analyses will not necessarily have to be confined to intergenerational transactions, but may be applied equally well to extended kin of the same generation, for example, to transactions with brothers and sisters who established their own families of procreation, to transactions with cousins, and so on. Indeed, such research may determine whether or not there are differentiated patterns governing transactions between extended kin of the same generation as compared with kin in different generations. There is, then, still a great deal which can be learned concerning this area. It differs, perhaps, from the other transactional fields because enough work has already been accomplished so that it will be possible to begin at a higher level than the exploratory one in developing for test propositions derived from theory.

CONCLUSION

This chapter has attempted to demonstrate the value of the developmental theoretical framework for moving beyond the interactional analysis of family careers to an investigation of the relationships which exist outside the family system but which have an effect on it. Although the areas explored are not often adequately researched, the potentialities are high for increased explanatory power of family behavior. There are, of course, other transactional fields. One which has increasing importance in the present technological development of Western industrialized societies is leisure or, more broadly, nonwork time. With the reduction of time on the job which is occurring in many occupational areas, increased amounts of time are freed to be given over to other types of activities. There is a growing field of writing and research on leisure. Family behavior is bound to be affected by it (Cunningham and Johannis, 1960). We can anticipate, then, that analyses of nonwork time based on family developmental theory may be forthcoming.

With the conclusion of this chapter comes the completion of the treatment of what may be termed *modal family patterns*. Although some material from nonmodal situations has been cited, the central concerns have not been extended to any great degree beyond these limits. The analysis also has dealt primarily with American society. In the chapters to follow, however, our attention will turn to special problems for analysis. A major criticism of the developmental theory has been its tendency to deal with a limited range of examination. I shall attempt to show that this neglect is not a result of inherent limitations in the theoretical approach. I shall be suggesting ways to accomplish developmental analysis of atypical role structures, analysis of stress in family careers, and analysis of non-modal American and non-American family careers.

REFERENCES

Adams, Bert N.
 1970 "Isolation, function, and beyond; American kinship in the 1960's." *Journal of Marriage and the Family* 32 (November): 575–97.

Aldous, Joan
 1965 "The consequences of intergenerational continuity." *Journal of Marriage and the Family* 27 (November): 462–68.

——— 1969a "Wives' employment status and lower-class men as husband-fathers: support for the Moynihan thesis." *Journal of Marriage and the Family* 31 (August): 469–76.

——— 1969b "Occupational characteristics and males' role performance in the family." *Journal of Marriage and the Family* 31 (November): 707–12.

————, AND REUBEN HILL

1967   *International Bibliography of Research in Marriage and the Family, 1900–1964*. Minneapolis, Minn.: University of Minnesota Press.

BATES, FREDERICK L.

1957   "A conceptual analysis of group structure." *Social Forces* 36 (December): 103–11.

————

1960   "Institutions, organizations and communities: a general theory of complex structure." *Pacific Sociological Review* 3 (Fall): 59–70.

BOTT, ELIZABETH

1957   *Family and Social Network*. London: Tavistock Publications, Ltd.

COHEN, WILBUR J.

1966   "Social policy for the nineteen seventies." *Health, Education, and Welfare Indicators* (May): 8–19.

CUNNINGHAM, KENNETH R., AND THEODORE B. JOHANNIS, JR.

1960   "Research on the family and leisure: a review and critique of selected studies." *The Family Life Coordinator* 9 (September–December): 25–32.

DEUTSCHER, IRWIN

1962   "Socialization for postparental life." Pp. 506–25 in Arnold Rose (ed.), *Human Behavior and Social Processes*. Boston: Houghton Mifflin Company.

————

1964   "The quality of postparental life: definition of the situation." *Journal of Marriage and the Family* 26 (February): 52–59.

DUVALL, EVELYN M.

1954   *In-Laws: Pro and Con*. New York: Association Press.

ECKHARDT, KENNETH W., AND ELDON C. SHRINER

1969   "Familial conflict, adolescent rebellion, and political expression." *Journal of Marriage and the Family* 31 (August): 494–99.

FAIRCHILD, ROY W., AND J. C. WYNN

1961   *Families in the Church: A Protestant Survey*. New York: Association Press.

FARBER, BERNARD

1961   "The family as a set of mutually contingent careers." Pp. 276–97 in Nelson Foote (ed.), *Household Decision-Making*. New York: New York University Press.

GLOCK, CHARLES Y., AND RODNEY STARK

1965   *Religion and Society in Tension*. Chicago: Rand McNally & Company.

HERBERG, WILL

1955   *Protestant, Catholic, Jew*. New York: Doubleday and Company.

HESS, ROBERT D., AND JUDITH V. TONEY
1967   The Development of Political Attitudes in Children. Chicago: Aldine Publishing Company.

HILL, REUBEN
1970   Family Development in Three Generations. Cambridge, Mass.: Schenkman Publishing Company, Inc.

HOCHSCHILD, ARLIE
1969   "The role of the ambassador's wife: an exploratory study." Journal of Marriage and the Family 31 (February): 73–87.

JACOBSEN, R. BROOKE, ET AL.
1966   The Family and Occupational Choice: An Annotated Bibliography. Eugene, Ore.: Center for Research in Occupational Planning, Department of Sociology, University of Oregon.

KATELMAN, DORIS K., AND LARRY D. BARNETT
1968   "Work orientations of urban, middle-class, married women." Journal of Marriage and the Family 30 (February): 80–88.

KERCKHOFF, ALAN C.
1965   "Nuclear and extended family relationships: a normative and behavioral analysis." Pp. 93–112 in Ethel Shanas and Gordon F. Streib (eds.), Social Structure and the Family: Generational Relations. Englewood Cliffs, N.J.: Prentice-Hall, Inc.

KOMAROVSKY, MIRRA
1962   Blue Collar Marriage. New York: Random House, Inc.

LANSING, JOHN B., AND LESLIE KISH
1957   "Family life cycle as an independent variable." American Sociological Review 22 (October): 512–19.

LITWAK, EUGENE
1958   "Primary group instruments for social control in industrialized society." Unpublished doctoral dissertation. New York: Columbia University.

————
1959   "The use of extended family groups in the achievement of social goals: some policy implications." Social Problems 7 (Winter): 177–87.

————
1960a   "Occupational mobility and extended family cohesion." American Sociological Review 25 (February): 9–21.

————
1960b   "Geographical mobility and extended family cohesion." American Sociological Review 25 (June): 385–94.

————, AND J. FIGUEIRA
1968   "Technological innovation and theoretical functions of primary groups and bureaucratic structures." American Journal of Sociology 73 (January): 468–81.

————, AND HENRY J. MEYER
1967 "The school and the family: linking organizations and external primary groups." Pp. 522–43 in Paul F. Lazarsfeld et al. (eds.), *The Uses of Sociology.* New York: Basic Books, Inc., Publishers.

————, AND IVAN SZELENYI
1969 "Primary group structures and their functions: kin, neighbors, and friends." *American Sociological Review* 34 (August): 465–81.

MIDDLETON, RUSSELL, AND SNELL PUTNEY
1963 "Political expression of adolescent rebellion." *American Journal of Sociology* 68 (March): 527–35.

MUDGE, LEWIS S., ED.
1970 *Model for Ministry.* Philadelphia: The United Presbyterian Church in the United States of America.

NELSON, JOEL I.
1966 "Clique contacts and family orientations." *American Sociological Review* 31 (October): 663–72.

NYE, IVAN, AND LOIS W. HOFFMAN
1963 *The Employed Mother in America.* Chicago: Rand McNally & Company.

PARSONS, TALCOTT
1943 "The kinship system of the contemporary United States." *American Anthropologist* 45 (January–March): 22–38.

1953 "Revised analytical approach to the theory of social stratification." Pp. 92–128 in R. Bendix and S. M. Lipset (eds.), *Class, Status, and Power.* Glencoe, Ill.: The Free Press.

1959 "The social structure of the family." Pp. 241–74 in Ruth N. Anshen (ed.), *The Family: Its Function and Destiny,* 2nd ed. New York: Harper and Brothers.

————, AND ROBERT F. BALES
1955 *Family, Socialization, and Interaction Process.* Glencoe, Ill.: The Free Press.

RAPOPORT, ROBERT, AND RHONA RAPOPORT
1965 "Work and family in contemporary society." *American Sociological Review* 30 (June): 381–94.

RODGERS, ROY H.
1966 "The occupational role of the child: a research frontier in the developmental conceptual framework." *Social Forces* 45 (December): 217–24.

1967 "Planned and unplanned aspects of occupational choices of youth: family and occupational choice." Eugene, Oregon: Center for Research in Occupational Planning, Department of Sociology, University of Oregon (mimeographed).

SCANZONI, JOHN
1965a "Resolution of occupational-conjugal role conflict in clergy marriages." *Journal of Marriage and the Family* 27 (August): 396–402.

1965b "A reinquiry into marital disorganization." *Journal of Marriage and the Family* 27 (November): 483–91.

SCHOTTLAND, CHARLES I.
1967 "Government economic programs and family life." *Journal of Marriage and the Family* 29 (February): 71–123.

SHOSTAK, ARTHUR B.
1967 "Education and the family." *Journal of Marriage and the Family* 29 (February): 124–39.

STREIB, GORDON F.
1965 "Intergenerational relations: perspectives of the two generations on the older parent." *Journal of Marriage and the Family* 27 (November): 469–76.

SUSSMAN, MARVIN B.
1951 "Family continuity: a study of factors which affect relationships between families at generational levels." Unpublished doctoral dissertation. New Haven, Connecticut: Yale University.

1953a "The help pattern in the middle-class family." *American Sociological Review* 18 (February): 22–28.

1953b "Parental participation in mate selection and its effect upon family continuity." *Social Forces* 32 (October): 76–81.

1954 "Family continuity: selective factors which affect relationships between families at generational levels." *Marriage and Family Living* 16 (May): 112–20.

1955 "Activity patterns of post-parental couples and their relationship to family continuity." *Marriage and Family Living* 17 (November): 338–41.

1959 "The isolated nuclear family: fact or fiction?" *Social Problems* 6 (Spring): 333–40.

1960 "Intergenerational family relationships and social role changes in middle age." *Journal of Gerontology* 15 (January): 71–75.

———, ED.
1967 "Government programs and the family." Special issue of *Journal of Marriage and the Family* 29 (February).

————, AND LEE BURCHINAL
1962a "Kin family network: unheralded structure in current conceptuali-
zations of family functioning." *Marriage and Family Living* 24
(August): 231–40.

1962b "Parental aid to married children: implications for family functioning." *Marriage and Family Living* 24 (November): 320–32.

————, AND SHERWOOD B. SLATER
1962 "The family life cycle and the kinship network: an empirical test."
Unpublished paper presented at the annual meeting of the
National Council on Family Relations, Storrs, Connecticut.

————, AND R. CLYDE WHITE
1959 *Hough, Cleveland, Ohio: A Study of Social Life and Change.*
Cleveland, Ohio: Western Reserve University Press.

SWEETSER, DORRIAN A.
1968 "Intergenerational ties in Finnish urban families." *American
Sociological Review* 33 (April): 236–46.

TOWNSEND, PETER
1957 *The Family Life of Old People: An Inquiry in East London.*
London: Routledge and Kegan Paul, Ltd.

TROLL, LILLIAN E.
1971 "The family of later life: a decade review." *Journal of Marriage
and the Family* 33 (May): 263–90.

TROPMAN, JOHN E.
1968 "The married professional social worker." *Journal of Marriage
and Family Living* 30 (November): 661–65.

VINCENT, CLARK E.
1967 "Mental health and the family." *Journal of Marriage and the
Family* 29 (February): 18–39.

WASBY, STEPHEN L.
1966 "The impact of the family on politics: an essay and review of
the literature." *The Family Life Coordinator* 15 (January): 3–23.

WHYTE, WILLIAM H.
1956 *Organization Man.* New York: Simon and Schuster, Inc.

WILENSKY, HAROLD L.
1961 "Life cycle, work situation, and participation in formal associations." Pp. 213–42 in Robert W. Kleemeier (ed.), *Aging and
Leisure.* New York: Oxford University Press.

WINCH, ROBERT F., ET AL.
1967 "Ethnicity and extended familism in an upper-middle-class
suburb." *American Sociological Review* 32 (April): 265–72.

YOUNG, MICHAEL, AND PETER WILLMOTT
1957 *Family and Kinship in East London.* London: Routledge and
Kegan Paul, Ltd.

8

Atypical
Role Complexes
and Family Careers

I am dissatisfied with the connotations of the term *atypical* as applicable to the material to be discussed in this chapter. Whenever a person encounters this term and similar ones, he tends to assume that the matters to be discussed are either of an "abnormal" variety or are so infrequent as to be of less significance than "typical" phenomena. I hope to demonstrate that such a conclusion is invalid. It is true that the areas of concern in this chapter are associated either with phenomena which are infrequent or which involve certain types of normative deviation. The events occur, however, with sufficient frequency in the social organization of most societies as to merit major attention from any theorist interested in developing an adequate explanation of human behavior. Most of them have long been the concern of the various helping professions of medicine, social work, counseling, and law. Attention by persons with applied interests has not been balanced to a similar degree by individuals with theoretical concerns, particularly by family analysts. A partial explanation for this lack may be that family sociologists are still seeking adequate explanations of "normal" behaviors. It may be argued that, until such explanations are pretty well in hand, interpretations of behavior lying outside that range should not be attempted. An alternative approach, one which I tend to hold, takes the position that it is possible to derive a theory which accounts for both types of phenomena. It is my intention, therefore, to attempt to demonstrate in the discussion to follow that the developmental theory has this potentiality.

This chapter will deal with three general types of phenomena. First to be treated will be the structural characteristics of the family: excess in structure, deficit in structure, and certain types of atypical formations resulting from the accession of members through adoption and through remarriage. Second, an examination will be made of the general area of the inability to play roles resulting primarily from physical and mental disabilities of various types. Third, a topic will be presented which I have labeled somewhat arbitrarily, and perhaps inaccurately, the unwillingness to play roles, under which I place such topics as desertion, runaways, infidelity, and suicide.

In an article published some years ago, Reuben Hill (1958) presented a conceptual framework for the general study of social stress and of crisis in families. In his classification of various types of stressful events, he included the kinds of matters which appear in this chapter and in the next one.

I have distinguished the areas of atypical role structures from the topics dealing with stresses in role complexes and in familial careers on the following basis: Although each of the types of atypicality to be analyzed certainly produces stress in the family structure, this pressure tends to be restricted only to families in which the particular atypical phenomena occur. In discussing the specific types of stress, I am concerned with general phenomena affecting families that are otherwise typical (in the structural and statistical sense) and families that may be atypical. The legitimacy of such a rationale, hopefully, will become apparent from reading the two chapters.

The general treatment of atypical role complexes and familial careers from a developmental perspective begins with the fundamental recognition that there are broad societal-institutional normative structures to which all families are expected to conform within somewhat ill-defined limits. In addition, there may be group-interactional and individual-psychological normative expectations. The existence of this normative structure precipitates the analytical focus when it is determined that a particular family or positional occupant of a family falls beyond the acceptable limits in some area of that normative structure. Such deviations have both interactional and transactional implications, though the relative effect may differ with the kind of atypicality and/or with the particular situation. I am not going to attempt to discuss all the possible implications of a given kind of atypical phenomenon but will be content to provide some of the major consequences resulting from an application of developmental theory to an explanation of the familial behavior arising from it.

ATYPICAL STRUCTURES

Developmental theory posits a basic normative structure with respect to the composition of the family over its career. Simply stated for the American family the norms would be that a nuclear unit should be established by the marriage of two people in their early twenties who should establish a separate domicile and who should bear from two to three children with at least one of each sex within the first decade of marriage. These children should live to maturity, should depart the family in their early twenties to establish their own families of procreation, which leaves the parents to live again by themselves, with the husband retiring from his occupation at about sixty-five, and the ultimate death of one partner leaving the remaining partner to live on in widowhood until his or her death. Any variation from this pattern constitutes an atypical family structure. It may be atypical in one of three ways: by having an excess in structure, by having a deficit in structure, or by an irregular method of forming an otherwise normal structure.

Excess in Structure

The Presence of Extra Household Occupants. The most obvious type of excess in structure, at least for American families, is violations of the neolocal norm: married children living in the parental home, parents living with one of the married children, or less frequently, married siblings sharing a common dwelling. One may easily determine the existence of this norm and become aware of its violation by listening to families explain the reasons for their deviation. Parents whose married children have moved into their home will frequently explain that the situation is only temporary until the young couple gets established or find their own home; or because the husband will soon be entering the military service and his wife will be unable to accompany him immediately. Children whose parents have moved in will explain that the temporary nature of the stay is related to the illness of one parent, will last until they can find a place in the same locality, or will continue while one parent enters the hospital for treatment. These and other explanations are not necessarily rationalizations, though the temporary nature of such arrangements often stretches over several months and even years and is more likely to do so, in all probability, in the case of a single individual moving into the household—a widowed parent, a recently divorced child, or an unmarried adult offspring or sibling. Although it is far less frequent to find the maiden aunt occupying the spare bedroom (probably because there are fewer of both the former and the latter), such extra relatives are found in many households. One may see how strongly this situation is resisted by observing the number of single-person households, the popularity of efficiency apartments, and the great increase in the number of nursing homes, of retirement villages, and of retirement apartment homes, which are all relatively recent phenomena (Stehouwer, 1965; Belcher, 1967).

The presence of extra household occupants presents the family with an immediate issue. Since the standard normative structure has no regular latent position with attendant roles, such a position must somehow be created. It is possible, of course, for a period of time to invoke the position of guest. Indeed, this method is probably a frequent way of meeting the matter at the outset; however, certain limits are attached to the tenure of a guest, though they are usually not well defined. To my knowledge, there has been little systematic analysis of such a position. Bossard and Boll (1947) published an article on the subject in the forties. Their data, however, were drawn from autobiographical sources and were concerned with guests making short visits of a few hours or brief overnight stays. Their central findings may best be expressed by stating that they detailed a series of socialization effects which guests had on children. Predictably, they ended the article with a plea for more research on this area, but I have found no followup. Bossard and Boll's guests, of course, were not family members for the most part, nor were they considered to be potential long-term residents in the household. The essential point is, therefore, that extra actors probably cannot continue to occupy a guest position for an unlimited length of time. This assertion implies that the family, with very little in the way of societal-institutional guidance, must create a new position, must endow it with role content and must provide for a set of reciprocal roles in all other positions by which the newcomer can be integrated into the family. Since most of the rights and the duties required for the daily functioning of the family have already been allocated to the roles of the basic four positions in the family, some sort of reallocation or creation of new roles must take place.

Developmental analysis, then, will center on how this process takes place and the way it differs at varying periods of the family career. It is clear that the former positions and roles which the outsiders may have occupied will not fit well into the nuclear structure. An aging set of parents cannot continue to play parent roles with respect to their now-married child, and there are probably some genuine limits on the degree to which they can continue to play their accustomed roles of grandparents to the offspring of their married children. Such roles tend to emphasize expressive kinds of interaction (the familiar pattern of grandparents "spoiling" their grandchildren), which probably operate better on an intermittent basis during short-term visits than on a continuing basis (Neugarten and Weinstein, 1964). This arrangement probably is true both because the grandparents may find such roles restricting and also because the parents may find that they conflict with their own expressive roles and disciplinary roles with the children. Other roles which the grandparents may have been accustomed to holding, for example, homemaker or wage earner, also raise potential conflicts. In the same manner, an adult offspring who has returned to his family of orientation, or who may have never left it, cannot recapture his accustomed child position. The reason is that the normative structure of this role combines the expectation that he will leave the family of orientation. Therefore, there are no roles in the position beyond a certain period in its career.

All these instances relate to interactional issues. There are also the transactional patterns to be considered. The family is faced with having to define to others the position occupied by the outsider so that actors in other systems will have some way of determining their reciprocal roles toward this extra family member. In addition, there is a problem as to what transactional roles may be appropriate for the extra member to play in other systems as a representative of the family. Once again, most of these transactional roles already have been allocated and the reallocation of them may open up areas of potential conflict.

How are these matters resolved? What considerations are taken into account in the creation of a position and in the assignment of particular roles to it? We really do not know. Perhaps it should be said that the development of such positions and roles does not necessarily mean that conflict is inevitable. It undoubtedly is true that families do restructure their familial roles in a way that makes it possible to live with extra members; however, a developmental theoretical orientation will anticipate that these arrangements differ according to the composition of the nuclear family and the period of the career in which that family is found. It will also predict some degree of disorganization in the process of reorganizing. This area is one in which exploratory research at the outset may only describe the process of accommodation of extra family members. Later research may then be able to begin to explain the differing kinds of patterns observed (Kosa et al., 1960; Monahan, 1956).

Before this chapter continues to another type of excess in structure, it may be noted that nonrelatives may also be found as extra residents in the family. Though this phenomenon may be considerably less common, hired hands, domestic employees, boarders, or friends may be found living with a family. The fact that these residents are not related to the family may provide a different kind of positional structuring, since the nonrelatives do not already have a prescribed position denoted by their familial ties. Pseudorelationship terms (such as *uncle* or *aunt*) may well be invoked to facilitate the transition; however, we really know very little about the characteristics of such situations, so that it is difficult to speculate how they may differ from ones involving the presence of nonnuclear family members.

Out-of-Wedlock Births. Out-of-wedlock births provide another sort of excess in structure. Such births may be wanted or unwanted. Beyond this factor, there are a number of considerations. Whether the unwed mother is part of a family group, probably her own family of orientation; whether she is living alone or with someone, not necessarily the father of the child; whether the child is kept by the mother, is given up for adoption, or is cared for by some relative; these and other matters will all form part of a potential analysis of such a situation. There is, of course, a great deal of material on the subject. Aldous and Hill (1967:271–72) list about seventy references through 1964 under the subject heading "Illegitimacy." Added to this topic may be some additional references dealing with premarital pregnancy. A review of this literature, however, reveals heavy emphasis on demographic reports of the incidence of illegitimate birth, attitudes toward illegitimacy, analyses of decisions with respect to surrendering the child for adoption, characteristics of unwed mothers (and, less frequently, of unwed fathers), and the like. Studies of the impact of such an event on the family career do not stand out in the same way as do studies of the impact on personal adjustment of the mother, primarily, and of the child, secondarily. Indeed, there seems to be some sort of covert assumption which tends to ignore the familial implications of unwed motherhood. Again, it must be recognized that, with the general stigma which has been attached to out-of-wedlock births in the past, this area is a somewhat difficult one in which to carry out research of the type called for from a developmental perspective.

The Return of a Family Member. A final type of excess in structure is the return to the family of a member who has absented himself for some period of time. Such events as the return of a deserting spouse, of a husband who has been absent for military service, of an imprisoned family member, of a former mental patient, of a runaway child are examples of this phenomenon. The area of interest from a developmental perspective hinges on the degree to which the roles which were part of the position formerly occupied by the returnee had been reallocated to other positions in the family. The necessity to reassign these roles to the reoccupied position and the processes which take place in such a reorganization provide some interesting possibilites. The particular period of the family career, the implications for the future career of the family and similar matters are involved.

There are two studies which illustrate this last type of excess in structure. At the end of World War Two, Reuben Hill (1949) undertook a study of family adjustment to the crises precipitated by war separation and by reunion. Though no analysis exists which differentiates families by family career period (all families studied had children in the home), a major emphasis is on the role relationships existing in these families before separation, during separation, and upon reunion. Hill (1949:298–99) cites the following elements as essential in developing a scale for classifying families into various adjustment types:

> The scale touched on husband-wife relationships, the division of labor in the home, the reallocation of roles, the father-child relationships, and the areas of conflict which are apt to crop up in reunion. . . . Effective role reorganization was one clue to good adjustment. The reopening of the family circle to absorb the father, renewal of husband-wife marital ties, and the growth and development of all family members were also items important in classifying families by type of adjustment to reunion.

The essential basis of the analysis, then, followed from a developmental theoretical perspective by viewing the adjustment to reunion as following from the role sequences which had existed in the family career over some time previously.

Similarly, Freeman and Simmons (1963) studied the degree of success in reentering the community on the part of former mental patients. Dividing the types of families to which the patient returned into parental, conjugal, sibling, and others (for example, cousins), the researchers determined both the level of functioning and whether the patient returned to the hospital within a twelve-month period. Neither male nor female patients were likely to return to the hospital if they reentered a conjugal relationship. Men were somewhat more successful in sibling settings than in parental settings, whereas women were almost as successful in other settings as in conjugal ones, with parental settings being slightly more favorable than sibling settings. With respect to level of functioning, however, the findings are strikingly differentiated. Both men and women were most likely to have low functioning levels in parental settings. Both were most likely to have high-level functioning in conjugal settings, but men were somewhat more successful than women here. Sibling settings provided intermediate functioning levels for both (Freeman and Simmons, 1963:92–93).

The explanation of this differential in level of functioning is very significant from a developmental theoretical perspective. Although the investigators had begun with a proposition that adjustment to a return to the community would be related to the differential degree of tolerance of deviant behavior in the families, they were forced to reevaluate and to modify this proposition (Freeman and Simmons, 1963:99):

> Our reformulated position maintains that the variables we derived from the proposition of tolerance of deviance reflect the extent to which the role expectations of significant others account for level of instru-

mental performance. In simplest terms, we can say that persons do what their relatives expect them to do; that wives have higher expectations than parents; and that differential performance levels represent the adaptation of the patients to the expectations of their family members.

Freeman and Simmons's findings tended to support the revised view. They found that the expectations of family members, particularly ones who showed that they would insist on certain levels of performance, were congruent with the performance of the return patients. Furthermore, there was no congruence between the level of expectations placed on performance and rehospitalization; that is, one could not explain returning or not returning by either having high or low expectations placed on patients (Freeman and Simmons, 1963:142–48). In effect, this finding suggests that if families reallocate to the returning patient the roles which he played before hospitalization, he is likely to meet those expectations. It is also important to note, however, that these expectations have been for a relatively inadequate level of functioning, particularly in parental settings. As Freeman and Simmons note, this fact has some significant applied implications concerning successful rehabilitation of mental patients. The researchers argue that permissive treatment of former mental patients tends to insulate them from the family and from the community and, thus, tends to result in less adequate performance. Whether a patient is rehospitalized or not relates not so much to his level of performance but to independent manifestations of certain symptoms of behavior, such as getting into debt, damaging things, and appearing nervous. For our purposes, then, it appears that further developmental exploration of the kinds of roles expected and played by mental patients in the family *before* hospitalization, as well as following it, will be a more significant part of the explanation of the family's behavior in such a structural excess situation. The findings of Freeman and Simmons certainly stimulate the desire to explore further this dimension of family behavior. It must be noted, however, that the period of the family career was not a variable examined in their research. It is possible that clear differentials may be expected if such an additional element were introduced.

In general, we must conclude that the impact of excesses in structure in the family career has not been investigated adequately, but that it has a major effect on the behavior of families and, therefore, merits considerably more attention.

Deficit in Structure

Deficit in structure presents, in effect, the converse of the kinds of situations with which we have just been concerned. We are now dealing with phenomena in which one or more of the normatively defined positions is vacant. The role content of these positions must be accounted for in some manner by the family. In their day-to-day experience, family members continually will encounter societal-institutional normative pressures and, perhaps to a lesser extent, group-interactional and individual-psychological expectations associated with the vacant position. This phenomenon is particularly true of those obligatory, dominant, and manifest roles which normally will be attached to such a position. The process by which families deal with the reallocation of these roles at various periods of the family career in both the interactional and transactional dimensions becomes, therefore, a central concern of developmental theory.

The varieties of structural deficit stem from the location and role content of the vacant position and of the circumstances accounting for the vacancy. The husband-father position may be vacated for the following reasons, among many: military service or other employment requiring an extended period of absence (employment as a merchant seaman, for example); imprisonment or some other sort of institutionalization; divorce; or premature death. The wife-mother position may be vacated for similar reasons. Child-position vacancies arise from voluntary or involuntary childlessness, from having all children of the same sex, as well as death.

The material which examines the *family* dynamics of absentee husband-fathers and wife-mothers is quite limited. This fact is particularly interesting, since one out of eight families in the 1960 census was a single-parent family with at least one child under age eighteen. Aldous and Hill (1967: 281–83) list over two hundred references under the heading "Families with Incomplete Structure," which includes all types of situations involving a deficit of structure. Titles dealing with absentee parents, however, tend to emphasize the effects on children, primarily from a psychological adjustment perspective. A similar emphasis is found in Schlesinger's (1966) forty-three item bibliography. I already have referred to Hill's (1949) study of war separation, which remains one of the few works to deal with adjustment to dismemberment in the family system. Goode's (1956) study of divorce provides some analysis of family adjustment to divorce (though the major thrust is on individual adjustment), and Pauline Morris (1965) has analyzed the family life of imprisoned men. Studies concerned about deficit of structure through death deal heavily with the bereavement process and with psychological adjustments to death. Another emphasis in the latter area deals with adjustments to living alone which are obviously relevant to the latter portion of the family career (Berardo, 1968, 1970). A developmental analysis of these phenomena will launch research with a somewhat different focus than most studies now available.

First, one of the central issues from a developmental perspective will be the varying impact of unoccupied positions according to the particular period in the family career. For example, the term *premature death* has been used to refer to the vacating of parental and child positions. Although death is accounted for in the normative system of families, it usually is considered to be normal only in the latter portion of the family career. Thus, the death of a parent during the childrearing years or the death of a school-aged child is premature or atypical, since the norms of the family system do not anticipate death at this point in the family career nor do they provide alternative structural arrangements of succession to fill a positional vacancy due to death. This fact probably is more applicable to child positions than it is to adult positions. Death is not a phenomenon that applies only to married couples in the later years of the family career. Similarly, divorce is a matter which involves more than a married couple, since over half of all divorces include minor children. A complete developmental analysis will examine, then, the reallocation of roles when required over the various periods of the family career.

Second, developmental theory will be particularly interested in the reallocation of roles when there is anticipation that the vacated positions may be reoccupied at a later point in the family career. Sensitivity to the fact that current behavior is influenced not only by past behavior and current situations but also by anticipations of future situations remains a somewhat unique perspective of the developmental approach. Families of war absentees or with positions vacated due to certain types of employment certainly tend to anticipate that the abandoned position is only temporarily so, in spite of their awareness of the possibility that the absentee may never return. Divorced and widowed families often consider the possibility of remarriage. This view seems realistic, since available data show that divorcees have the highest probability of marriage, widows the second highest, and the never married the the third highest. Couples who have lost a child in death may also anticipate the reoccupying of the vacated position by having other children.

Third, the focus may be on situations in which the families do not particularly desire the vacated positions to be filled and structure the family in terms of such a consideration. Some couples remain childless voluntarily, for example. They are faced, nevertheless, with the societal-institutional expectations to do otherwise. As they move through their career, although they may have resolved the interactional implications of their childlessness, they are still faced with the transactional implications. Families with children of only one sex may also be faced with similar kinds of situations, especially one-child families. Finally, it is possible that divorced or widowed families may determine to restructure their family system without seeking to fill the vacant spouse-parent position.

Fourth, analyses with a developmental perspective may center on individual-psychological factors, with the theoretical framework tending to orient the studies toward the impact on the role relationships of the family rather than the impact on the individual per se. Studies of death in the later portion of the family career, as well, fall within the developmental rubric. The discussion above attempted to identify areas of analysis which appear to have received less attention than they merit. Adequate explanation of behavior associated with these situations cannot be reached by minimal attention to the family context in which they occur.

Atypical Formations

Most family units are formed and positions are occupied through the process of marriage between relatively young people of similar ages and through biological reproduction. There are, however, at least three modes of formation of family units or of filling familial positions which do not follow this typical pattern. The remarriage of one or both partners who often bring offspring from a previous marriage to this new unit is one mode. Child positions may be filled through the adoption of children at any age from infant to adolescent. Finally, there are the so-called "May-December" marriages between partners of dissimilar ages and the first marriage of a couple well advanced in years. Each of these has a common characteristic. The career of the family, in effect, begins at some point other than the typical establishment point. It is as if the unit breaks into the stream of the career, not at its source but somewhere down-river. Although the structure of these family units is otherwise typical, that is, the positions are all filled with neither excess nor deficit in structure, the creation of the structure has occurred in an atypical fashion. This circumstance has some profound implications for developmental theoretical considerations.

The basic formulation of developmental theory emphasizes the fact that the family career is influenced by what has gone before, as well as what exists at the present and by what is anticipated in the future. In these situations, however, the actors in the system have sometimes extensive histories in one or more other family careers. Particularly in the case of remarriage, then, there is an additional major factor to contend with: the merging of two previous careers into a new common career. If only one partner has been previously married, this process is of a different order. The merging process may take on different characteristics in the adoption of infants or very young children as compared with the adoption of older children. In marriages of two individuals in their mature years, the probability exists that roles have been played which were of a nonfamilial type. Now adaptation to a familial setting of a somewhat deviant variety must occur. Such couples are probably less likely to anticipate having children, since they have begun their family career at a point in chronological age which is analogous to the postparental period. In this sense, they also fit into the deficit-in-structure category. In the dissimilar age situation, only one partner may be at such a point, further complicating the fitting of the normative structure to the typical family career.

Material is scarce in this general area. Studies of remarriage center heavily on the demographic analysis of probabilities for remarriage and probability of success of remarriages. Bernard (1956) has examined remarriage in what remains the single most comprehensive study, along with a somewhat less extensive treatment by Goode (1956). Though methodological purists may feel disturbed by the fact that Bernard gathered her data on 2,001 cases of remarriage through questionnaires completed by nonrandomly selected informants who knew the marriages, rather than by participants who were themselves in the marriages, the fact remains that there exist no comparable data on this subject. Bernard's data, augmented by statistical and other kinds of case materials, has at least provided some foundation from which to begin. Her analysis is a careful attempt to sort out the differences found within remarriages according to the following themes: the previous marital status of the spouses, the presence or absence of children by previous marriages, and the relative significance of the first and subsequent marriages. Bernard has carefully explored each of these major themes further along a number of dimensions. There is much in this study, therefore, which may provide propositions for further research within a developmental persepective, since Bernard has recognized the major impact of previous family history on current family experience.

Regarding another aspect related to remarriage, the research on the position of stepchild and stepparent is similarly sparse. The Aldous-Hill (1967: 179) bibliography lists only seven items published between 1950 and 1964 with the term *step child* or *step parent* in the title. Two of these are books, one a chiefly descriptive scholarly work by Smith (1953), the other a more popular treatment by Simon (1964). Of the remaining five articles, one was published in Japan (Yamazaki and Imada, 1959); there is a chapter by Smith (1957) which condenses material from his book, a study by Podolsky (1955) on the emotional problems of stepchildren, a short article by Bowerman (1956), and a more extensive article by Bowerman and Irish (1962) which apparently incorporates data from the original study along with new data. Both Smith and Bowerman cite some other works, a number of which were published by German students of the subject. There has been, therefore, only a small amount of systematic study of the ways the family goes about restructuring itself when there is remarriage of at least one partner with children. Without going into any detail, we may observe that the situation is the same for adoption, foster-child, and foster-parent experiences. Indeed, as Smith (1953:3) points out, there has tended to be so little systematic attention to these areas that the two, step relationships and foster relationships, are frequently confused or are treated as if they were identical. Lack of clear terminology is often an excellent indication of an area which has yet to be explored adequately.

INABILITY TO PLAY ROLES

Under this general heading, attention turns to analyses of family careers in which the structural characteristics of the family may be quite typical, but one or more actors are unable to meet the normative expectations attached to the roles in the position occupied. In these situations, therefore, a deficit in structure exists in that, whereas actors are present who hypothetically should occupy certain positions, one or more roles of those positions may not actually be played or may be played in a deviant manner. The deviancy may be related to societal-institutional normative standards or it also may include departures from group-interactional and from individual-psychological expectations.

Physical Disability and Chronic Illness

This general category includes all the types of disability which arise from physical sources, for example, from various types of paralysis or loss of limbs, from blindness, deafness, from cerebral palsy, from epilepsy, from chronic heart disease, from asthma, and from other types of chronic illness. In effect, any kind of condition of a physical sort which results in defining a person as handicapped or as disabled is included.

There has been a moderate amount of attention paid to disability and the family in the research material. Aldous and Hill (1967:225–26) list under the heading "Family Transactions with Groups and Formal Organizations, Health Services" between fifty and sixty items which appear to fall in this area. Additional items were published since 1964, some of which will be cited in this discussion. Two types of limitations appear in this literature. First, the topics of cerebral palsy and asthmatic conditions are the predominant kinds of disability covered. Second, as in some other areas, the analyses focus heavily on parental emotional and attitudinal reactions to the handicap in children, on psychological characteristics of both the disabled actor and of other family members, and on the individual adjustments of the disabled persons. There is far less analysis of the restructuring of the roles in the family system as a result of disability; however, some major exceptions exist.

Gibson and Ludwig (1968) analyzed data from a study of applicants for social security disability benefits with respect to the basic family structure of the applicants. Noting that the typical statistical treatment fails to reveal adequately the structural characterisics of the family settings of disabled persons, the investigators developed a typology based on marital status, presence of dependent and independent children, and presence of other related and nonrelated household members. Applying these criteria to the data resulted in nineteen empirically observed types and in a residual category. Since over 70 percent of the applicants were more than fifty years old, it is not surprising to find that only about 30 percent of the males and 11 percent of the females live with dependent children (2.1 percent of the disabled females have dependent children but have no husband present). On the other hand, 73 percent of the males and 57 percent of the females live with their spouse. An additional 13 percent of the males and 16 percent of the females live with some other relative. Thus, 86 percent of the males and 73 percent of the females live in some sort of family setting. These data, though limited to a population which is peculiar in that they were seeking financial assistance for their disability, give at least some foundation from which to speculate concerning family structural settings. Additional data are needed from populations composed of families of disabled children and from families affected by disability but not seeking public financial assistance.

Studies analyzing role adjustments in the family include the following: Crain et al. (1966) found that marital integration suffered among families with a diabetic child. The researchers reported no analysis that might have revealed differences according to the period of the family career or concerning the effects on healthy siblings. Litman (1962, 1964) has analyzed some of the family dynamics associated with paraplegia. Fred Davis (1963) analyzed both parental and sibling relationships of a small sample of children partially paralyzed by polio. Both these studies also have relevance for transactional relationships with the medical system and for deficits in structure due to institutionalization. Of particular interest from a developmental perspective are the important interrelationships among the transactional roles of both the patient and the family with medical personnel, the interactional roles played by both patient and family members during hospitalization, and the kinds of roles developed on the return of the disabled person to the family. In addition, Davis found evidence similar to data discovered by Freeman and Simmons and by Hill that the role structures prior to the child being stricken with polio have considerable impact on the post-hospital family dynamics. Ludwig and Collette (1969) examined certain aspects of the husband-wife relationship in a disabled-male sample, and Fink et al. (1968) studied the same relationship in a disabled-female sample. Neither analysis took much account of the previous marital history of the couple. In both situations, there were clear findings that the disability resulted in less involvement in roles or in less adequate performance in roles normally expected of both the disabled and normal partner.

The research already carried out has the capability of providing some basis on which to begin studies beyond the exploratory level. A review of this literature should provide propositions which may be subjected to analysis from a developmental theoretical standpoint. Taking into account transactional as well as interactional elements is clearly indicated in this area, since there is an almost inevitable involvement of some outside system with the family. Such systems include hospitals or other health-care organizations, rehabilitation organizations, and ones which deal with financial aid for disabled persons.

Mental Illness and Mental Exceptionality

The customary approach has been followed of dividing psychological disorders which may lead to the inability to play roles into two categories: mental illness and mental exceptionality. The first classification refers to the various kinds of psychopathological conditions arising in the lives of otherwise psychologically normal individuals which disturb their emotional and other functioning so that they are defined as ill. Many of these conditions may be corrected through appropriate therapy. Mental exceptionality, on the other hand, refers to basic conditions of the individual's mental equipment which result in his falling outside the normal range in his ability to carry on the various mental processes. The general label *mentally retarded* is applied to those who fall below the normal range and the label *gifted* is often applied to those who fall well above the normal range. Mental retardation refers both to conditions which are congenital and ones which may arise out of some trauma occurring during pregnancy, birth, or later in life. There may be differences in the meaning attached to these different types by the family which may affect its behavior. In general, no therapeutic approach with the goal of bringing the individual into the normal range is appropriate. Rather, treatment is oriented toward helping the individual to cope with life within his limited range of ability.

Mental illness and the family is one of the most extensively researched of all the areas considered thus far. Undoubtedly, this situation results from the impact of the writings of Freud and other theorists asserting that mental illness and family relationships are closely intertwined. Thus, Aldous and Hill (1967:276–80) list in the neighborhood of five hundred references published through 1964 under their heading "Special Problems, Family of the Mentally Ill." Without undue oversimplification, the general stance of these articles may be divided between the ones analyzing the impact of the family as a cause of the mental illness and the ones analyzing the effect of the mental illness on the family. At some point the two perspectives are very much interrelated. Without making any evaluations about the relative significance of the two stances, we can say the matter of the impact of mental illness on the family is the most relevant for this discussion; that is, the interest at this point is in how the family copes with the fact that they have an actor who, as a result of some sort of emotional disturbance, is unable to play the roles of his position in the manner defined as appropriate.

The kind of general approach which developmental theorists would take to this problem has already been outlined in the discussion of Freeman and Simmons's (1963) study dealing with the return of the mental patient to the family. Their study dealt specifically with mentally ill family members who had been hospitalized. Work also has been done on families with noninstitutionalized mentally ill members. One single source, *The Psychosocial Interior of the Family* (1967), presents an anthology of articles edited by Gerald Handel. Not only does Handel present some of his own work, carried out with Robert D. Hess, but he also brings together other significant articles which attempt to deal with various types of mental illness in the family context. Although it deals heavily with the individual-psychological facet, Handel's approach of studying "whole families" caused him to select literature which also emphasizes the group-interactional facet. He clearly considers this aspect as indispensable to an explanation of psychological disturbance. The volume, then, can be seen as a basic source for the prospective researcher with a developmental orientation. In addition, there is an interesting monograph by Rogler and Hollingshead (1965) which reports a comparative study carried out in Puerto Rico of twenty normal couples and twenty couples in which one or both partners was schizophrenic. None of the mentally ill individuals had ever been a patient in a clinic or in a hospital for treatment of the psychotic condition. This study, although concerned to a great extent with attempting to discern the underlying bases of the mental illness, also reports a great deal of information on the family dynamics. There is retrospective information on the family of orientation experience as well as data on the interactions of the family of procreation and on transactive behavior with the extended family and with other systems in the community. Such a study provides the prospective researcher with extensive comparative data which may suggest propositional areas for further developmental research.

The area of mental illness is a particularly interesting one for highlighting the impact of the individual-psychological facet on family careers. Not only is there the factor of the basic inability of the individual to meet role expectations, but there is also the complicating factor that the mentally ill actor frequently behaves in ways which disrupt the role complexes of sets of actors in other positions. Thus, the mental illness circumstance particularly underscores the distinction between vacancy of a position and having the position occupied by an actor who cannot meet the role expectations. Although there may be both societal-institutional and group-interactional norms for defining the role of such an actor, the dominating effect of individual-psychological characteristics becomes especially apparent. The consequences for the way family roles are played among the nondisturbed family members as well as toward the disturbed individual are of considerable import. They may serve only to intensify the mental illness by locking the person into a kind of role which prevents him from beginning to act in a more acceptable manner. Such a situation is illustrated in Vogel and Bell's (1968) analysis of families in which the emotionally disturbed child becomes a scapegoat.

The topic of mental exceptionality has also developed a considerable body of material in one of the two areas. Aldous and Hill (1967:275–76) list over seventy-five references published through 1964 under the heading "Special Problems, Family of the Mentally Retarded." Undoubtedly, this great amount of attention results from the fact that retardation is usually discovered during childhood and, thus, inevitably involves the family. Special attention should be directed to the work of Bernard Farber in this area. His idea of the family as a set of mutual contingent careers is one of the basic conceptual elements in the developmental theory. Farber (1959, 1960; Farber and Jenne, 1963) has used this basic idea in his extensive analysis of the dynamics of families containing a severely retarded child. Three monographs, one dealing with husband-wife marital integration, one dealing with general family integration, and one dealing with parent-child interaction, are of particular interest. In these analyses, Farber not only deals with emotional reactions to the fact of mental retardation but particularly considers the impact of retardation on the role sequences and complexes of all family members. His examinations are truly developmental ones. For example, Farber analyzes the way the roles of a sibling of a retarded child change as both grow older. Since the retarded child's ability to perform in line with age-role expectations decreases relatively as he becomes older, a widening gap exists between the two actors. Or, in the case of the normal sibling being younger than the retarded child, the sibling has the unusual experience of overtaking and of surpassing the retarded child in his ability to play the appropriate roles. Thus, the sibling finds himself actually changing his ordinal position vis-a-vis the position of the retarded child during his own positional career. In other analyses, the finding is that female retarded children generally disrupt the family less than male retarded children, apparently because with aging, male children are normally expected to take on nondomestic roles whereas female children tend to continue with domestic roles. Thus, it is somewhat easier for female children, though retarded, to meet at least some of the normal expectations, such as helping with the dishes and doing other sorts of household chores.

Another aspect investigated is the process by which the decision to institutionalize the retarded child is made (Farber et al., 1960). Again this matter is handled within the family career context, not simply situationally. Thus, while there are other references to which a potential researcher will wish to turn, Farber's work is an excellent model upon which to build and further extend a developmental approach in this area. This is particularly true since much of his material has followed the pattern observed in mental illness research by dealing more narrowly with attitudes, psychological reactions, and other characteristics of the parents and of the retarded child. These studies contribute little to an understanding of the reorganization of the role content of positions in the family career.

At the other extreme in the area of mental exceptionality, analyses of families with gifted chlidren are not nearly as numerous. Aldous and Hill (1967:283) list only nineteen references under this subject heading, no more than a third of which were published between 1960 and 1964. A survey of the major sociological journals since 1964 reveals no further treatments. This lack of research is probably due in great part to the problem orientation of much behavioral research. Gifted children tend not to be viewed as problems for the society or for their families; yet, from a theoretical point of view, the probability is that families modify the role expectations for such actors because they find them unable to play the roles as normally defined. The effect of this modification in the one position, then, inevitably affects the other positions and, thus, the career of the family. While, by definition, such families constitute a very small proportion of all families, they present a particularly interesting area for research and theory, since they represent the deviancy of overachievement in role behavior about which we have far less information than about underachievement.

Addiction to Alcohol and to Drugs

Still another kind of phenomenon which has an effect on the ability of individuals to meet their role expectations in the family and in other situations is addiction to alcohol or to various types of drugs. Such compulsive dependence may be psychological or physiological, but for analytical purposes the effect remains the same. Particular interest lies in how this addiction may affect the dynamics of the family, rather than in how the family may be a source of the condition. Of course, the two aspects may well be closely interrelated, and the investigation of one may provide insights into the other.

With respect to alcohol addiction, a considerable body of literature has accumulated (Bailey, 1961; Day, 1961). Much of it deals with the individual-psychological characteristics of alcoholics and of family members associated with them. In this area, the work of Joan K. Jackson stands out because of her attempt to trace the processes by which families of alcoholics adjust to the phenomenon. Three publications provide her basic approach (Jackson, 1954, 1956, 1958), though she and her colleagues have continued to investigate the area since this early work. Jackson identifies a seven-stage process in which the family moves from denial of a problem, to attempts to eliminate the problem, to disorganization, to attempts to reorganize in spite of the problem, to attempts to escape the problem through separation, to reorganization of the family during separation, to reorganization of the whole family. This approach certainly contains the basis for a developmental analysis. Jackson did not take into systematic account the differing patterns which might occur depending on the point in the family career when alcoholism became identified as a problem. Furthermore, her analysis is based on alcoholism in the husband-father position only, since she gathered her data through association with an Alcoholics Anonymous Auxiliary group. Indeed, a great share of the material seems to carry the implicit assumption that alcoholism strikes only the adult male head of the family. In 1961, Day (1961:257) stated that there was a need to examine the applicability of the developmental framework, as well as of other sociological approaches, to the study of alcoholism. That need seems to be no less today than it was then. Such an application appears to provide a considerably broader base for the explanation of behavior in families with one or more alcoholic members than has been achieved to date.

The subject of drug addiction took on new significance in the latter part of the 1960s. That it did not carry similar importance earlier is amply testified to by the fact that Aldous and Hill (1967) cite only two studies using the key word *drug* in the title (Hirsch, 1961; Wolh and Driskind, 1961). With the appearance of the "hippie" culture around 1967, however, there was included in that cultural pattern a routine use of addictive drugs as well as of marijuana. (Around the latter, while this book is in press, a controversy continues to boil concerning its addictive nature.) The "drug scene," as it came to be called by many people, soon spread well beyond the confines of hippiedom and into the broad youth culture of every social-class level. At this writing, the entire phenomenon represents what is undoubtedly the single most discussed so-called youth problem, with the attention of the mass media, government and education officials, and parents being drawn to it on an almost daily basis. There is, however, a great deal of conflicting information to be gained from these popular sources. Such basic matters as the incidence and prevalence of usage, the effects of usage, and the like are still in a state of confusion. As to the professional material, the lag between research and publication (assuming that research is being carried on) is such that no publications of consequence analyzing family dynamics and drug usage have appeared in the major journals to date (late 1971).

One focus of this phenomenon has been on youth and the reactions of parents. Some estimates given in national periodicals assert that well over 50 percent of the high school students in the United States have used marijuana. The estimates for the "hard" drugs are considerably lower, though the estimates for all types of drug usage increase when applied to the college-age population. The impact on the family, whether members have been revealed to be users or not, has been profound. Most parents express among themselves considerable anxiety over the possibility that their children may become involved with drugs. As is often the case, the lack of knowledge and information only heightens the anxiety. Almost daily, news reports appear about arrests of young people for drug violations—the children of people in prominent places as well as offspring of ordinary citizens. Less frequent, though no less alarming, are the reports of serious illness or deaths resulting directly or indirectly from drug use. Assuming that the phenomenon continues, we can postulate that there are bound to be profound effects on the family. Thus, from both theoretical and applied perspectives, this area represents a significant one for the potential contributions of family research. At this point, however, we can do little more than to identify the existence of the drug phenomenon.

Cultural Deprivation

Another area in which a new kind of emphasis has emerged in the decade of the sixties consists of *culturally deprived* groups. Generally, this term is applied to the poor and to certain ethnic groups: the Black American, the Spanish American, and the American Indians, particularly. From the societal-institutional normative standard of the dominant White Anglo-Saxon Protestant culture, such groups do represent a kind of deprivation. The trend in a great deal of the analysis of the situation toward the end of the decade, however, turned to distinguishing between economic disadvantage and cultural patterns which deviated from this dominant normative structure. Many assumptions concerning the so-called cultural inadequacy of these groups in terms of family strength, sense of identity, and the like where challenged. Some of this material will be cited in the chapter on cross-cultural applications of the developmental theory. For the present, it is enough to point out that, to the extent that the dominant culture defines familial roles in a certain manner, there remains an impact of the dominant culture on families in these American subcultures. Such classic studies as Thomas and Znaniecki's (1958) monumental work on the Polish peasant sensitized social scientists to this fact. Until recently, however, the emphasis has been on the ultimate incorporation of such subcultural groups into the dominant culture through the process of assimilation. The new emphasis on subcultural identity and autonomy as expressed in the ideas of Black Power, Red Power, and the like provide a new kind of phenomenon. Indeed, there is a fascinating twist from the issues identified by Thomas and Znaniecki of the children of immigrant parents struggling to free themselves from the ethnic cultural standards and to assimilate themselves into the dominant culture. In the contemporary situation, it appears to be the youth who are emphasizing the maintenance of their unique cultural identity in the face of long-standing striving on the part of the older generations to lose their ethnic identity. The normative confusion precipitated by such a state of affairs provides yet another area for analysis of the role structures of families caught up in such a struggle.

UNWILLINGNESS TO PLAY ROLES

The title selected for this section may be open to some debate. My intention is to cite briefly certain phenomena which involve in one way or another a particular kind of deficit in structure. These particular matters, however, appear to differ from the ones already discussed because there is a quality of volition on the part of the positional occupants in vacating one or more roles of the position or the entire position. There is another quality to the subject matter of this section. Each of the attributes has attracted little attention of a systematic nature from contemporary family theorists and researchers. Consequently, I shall attempt little more than to introduce them and to indicate some of the characteristics which appear to make them of interest from a developmental analytical perspective. One reason for this lack of attention is that the behavior involved represents an area which is difficult to research. Either it is of such a deviant kind, it is carried on under such covert circumstances, or it represents such trauma that gaining data by the methods usually employed by behavioral scientists is difficult.

Marital partners may be separated either through mutual agreement or through the unilateral decision of one partner. The former is usually labeled separation and the latter desertion. In either case, regardless of whether the ultimate recourse is formal divorce, a period occurs in which one partner has abandoned his position in the family. In contrast to divorce, however, the formal legal bond between the marital partners and the potentiality for reconciliation still exist. This factor contributes to a particular kind of anomie with respect to the roles of the family. Such people are neither married nor unmarried from a normative point of view. As Kephart (1966) has noted, the deserted wife can neither orient herself toward the potentialities of continuing in a single state nor toward the possibilities of entering a new marital situation, since a common phenomenon of desertion is the recurrent return of the deserting husband. The effects of such a situation probably vary according to the point in the career of the family at which it occurs. The results may be less profound during periods in which only the couple constitute the family at the beginning or in the latter part of the career. During that period when the child positions of the system are occupied, there are other implications. The role prescriptions for parent-child role complexes are considerably more clearly defined in the divorce situation. Separation, as compared to desertion, may be less anomic in its effects, since such a situation involves some kind of interaction between the partners over the decision to separate during which certain redefinitions of roles may take place. Separated persons, of course, still must cope with societal-institutional norms which tend to have the effect of pressuring them either toward reconciliation or toward divorce. In sum, then, desertion and separation have a special character not found in deficit of structure situations arising from divorce.

Vacating a child position as a result of the occupant running away from home is still another situation in which some volition on the part of the positional occupant is involved. Statistics on the extent of the runaway phenomenon are not easily obtainable; however, the hippie phenomenon of the late sixties brought to light that a large proportion of the residents of such areas as the Haight-Ashbury district of San Francisco were legally minor children who were runaways. Again, little data exist on the effect of such a situation on the family. Only two modern studies of runaways are listed by Aldous and Hill (Hildebrand, 1963; Robey et al., 1964). There are some parallels between runaways and deserters, since in both cases the possibility of returning is always present. As compared with the process of launching a maturing child into his own family of procreation or into an independent status in the society, running away carries with it few normative prescriptions. Parents, of course, are expected to attempt to find and to persuade the child to return to the home. The child, in turn, is expected to acquiesce to such persuasion. Indeed, a somewhat romantic view has the child longing for the parents to seek reconciliation and the child eagerly responding to such parental attempts. The extent to which role behavior follows these normative prescriptions, however, is unclear. Significantly, few clear normative prescriptions prevail for the ongoing behavior of the family in the face of such voluntary absenteeism. A developmental analysis of this situation will involve an investigation of the history of the parent-child and sibling-sibling role complexes prior to the vacating of the position as one way of explaining the kind of behavior followed during the absence. Such an approach will not only serve to provide some explanations of the reasons behind the decision to run away but also some reasons for the intrafamilial behavior of the remaining members and toward the runaway after the event.

Another type of unwillingness to play roles is represented by infidelity on the part of one or both partners. Such a pattern is, of course, institutionalized in some societies, most typically for the male partner. Spanish, Latin-American, French, Italian, and Japanese cultures come readily to mind in this context. In such situations, however, a distinction still is made between the husband who continues to meet his familial role obligations and one who does not. In the latter case, the situation may be similar to the general normative posture of American culture toward unfaithfulness, though probably lacking some of the moral implications deriving from the Protestant Pietistic and Puritan heritage.

Again, we have little data on the impact of such behavior on the family. Understandably, such behavior is carried on covertly and neither the party involved nor the uninvolved party is easily identified. Even if both were identifiable, their willingness to cooperate in research on the topic may be limited. One study has been published reporting interviews with over four hundred upper-middle-class men and women, most of whom were married (Cuber and Harroff, 1965). The report is chiefly anecdotal with extended case descriptions and with quotations used to illustrate five types of marriages which the authors developed. Although we are told that "probably a majority" have "ignored the monogamous prescriptions about sex (especially premaritally)," (Cuber and Harroff, 1965:193) at no time do the authors provide any quantitative data on the extent of infidelity. This lack is particularly puzzling and, frankly, frustrating to the reader, since such data obviously were available to the investigators and the overall impression given by them is that it was a very common element.

For the developmental investigator, there may be some profit in this study in suggesting areas in which familial roles are affected by or lead to infidelity; however, the work will provide little more. If Cuber and Harroff's experience can be generalized, research in this area may not be as difficult as we have assumed. The investigators report (Cuber and Harroff, 1965:9): "We had anticipated that many of the people we intended to approach would be unwilling to discuss the subject of men and women with candor and originality. We could not have been more wrong. There were only two refusals; the rest talked freely and at great length." It is possible, of course, that the investigators practiced some selectivity in making their approaches, so that an examination which attempted research on a more representative and on a more random basis would meet with greater difficulty. In any case, the fact of infidelity cannot be denied, nor can the probably profound effect on role relationships which infidelity may bring about. Since it has been suggested earlier that the sexual relationship in marriage may be an important indicator of the more general maintenance of meaning in marriage, it may be anticipated that some significant explanations of the general role behavior of family members, particularly of husbands and wives, will result from a more systematic investigation of infidelity. In this respect, the Cuber and Harroff study is supportive of such a general proposition.

Finally, suicide may be viewed as a special case of vacating a position through death. Much study of suicide is demographic in approach. Since Durkheim's (1951) classic study in 1897, however, some students have attempted, even when utilizing demographic data, to derive explanations based on the role characteristics of persons who take their own lives (Gibbs and Martin, 1964). The fact that single persons and those who have been divorced or have been widowed are more likely to commit suicide seems to support the proposition that the role relationships of families have an important bearing on the event. Again, however, the primary interest is not in explaining the cause of suicide, but in exploring the consequences of suicide for the family. From this perspective, it appears that the knowledge that an actor had vacated his position in the family by choosing death will effect significantly the role adjustments of the family. Until we have more data, such speculations cannot be carried very far.

SUMMARY

In this chapter, I have cited a variety of situations in which the essential characteristic involved various types of atypicality in role complexes as well as in positional and familial careers. Some of these areas are clear-cut, well researched, and only need to have the researcher-theorist consciously design studies which will test propositions derived from a developmental perspective. Others are areas in which little investigation and theorizing has been done from any perspective. Some are extremely difficult fields for gathering data, others seem only to want for researchers to direct their attention to an easily available body of information. Some involve a relatively small proportion of the total population, whereas others appear applicable to a substantial minority, if not to a majority, of the population. In spite of these variable qualities, my view is that all the areas are worthy of investigation and are particularly appropriate for application of the developmental perspective.

REFERENCES

Aldous, Joan, and Reuben Hill
1967 *International Bibliography of Research in Marriage and the Family, 1900–1964.* Minneapolis: University of Minnesota Press.

Bailey, M. B.
1961 "Alcoholism and marriage: a review of research and professional literature." *Quarterly Journal of Studies of Alcohol* 22 (March): 81–97.

Belcher, John C.
1967 "The one-person household: a consequence of the isolated nuclear family?" *Journal of Marriage and the Family* 29 (August): 534–40.

Berardo, Felix M.
1968 "Widowhood status in the United States: perspective on a neglected aspect of the family life-cycle." *The Family Coordinator* 17 (July): 191–203.

———
1970 "Survivorship and social isolation: the case of the aged widower." *The Family Coordinator* 19 (January): 11–25.

Bernard, Jessie
1956 *Remarriage: A Study of Marriage.* New York: Dryden Press.

Bossard, James H., and Eleanor S. Bell
1947 "The role of the guest: a study in child development." *American Sociological Review* 12 (April): 192–201.

Bowerman, C. E.
1956 "Family background and parental adjustment of step children." *Studies of State College of Washington* 24 (1956): 181–82.

———, and Donald P. Irish
1962 "Some relationships of stepchildren to their parents." *Marriage and Family Living* 24 (May): 113–21.

Crain, Alan J., et al.
1966 "Effects of a diabetic child on marital integration and related measures of family functioning." *Journal of Health and Human Behavior* 7 (Summer): 122–27.

Cuber, John F., and Peggy B. Harroff
1965 *The Significant Americans.* New York: Appleton-Century-Crofts.

Davis, Fred
1963 *Passage Through Crisis: Polio Victims and Their Families.* Indianapolis: The Bobbs-Merrill Company, Inc.

DAY, B. R.
 1961   "Alcoholism and the family." *Marriage and Family Living* 23
        (August): 253–58.
DURKHEIM, EMILE
 1951   *Suicide.* Glencoe, Ill.: The Free Press. Originally published in
        1897.
FARBER, BERNARD
 1959   "Effects of a severely mentally retarded child on family integra-
        tion." *Monographs of the Society for Research in Child Develop-
        ment* 24 (1959).

———
 1960   "Family organization and crisis: maintenance of integration in
        families with a severely mentally retarded child." *Monographs of
        the Society for Research in Child Development* 25 (1960).
———, ET AL.
 1960   "Family crisis and the decision to institutionalize the retarded
        child." *Council of Exceptional Children Research Monograph
        Series.* Washington, D.C.: National Education Association, Ser.
        A, No. 1.
———, AND W. C. JENNE
 1963   "Family organization and parent child communication: parents
        and siblings of a retarded child." *Monographs of the Society for
        Research in Child Development* 28 (1963): 3–78.
FINK, STEPHEN L., ET AL.
 1968   "Physical disability and problems in marriage." *Journal of Marriage
        and the Family* 30 (February): 64–73.
FREEMAN, HOWARD E., AND OZZIE G. SIMMONS
 1963   *The Mental Patient Comes Home.* New York: John Wiley & Sons,
        Inc.
GIBBS, JACK P., AND WALTER T. MARTIN
 1964   *Status Integration and Suicide.* Eugene: University of Oregon
        Press.
GIBSON, GEOFFREY, AND EDWARD G. LUDWIG
 1968   "Family structure in a disabled population." *Journal of Marriage
        and the Family* 30 (February): 54–63.
GOODE, WILLIAM J.
 1956   *After Divorce.* Glencoe, Illinois: The Free Press.
HANDEL, GERALD, ED.
 1967   *The Psychosocial Interior of the Family.* Chicago: Aldine Publish-
        ing Company.
HILDEBRAND, J. A.
 1963   "Why runaways leave home." *Journal of Criminal Law, Crimi-
        nology, and Police Science* 54 (1963): 211–16.

HILL, REUBEN
1949   *Families Under Stress.* New York: Harper and Brothers.

1958   "Generic features of families under stress." *Social Casework* 39 (February–March): 139–50.

HIRSCH, R.
1961   "Group therapy with parents of adolescent drug addicts." *Psychistric Quarterly* 35 (October): 702–10.

JACKSON, JOAN K.
1954   "The adjustment of the family to the crisis of alcoholism." *Quarterly Journal of Studies on Alcohol* 15 (December): 562–86.

1956   "Adjustment of the family to alcoholism." *Marriage and Family Living* 18 (November): 361–69.

1958   "Alcoholism and the family." *Annals of the American Academy of Political and Social Science* 315 (January): 90–98.

KEPHART, WILLIAM
1966   *The Family, Society, and the Individual,* 2nd ed. Boston: Houghton Mifflin Company.

————, AND THOMAS P. MONAHAN
1952   "Desertion and divorce in Philadelphia." *American Sociological Review* 17 (December): 719–27.

KOSA, JOHN, ET AL.
1960   "Sharing the home with relatives." *Marriage and Family Living* 22 (May): 129–31.

LITMAN, THEODOR J.
1962   "Self-conception and physical rehabilitation." Pp. 550–74 in Arnold Rose (ed.), *Human Behavior and Social Processes.* Boston: Houghton Mifflin Company.

1964   "An analysis of the sociological factors affecting the rehabilitation of physically handicapped patients." *Archives of Physical Medicine* 45 (1964): 9–16.

MONAHAN, THOMAS P.
1956   "The number of children in American families and the sharing of households." *Marriage and Family Living* 18 (August): 201–3.

MORRIS, PAULINE
1965   *Prisoners and Their Families.* London: Allen and Unwin, Ltd.

NEUGARTEN, BERNICE L., AND K. K. WEINSTEIN
1964   "The changing American grandparent." *Journal of Marriage and the Family* 26 (May): 199–204.

PODOLSKY, E.
1955   "Emotional problems of the step child." *Mental Hygiene* 29 (1955): 49–53.

ROBEY, A., ET AL.
1964   "The runaway girl: a reaction to family stress." *American Journal of Orthopsychiatry* 34 (1964): 762–67.

ROGLER, LLOYD H., AND AUGUST B. HOLLINGSHEAD
1965   *Trapped: Families and Schizophrenia.* New York: John Wiley & Sons, Inc.

SCHLESINGER, BENJAMIN
1966   "The one-parent family: recent literature." *Journal of Marriage and the Family* 28 (February): 103–9.

SIMON, ANNE W.
1964   *Stepchild in the Family: A View in Remarriage.* New York: The Odyssey Press.

SMITH, WILLIAM C.
1953   *The Stepchild.* Chicago: University of Chicago Press.

1957   "Remarriage and the stepchild." Pp. 457–75 in Morris Fishbein and R. J. Kennedy (eds.), *Modern Marriage and Family Living.* New York: Oxford University Press.

STEHOUWER, JAN
1965   "Relations between generations and the three-generation household in Demark." Pp. 142–62 in Ethel Shanas and Gordon F. Streib (eds.), *Social Structure and the Family: Generational Relations.* Englewood Cliffs, N.J.: Prentice-Hall, Inc.

THOMAS, W. I., AND FLORIAN ZNANIECKI
1958   *The Polish Peasant in Europe and America.* New York: Dover Publications, Inc.

VOGEL, EZRA F., AND NORMAN W. BELL
1968   "The emotionally disturbed child as the family scapegoat." Pp. 412–27 in Norman W. Bell and Ezra F. Vogel (eds.), *A Modern Introduction to the Family,* rev. ed. New York: The Free Press.

WOLH, R. L. AND M. H. DRISKIND
1961   "Personality dynamics of mothers and wives of drug addicts." *Crime and Delinquency* 7 (April): 148–52.

YAMAZAKI, M., AND Y. IMADA
1959   "A study of the step parent, step child relation." *Seishin Eisei Kenkyu* 7 (1959): 155–98.

Role Complex and
Family Career Stresses

The old saying "True love never runs smooth" may be appropriately extended to "True family life never runs smooth." The career of every family, whether the household is typical or atypical in structure or in characteristics of its actors, inevitably faces periods in which it must deal with stresses of one variety or another. Because the family is located in a larger community and society, it is subjected to the effects of the varying levels of organization-disorganization of these social systems. There are, in addition, certain inherent types of stresses which arise out of the very nature of the family career itself. This chapter directs attention to the developmental analysis of such stresses on family careers.

Studies of families in stressful situations were, as Hansen and Hill (1964:786) note, one of the earliest concerns of sociologists. Studies by Angell (1936), by Cavan and Ranck (1938), by Komarovsky (1940), by Koos (1946), and by Hill (1949) remain classics arising from the economic depression of the thirties and from World War Two. Indeed, they stand alone even today as the major monographs dealing with family stress. Perhaps the only more modern work which approaches them are the studies of anthropologist Oscar Lewis (1959, 1961, 1965) dealing with Mexican families and of Rainwater (1959, 1960, 1965) dealing with the modern poor.

Out of this early work, there developed in the fifties an attempt to create a systematic theoretical approach to the study of family and stress. The chief architect of this approach was Reuben Hill (1958), later joined by his colleague Donald A. Hansen (Hill and Hansen, 1962; Hansen, 1965). Their fullest statement of the viewpoint remains their joint effort in the *Handbook of Marriage and the Family* (Hansen and Hill, 1964). I shall not attempt to detail all its aspects here, since anyone interested in this area should refer to the original work. For our purposes, the important factor is that the theoretical approach attempts to deal with the family in terms of its organizational character before the group encounters a stressful event; then the approach follows through the adjustments in the system by taking account of both the internal and the external resources on which the family draws as it moves through disorganization and reorganization (or possibly to dissolution); and, finally, the perspective includes the level of organization which it may attain after the event. Thus, interactional and transactional factors are clearly recognized, as well as the importance of the previous career of the family in an explanation of the family's response to stress.

If we recognize the central role which Hill has played in the history of the developmental theoretical approach, this orientation to family stress should come as no great surprise. Calling on the central theoretical perspectives of symbolic interactionism and of social system—structure-functionalism, the conceptual approach to family stress is essentially a special case of general developmental theory. I have dealt with material identified by Hill and Hansen as "stressor events" in two separate chapters because I have treated them according to whether they were applicable to all families or only to families with atypical characteristics. The essential point remains that in accounting for a family's reaction to stressful events, the developmental theoretical perspective takes into account the previous career of the family and its anticipations for its future course, as well as the characteristics of its career at the time the stressor event is encountered.

The basic conceptualization of the family as a *semiclosed* system allows for events occurring in the larger society to have effects on the family system. This perspective includes a variety of phenomena, their source being external to the family system but imposing stress on the career of the family. Such factors as ones arising from nature (broadly conceived), as well as ones originating in the social and cultural environment are pertinent here (Martin, 1965). Turning from the external sources, we can see that there are two types of internal matters which may provide for stressful events. The first kind arises from the very nature of the family career itself. Central to the conceptualization is the view that the key transitional points in the family career represent significant points restructuring the system. Such restructuring may also be a source of critical stress for this system. The second kind springs from certain periods of the family career which find the family less adequately staffed to meet the daily demands of life than at other stages.

Hill (1965) once characterized the nuclear family as a "puny group" by which he meant to point out the basic weakness in its personnel composition. First, inherent in the age and sex structure of the family and in its changes over its career are the seeds of stress. Second, the nature of the family as a set of mutually contingent careers directs attention to the factor that each position carries within it certain potentialities for stress. Third, not only do certain transitions of the total system provide such opportunities, but also the transitions of each separate positional career may so dominate the family as to provide critical periods. These latter characteristics have been especially identified by the Rapoports (1963, 1964, 1965) and by Rossi (1968), as we saw previously.

These three sources of stress should have a ring of familiarity about them. They follow, quite obviously, the outline of the three major facets of analysis of family careers, societal-institutional, group-interactional, and individual-psychological. Therefore, this familiar outline will be followed as the interactional and transactional implications of stress for the family career are examined somewhat more in detail.

SOCIETAL-INSTITUTIONAL SOURCES

Natural Disasters

Natural disasters tend to be no respecters of persons. It is true, however, that certain types of natural disasters may affect some groups more than others. Thus, flooding often has a greater impact on the lower classes primarily because they are more likely to live in the older areas of a community which, when situated on a river, tend to be in or near the low-lying areas closest to the river. Likewise, fires are more likely in older buildings with inadequate wiring or heating systems, thus making lower-income people more vulnerable. However, tornadoes, hurricanes, blizzards, and other weather phenomena are less selective, although again they may do more damage to older or to less adequately constructed buildings of a community in which the poor dwell.

Hill and Hansen note in their various writings that a key issue in meeting stressful situations is associated with the definition which the family makes of the stressful event. It may well be that the relative material loss of lower-income families is higher as compared with middle- and upper-income families. This result may be offset, however, by another factor cited by Hill and Hansen: the organizational and material resources to which the family may have access. It is conceivable that low-income families, accustomed to living on "the edge of crisis" on a day-to-day basis, may both define the situation as less of a disaster and may also be more organizationally prepared to deal with it in spite of having less adequate material resources at their disposal. For example, Drabek and Boggs (1968) found that families affected by the 1965 flash flood in Denver were more likely to evacuate to the homes of extended kin if they were of lower socioeconomic status. It may be that lower-class families in general have more ready access to the organizational support of extended kin in crisis situations, since a partial explanation of the greater use in Denver was that a greater proportion of middle- and upper-income families had no relatives living in the area. The view seems reasonable since, in general, lower-income families are probably less geographically mobile (Slater, 1967). Thus, the ultimate impact of a natural disaster, although being explained at one level by socioeconomic status, is more adequately explained by examining the dynamics of interaction and of transaction of which socioeconomic status is one partially valid measure.

Economic and Political Events

Much of the basic material on family stress arose out of studies dealing with family life during the economic depression of the thirties. Cavan (1959) has summarized some of the findings of those works with respect to the impact of unemployment on various types of families. She notes that both the very lowest socioeconomic class, characterized by regular repetitive unemployment, and the upper-middle class, characterized by relatively stable employment even during the depression and possessing additional resources for surviving the crisis, were far less affected than were the upper-lower and the lower-middle classes, which had little experience with unemployment but also less in the way of emergency resources when unemployment occurred. Thus, the proposition above that the differential impact felt in natural disasters is related to the previous experience of the family as well as to its organizational and material resources is supported further. The interrelation of transactional and interactional circumstances is well illustrated by the finding that a particularly major impact on the husband's role within the family system resulted from his loss of employment in the upper-lower and in the lower-middle class. Not only did his personal status tend to fall in the eyes of the other family members, but his own self-evaluation seemed to suffer, especially if the economic contributions of other family members to the family tended to be greater than those he was able to make. In addition, he tended to be unable to work out other internal family roles for his position and, thus, found himself in an anomic situation both within the family and in the community. These findings parallel some of the ones reported by Nye and Hoffman (1963) on the impact of wife-mother employment on families in which the husband is employed.

Few data have been reported on the opposite experience of sudden achievement of wealth. The popular press from time to time publishes reports of the difficulties which individuals, and presumably their families, have experienced as the result of receiving a large unanticipated bequest or winning a large sum of money in a contest, from a sweepstakes, or some other form of gambling. The folk tale ending that they lived happily ever after does not seem always to be the outcome. The explanation, developmentally, would be sought in the way previous role organization in the family either aided or hindered the structuring of new roles under the condition of sudden affluence.

Major political changes also may have a striking impact on the family career. Revolutions which displace certain classes of people from political power and which install others in their place are an obvious example; however, other kinds of political change may be no less dramatic in their consequences. Thus, the changes in the status of black Americans arising from the series of judicial, administrative, and legislative actions of the fifties and sixties had a widespread and not totally positive effect. A key factor cited by many analysts for much of the upheaval of this period lay in the differential experienced by blacks between rising expectations of social and economic equality and the lag in realization of such equality. Some of the consequences of this period for black families have been analyzed by Billingsley (1968) and some of the individual-psychological consequences have been reported most dramatically by Grier and Cobbs (1968).

Another example of stress arising out of political change may be seen in the experience of groups who are suddenly thrust into a politically disfavored position. The cases of the Jews in German-controlled areas during the Hitler era or of Japanese-Americans who were "relocated" during World War Two come immediately to mind. The literal stripping of property and other rights of legal American citizens which occurred as a result of what can only be termed the hysteria of the time had a long-term profound influence on Japanese-American families. Though it fell short of the genocide practiced by the Nazi regime, there were many parallels in the two experiences. Evidence exists that the strong family structure of both groups was a central factor in their ability to withstand total demoralization and destruction.

Technological Change

Some years ago, Ogburn and Nimkoff (1955) presented an institutional-historical anlaysis of the effect of technology on the family. No similar developmental analysis has appeared. Aside from the obvious impact of loss of employment particularly in the unskilled occupations, which may result from various technological innovations in production and in distribution of goods, there is the increasing recognition that technological change is having a pervasive effect on work at all levels. The necessity for persons in skilled, in semiprofessional, and in professional-managerial occupations to learn new skills or to take up whole new career lines is an increasing fact of modern life. Such necessity for change, unanticipated in the normal career projections, may represent major stresses for the family as it attempts to adjust to the adult male's efforts to reorient himself in his major transactional role.

Other factors related to technology include increased nonwork time for many employees through shorter work weeks, a host of changes in the kind of consumer goods available for domestic use which tend to change the standards of excellence in the homemaker role (detergents which wash clothes "whiter than white," floor waxes and mechanical polishers which make floors shine brilliantly, etc.), and a great increase in consumer goods developed especially to fill all the time supposedly released by the increased mechanization in both the work and domestic realms. Indeed, a casual look at the current Sears, Roebuck mail order catalog will quickly reveal how nonwork oriented the society has become. Even the tools available tend to be oriented toward nonwork time activity, rather than toward use in earning a livelihood.

Analyses of these kinds of effects of technology on the family career remain essentially nonexistent, though as noted in the chapter on transactional roles, increasing attention is being directed to this topic. Whether these effects merit the label "stress" is probably still an open question. It may be that the changes thus far have been slow enough that adjustment to them has been accomplished without major difficulty. On the other hand, should the present trend continue, a major crisis may occur over the basic definitions of roles while the value of work as a central meaning in life diminishes (Litwak and Figueira, 1970). Indeed, such a possibility has the potentiality for a complete restructuring of the family career as we know it today.

GROUP-INTERACTIONAL SOURCES

At various points previously, the different types of change have been discussed which take place in the family as a result of adding or of losing actors, as a result of the changing roles of members as they mature, and the like. Thus, the critical structural transitions—which have traditionally characterized the stages of the family life cycle—become potential points of stress for the family system. Marriage, the birth of a child, the entry of a child in school, the adolescent transition, the placing of members into the larger society or into their own families of procreation, the postparental experience, retirement, and widowhood all represent such periods. These matters are not simply ones for the individual actor to cope with, since the basic theoretical approach emphasizes the reciprocal nature of these experiences. Developmentally it may be anticipated that, as in the case of the other types of crisis and stress, the way the family had organized itself previously and the degree to which it had anticipated these transitions would form a major element in the explanation of the quality of the family's coping with them. The experience of the postparental wife-mother actor in being "lost without her children" or of the retired husband-father being similarly "lost without his work" represents some kind of failure to anticipate and to prepare for the necessity to take on new roles or to enlarge the scope of already existing ones on the part of the family as a whole. Such transitions are not necessarily stress producing, of course. Indeed, they may have the effect of resolving a continuing problem of disorganization for the family system through the process of removing an actor or of restructuring the roles in some more compatible manner.

Particular periods of the family career, because of the structural makeup, because of the positions occupied, and the like, may be potentially more vulnerable to stress than others. The family with three preschool children may exemplify such a period. The typical childhood illnesses; the demands on the physical and emotional energy of the wife-mother which children at this age require; the probability that the husband-father is in the early part of his occupational career with relatively minimal income and without having had the opportunity to accumulate savings or other material resources to cope with unusual financial stress; the high financial demands associated with housing, feeding, and clothing a growing family, which almost inevitably leads to deficit financing; the reduced time and money available for the husband and the wife to invest in their own relationship—such a picture provides all the ingredients of incipient crisis. In contrast, the postparental period appears as a time of relative calm, with the possibility of some financial and occupational stability, even the opportunity to liquidate the debts associated with the costs of childrearing and to accumulate some assets in preparation for retirement, and the chance to reestablish the husband-wife relationship as a basic foundation for the final years of the family career. The extent to which either period realizes its potentialities for stress or calm, of course, depends heavily on how the roles are defined and whether the role behavior conforms to these definitions. The tables reproduced here (see Tables 9.1–9.3), which were developed by Aldous and Hill (1969) from several pieces of research, illustrate various kinds of vulnerability in the family career. For example, Table 9.1 shows that the adolescent, launching, and aging periods of the family career are the most vulnerable to lack of expressive resources in the family. On the other hand, vulnerability is highest in the child-bearing, school-age, and

TABLE 9.1 · *The Family's Vulnerability to Stress Owing to Deficits in Expressive Resources* [a]

	FAMILY STAGE						
Deficit	Establish-ment	Child-bearing	School-age Children	Adoles-cents	Launch-ing	Post-parental	Aging
Incidence of divorce and separation [b]	5	3	2	2	1	1	1
Degree of marital dissatisfaction [c]	1	1	2	3	5	4	5
Dissatisfaction with love [d]	1	1	2	3	5	3	4
Dissatisfaction with companionship [e]	1	2	3	4	5	3	4
Lack of marital communication [f]	1	2	5	4	3	2	2
Segregation of marital roles [g]	1	2	2	3	5	4	5
Husband's alienation from home tasks [h]	1	2	5	5	5	3	3
Wife's failure to share problems with husband [i]	1	3	4	5	5	4	5
Total vulnerability score	12	16	25	29	34	22	29
Duration of marriage (in years)	0–1	2–7	8–14	15–21	22–29	30–43	44–50
Husband's age	22	24–30	31–37	38–44	45–52	53–65	66–72

Reprinted with permission of the National Association of Social Workers, from Joan Aldous and Reuben Hill, "Breaking the poverty cycle: strategic points for intervention," *Social Work*, 14 (July, 1969), Table 1, p. 7.

[a] The scores range from least vulnerable (1) to most vulnerable (5).

[b] Thomas P. Monahan, "When Couples Part," *American Sociological Review*, 27 (October, 1962), Table 1, p. 630.

[c] Robert O. Blood, Jr., and Donald M. Wolfe, *Husbands and Wives: The Dynamics of Married Living* (Glencoe, Ill.: Free Press, 1960), p. 265.

[d] *Ibid.*, p. 232.

[e] *Ibid.*, p. 156.

[f] Harold Feldman, *Development of the Husband-Wife Relationship* (Ithaca, N.Y.: Department of Child Development and Family Relationships, Cornell University, 1964), p. 126. (Mimeographed.)

[g] *Ibid.*, p. 70.

[h] *Ibid.*, p. 71.

[i] *Ibid.*, p. 188.

adolescent phases of the career if one analyzes the availability of instrumental resources, according to Table 9.2. Finally, Table 9.3 shows that dissatisfaction with instrumental resources increases the vulnerability of families in every parental period of the career. The developmental analyst, then, finds great interest in comparisons of families experiencing the same general period of the family career as a way of explaining the degree to

TABLE 9.2 · *The Family's Vulnerability to Stress Owing to the Insufficiency of Instrumental Resources* [a]

Deficit	FAMILY STAGE						
	Establish-ment	Child-bearing	School-age Children	Adoles-cents	Launch-ing	Post-parental	Aging
Income per member [b]	5	4	4	3	3	1	5
Size of family [c]	1	4	5	5	3	1	1
Adequacy of housing [d]	4	5	4	3	3	2	2
Medical expenses [e]	1	4	5	3	2	2	5
Family debts [f]	2	5	5	4	3	1	1
Job changes [g]	5	5	3	3	2	2	1
Wife in labor force supplementing income [h]	1	5	4	3	2	3	5
Total vulnerability score	19	32	30	24	18	12	20
Duration of marriage (in years)	0–1	2–7	8–14	15–21	22–29	30–43	44–50
Husband's age	22	24–30	31–37	38–44	45–52	53–65	66–72

Reprinted with permission of the National Association of Social Workers, from Aldous and Hill, "Breaking the poverty cycle," *Social Work*, 14 (July, 1969), Table 2, p. 8.

[a] The scores range from least vulnerable (1) to most vulnerable (5).

[b] Paul C. Glick and Robert Parke, Jr., "New Approaches in Studying the Life Cycle of the Family," *Demography* (1965), pp. 187–202.

[c] Reuben Hill and Nelson Foote, *Household Inventory Changes Among Three Generations of Minneapolis Families* (New York: General Electric Co., 1962), Chart 2.

[d] Nelson Foote et al., *Housing Choices and Housing Constraints* (New York: McGraw-Hill Book Co., 1960), Table 19, p. 99.

[e] John B. Lansing and James N. Morgan, "Consumer Finances Over the Life Cycle," in Lincoln Clark, ed., *The Life Cycle and Consumer Behavior* (New York: New York University Press, 1955), p. 49.

[f] *Ibid.*, p. 44.

[g] Hill and Foote, *op. cit.*, Chart 4.

[h] Robert O. Blood, Jr., and Donald M. Wolfe, *Husbands and Wives: The Dynamics of Married Living* (Glencoe, Ill.: Free Press, 1960), p. 98.

which the potentiality for stress is or is not averted. Such analyses have significant applied implications for persons in the helping professions as well as strictly theoretical interest for behavioral scientists.

INDIVIDUAL-PSYCHOLOGICAL SOURCES

Paralleling the recognition that certain periods of the familial career are more vulnerable to stress than others is the realization that certain periods in the individual career, both with respect to the characteristics of each unique actor and in terms of the unique position which he occupies in the

TABLE 9.3 · The Family's Vulnerability to Stress Owing to Dissatisfaction with Instrumental
Resources [a]

| | FAMILY STAGE | | | | | | |
Deficit	Establish-ment	Child-bearing	School-age Children	Adoles-cents	Launch-ing	Post-parental	Aging
Satisfaction with level of living [b]	1	3	4	4	3	5	2
Satisfaction with job [c]	1	3	5	5	3	1	1
Disagreements over money [d]	1	5	4	4	4	4	3
Worries about financial cost of children [e]	1	3	5	2	4	2	1
Total vulnerability score	4	14	18	15	14	12	7
Duration of marriage (in years)	0–1	2–7	8–14	15–21	22–29	30–43	44–50
Husband's age	22	24–30	31–37	38–44	45–52	53–65	66–72

Reprinted with permission of the National Association of Social Workers, from Aldous and
Hill, "Breaking the poverty cycle," Social Work, 14 (July, 1969), Table 3, p. 8.

[a] The scores range from least vulnerable (1) to most vulnerable (5).

[b] Robert O. Blood, Jr., and Donald M. Wolfe, Husbands and Wives: The Dynamics of Married
Living (Glencoe, Ill.: Free Press, 1960), p. 112.

[c] Harold L. Wilensky, "Life Cycle, Work Situation and Participation in Formal Associations," in
Robert W. Kleemeier, ed., Aging and Leisure (New York: Oxford University Press, 1961), pp.
228–229.

[d] Blood and Wolfe, op. cit., p. 247.

[e] Ibid., p. 143.

family system, are also more vulnerable to stress than others. During
these periods, the individual may demand an inordinate amount of the
attention of the other family members. It is not totally unjustified to
identify infant human beings as tyrants in the family. The demands which
they make on the family for attention to their needs and the fact that they
have not yet developed any awareness of or sensitivity to the needs of other
members does amount to a kind of tyranny. Other periods in the physical,
psychological, and/or social maturation of a family member may have
similar characteristics.

Stress as a result of the individual careers of family members is most
likely to develop when other family members are unwilling or are unable
to respond in their role behavior to the role expectations of the focal member. Another type of potential stress arises when two or more actors are
experiencing periods in their careers which place competing demands on
the other actors in the family. Still a third type of potential stress comes
about when the normative structure of the family or of the society begins
to place demands on the career of a given position to which the actor in

that position is unwilling or is unable to respond. These possibilities apply quite as much to the adult positions as to the child positions. There has been so much emphasis on the behavioral problems of children over the past forty years or more, that it frequently goes unrecognized that adult family careers may also be precipitators of family stress. Such behaviors are so frequently cloaked with the more sophisticated adult ability to legitimize their actions that they are often more difficult to identify as analogous to children's career developmental stress.

From a transactional perspective, individual career stress may arise as a consequence of some particular difficulty in a role being played by a family member as an occupant of a position in some extrafamilial system. We are quite familiar with the school problems of children or of their peer group difficulties. Similarly, there are the stresses which affect the family career resulting from the occupational career of the adult male or the adult female of the family. Difficulties in working out relationships in the extended family may have their effect on the nuclear family career. Such a strain may focus either on the positional career of a single actor, or it may be more general in nature and, thus, be more properly classified under the group-interactional sources of stress. If, for example, the husband-father is the sole remaining child from his family of orientation, he may experience unusual stress in his transactional roles with his family of orientation, particularly as he faces the expectations placed on him by aging and progressively less physically and economically able parents.

Rosenstock and Kutner (1967) have presented an interesting analysis of the appropriateness of the concept of alienation in dealing with family stress. Their treatment fits well with this particular area covering the developmental analysis of individual-psychological career sources of stress. By drawing together material on the concepts of alienation, of cognitive dissonance, of anomie, of role complementarity, and of family crisis, Rosenstock and Kutner develop an analytical paradigm identifying a number of alternative paths which may be followed in the family career for the resolution of stress resulting from individual-psychological sources. In effect, their model represents an extension of the pattern suggested by Hill and Hansen. Thus, in addition to the paths which lead from disorganization following crisis to either dissolution or to reorganization, Rosenstock and Kutner posit a path which leads to alienation of the individual actor. From this point, alternative paths lead to retreatism and then to dissolution or the possibility of a new form of role complementarity. Alternatively, alienation may lead to ultraconformity, ritualism, adjustment, innovation, or rebellion and thence to a new kind of role complementarity. Each option, of course, represents a somewhat different response to the redefinition of role expectations by the other actors in the system and by the focal actor with respect to the goals and the means for achieving these goals within that system. Although this model ultimately focuses on the individual career, it is equally applicable to stress situations which arise at the group-interactional and societal-institutional levels. The explanatory strength of the Rosenstock and Kutner analysis lies in its ability to deal with the individual positional career when a stress situation results in the major effect being placed on one particular position. The Hill-Hansen model tends to be more effective in explaining the family dynamics in response to stress at the family system level. Thus, this extension of that model represents an important contribution to developmental theory where the concern is to be able to derive explanations at all three facet levels.

SUMMARY

This chapter has dealt with the discussion of family stress which results not from some atypicality in individual actors or in familial structure but from the more general sources of the society, of the family system, or of the individual. In concluding the general treatment of family response to stress and crisis, I think that some basic, significant points from a developmental point of view merit emphasis.

First, it is quite probable that a family may experience stress or crisis arising from more than one source at the same time. The profession of social welfare and social work is thoroughly familiar with multiproblem families. It may be that the degree of difficulty encountered by a family is closely related to either the severity of a single stress or the compounding severity of a number of stresses found in close proximity. To illustrate the point, unemployment usually results in reduction or in loss of income, which in turn leads to less adequate nutrition, which may produce an increased susceptibility to illness, although the family has less adequate financial resources for proper treatment. There are other compounding elements which may be added without departing from the realm of credibility. The fatigue which arises from care of the sick, the anxiety over their welfare, the worry over lack of income, the loss of self-respect resulting from unemployment—these and other factors provide a fertile soil for major family crisis.

Second, families subject to crisis as a consequence of some atypical characteristic are not thereby immune from the more general sources of crisis. Again, the degree to which they have been able to restructure their roles to meet the basic stress may be a major factor in their meeting other types of stress.

Finally, these two chapters have attempted to demonstrate the ability of developmental theory to deal with something other than the norm—

statistically and culturally. Explanations of deviating, as well as of conforming, familial behavior are fully realizable within the theory. In order to completely demonstrate this point, however, there is one more area for attention. Thus far, the analysis has dealt chiefly with family systems which follow closely the American nuclear family ideal with all that the model represents in terms of structure, of values, and of behavior patterns. The potentiality for application of the developmental theory to family systems which do not fit this particular model, either because they represent a substantial subcultural pattern within the American system or because they form a distinctly non-American or non-Western pattern, is explored in the next chapter.

REFERENCES

ALDOUS, JOAN, AND REUBEN HILL
  1969 "Breaking the poverty cycle: strategic points for intervention." *Social Work* 14 (July): 3–12.
ANGELL, ROBERT C.
  1936 *The Family Encounters the Depression.* New York: Charles Scribner's Sons.
BILLINGSLEY, ANDREW M.
  1968 *Black Families in White America.* Englewood Cliffs, N.J.: Prentice-Hall, Inc.
CAVAN, RUTH S.
  1959 "Unemployment: crisis of the common man." *Marriage and Family Living* 21 (May): 139–46.
———, AND K. H. RANCK
  1938 *The Family and the Depression.* Chicago: University of Chicago Press.
DRABEK, THOMAS E., AND KEITH S. BOGGS
  1968 "Families in disaster: reactions and relatives." *Journal of Marriage and the Family* 30 (August): 443–51.
GRIER, WILLIAM H., AND PRICE M. COBBS
  1968 *Black Rage.* New York: Basic Books, Inc., Publishers.
HANSEN, DONALD A.
  1965 "Personal and positional influence in formal groups: propositions for research on family vulnerability to stress." *Social Forces* 44 (December): 202–10.
———, AND REUBEN HILL
  1964 "Families under stress." Pp. 782–819 in Harold Christensen (ed.), *Handbook of Marriage and the Family.* Chicago: Rand McNally & Company.

HILL, REUBEN
1949   *Families Under Stress.* New York: Harper and Brothers.

———
1958   "Generic·features of families under stress." *Social Casework* 39 (February–March): 139–50.

———
1965   "Challenges and resources for family development." Pp. 251–68 in *Family Mobility in Our Dynamic Society.* Ames, Iowa: Iowa State University Press.

———, AND DONALD A. HANSEN
1962   "The family in disaster." Pp. 185–221 in G. W. Baker and D. W. Chapman (eds.), *Man and Society in Disaster.* New York: Basic Books, Inc. Publishers.

KOMAROVSKY, MIRRA
1940   *The Unemployed Man and His Family.* New York: Dryden Press.

KOOS, EARL L.
1946   *Families in Trouble.* New York: King's Crown Press.

LEWIS, OSCAR
1959   *Five Families.* New York: Basic Books, Inc., Publishers.

———
1961   *The Children of Sànchez.* New York: Random House, Inc.

———
1965   *La Vida.* New York: Random House, Inc.

LITWAK, EUGENE, AND JOSEFINA FIGUEIRA
1970   "Technological innovation and ideal forms of family structure in an industrial democratic society." Pp. 348–96 in Reuben Hill and Rene Koenig (eds.), *Families in East and West.* Paris: Mouton.

MARTIN, WALTER T.
1965   "Socially induced stress: some converging themes." *Pacific Sociological Review* 7 (Fall): 63–69.

NYE, IVAN, AND LOIS W. HOFFMAN
1963   *The Employed Mother in America.* Chicago: Rand McNally & Company.

OGBURN, W. F., AND M. F. NIMKOFF
1955   *Technology and the Changing Family.* Boston: Houghton Mifflin Company.

RAINWATER, LEE
1960   *And the Poor Get Children.* Chicago: Quadrangle Books.

———
1965   *Family Design: Marital Sexuality, Family Size, and Contraception.* Chicago: Aldine Press.

———, ET AL
1959   *Workingman's Wife.* New York: Oceana Publications, Inc.

RAPOPORT, RHONA
    1963   "Normal crises, family structure and mental health." *Family Process* 2 (March): 68–80.
——, AND ROBERT RAPOPORT
    1964   "New light on the honeymoon." *Human Relations* 17 (1964): 33–56.
RAPOPORT, ROBERT, AND RHONA RAPOPORT
    1965   "Work and society in contemporary society." *American Sociological Review* 30 (June): 381–94.
ROSENSTOCK, FLORENCE, AND BERNARD KUTNER
    1967   "Alienation and family crisis." *The Sociological Quarterly* 8 (Summer): 397–405.
ROSSI, ALICE
    1968   "Transition to parenthood." *Journal of Marriage and the Family* 30 (1968): 26–39.
SLATER, SHERWOOD
    1967   "The function of the urban kinship network under normal and crisis conditions." Unpublished paper presented at the annual meeting of the American Sociological Association, San Francisco, California.

10 Cross-Cultural and Subcultural Applications

The more general a theory, the greater its explanatory power. Not only is it desirable to have a theoretical framework which will explain varying kinds of deviations from the norm, but it is also advantageous if the framework can be applied to subcultural variations and to cultures other than the one to which it is originally addressed. The goal in this chapter is to demonstrate that the developmental theory has such a potentiality, which is not to say that it has been applied in this direction. A few studies have been identified in which family life cycle analyses were a specific focus. These included work on French Canadian (Miner, 1938), on Burmese (Brant and Khaing, 1951), on Peruvian (Hammel, 1961), on Belgian (Delcourt, 1963–64), on East Indian (Collver, 1963), Japanese (Koyama, 1959; Morioka, 1953, 1967), on Chinese (Morioka, 1967) and on Danish (Noordhoek, 1969) families. Even these few references represent a remarkable range of cultures; however, most do not follow the kind of theoretical perspective presented in this volume. One outstanding exception to that generalization is the work of Professor Kiyomi Morioka (1953, 1967) in Japan. He has stated explicitly that his work follows "the approach which regards the life cycle as process, focusing attention on the role complex characteristic of each stage and tracing changes in it from the early stage to the later one mainly through a comparison of synchronic cross-sectional data on families in different stages" (Morioka, 1967:596). His work will be discussed in some detail since it is of considerable significance on several counts: First, it represents a clear demonstration that the developmental framework as presented in this volume may be utilized to analyze a nonnuclear, nonneolocal family system. Second, Morioka explicitly has rejected both the social anthropological approach of dealing simply with household composition as an indicator of family life cycle category and the narrow demographic analysis approach. Third, he has done some cross-cultural comparative analysis. Before considering Morioka's work, however, I would like to discuss how the developmental theory may be applied to these other cultural settings.

Return to the basic concepts of the theory set forth in Chapter 2, beginning with the definition of the family: "The family is a semiclosed system of actors occupying interrelated positions defined by the society of which the family system is a part as unique to that system with respect to the role content of the positions and to ideas of kinship relatedness. The definitions of positional role content change over the history of the group." First, I would like to emphasize that this definition does not in any way specify the necessary positional content of the family but only states that such content is "defined by the society of which the system is a part as unique to that system." This part means that the first task of any investigator wishing to use the theory is to determine the societal-institutional definition of family in the culture or in the subculture in which he wishes to work; that is, he must identify the group structure or structures which carry the normative identification of *family*, regardless of whether these group structures perform the same functions performed in other family systems of which he is aware and regardless of whether the positional content is equivalent or nearly so to other known family systems. Having made this basic determination, the definition demands, secondly, that the researcher identify the manner in which "those definitions of positional role content change over the history of the group." In carrying out these two basic tasks, he has at his disposal the other concepts set forth in Chapter 2. It may be that in the process of establishing the basic structural history of the family system of that culture, he will find these concepts inadequate to the task. I noted in the discussion of the three analytical facets some of my own concerns about the inadequacies, even for analysis of the American family system of that culture, he will find these concepts inadequate to the task. to devise additional concepts to incorporate into the theoretical system in order to account for what he finds. Thus, again the process of research results in the improvement of theory.

The two basic tasks of identifying the fundamental normative structure and its career changes lie within the societal-institutional facet of analysis. Note that for subcultural analyses, this initial approach suggests the way a *particular* subculture defines the family structure and career, rather than the way the larger society containing the subculture defines the family structure and career. Depending upon the degree of research data already available, this research task may be a relatively simple one. Having made the basic determinations, the researcher then may turn to the group-inter-actional facet to gather data on the normative expectations that prevail with respect to the role content of positions, to the definitions of roles, to the types of role complexes, and so forth which arise within the family experience. Next he may continue his investigations into the individual-psychological facet in determining the way actor-occupants of positions within the family system influence the definitions of their roles and the roles in positions reciprocal to theirs.

Having gained a body of data providing him with knowledge of the normative structure governing the interactional characteristics of the family system, he then may turn to the transactional relationships which pertain to the family system as it relates to the other systems in a particular society. Again, he deals with both the more general definitions of the links and with the changing definitions which apply at differing periods of the family career. Depending on the characteristics of the society, these transactional relationships may be rather limited or very widespread.

These investigations, which may represent many years of work, should yield the basic developmental analysis of the "normal" family structure of a given society. Having established such a base, the investigator now is prepared to delve into the kinds of issues which were discussed in the chapters on atypical family structures and on family stress. Again, depending on the society, he also may extend his studies into subcultural variations which he discovers in the society. Indeed, he may even discover such subcultural variations *within* what he may have defined as a subculture. An example of this kind of analysis is represented by the work which has been carried out on the American black family system. The black family in the United States is in no sense some kind of monolithic structure without significant variation. Thus, studies show important differences along religious or along ideological lines; they show social class, region, urban-rural differences; and they reveal dissimilarities in terms of such historical factors as whether the family came from a lineage of slavery or from the substantial group of free Negroes which existed from the beginning of the nation (Edwards, 1968; Billingsley, 1968; Donald, 1952; Bernard, 1966; Lewis, 1955; Clark, 1965; Rainwater, 1966). These works demonstrate that such intrasubcultural differences do exist and that a developmental analysis of them will be quite appropriate.

NON-WESTERN CULTURES

Kiyomi Morioka's (1967) work is an outstanding example of the cross-cultural application of developmental theory. This remarkable analysis, though not dealing in detail with every aspect discussed in the paragraphs above, does at least touch almost every issue mentioned. Initially, in the societal-institutional facet Morioka presents for study two nonnuclear family systems, the stem family system of Japan and the joint family system of China. The basic structure of the Japanese stem family calls for the system to be composed of the father, his wife, any unmarried children, and the oldest married son and his unmarried children. All other sons, when they marry, depart the family to establish independent families or, in some cases, to be "adopted" by their father-in-law should he have no son. Thus, three basic stages of this family are identified by utilizing the criterion of family headship: Stage 1 is composed of two nuclear families of successive generations, with the headship residing in the father; Stage 2 occurs when the father retires or dies and the headship passes to the oldest son; Stage 3 occurs with the death of the surviving parent and continues until the oldest son of the third generation marries and takes up residence with his father, at which time the structure returns to Stage 1 (Morioka, 1967:597–98).

In the Chinese joint family, a different pattern obtains. Here all married sons continue in the household of the father. Morioka identifies four basic stages to such a system: Stage 1 includes the nuclear family from formation until the marriage of the oldest son; Stage II involves a stem family structure existing until the marriage of the second son; Stage III constitutes a joint family system with all married sons and their families residing together with the parents until their death; Stage IV is composed of the joint family in the absence of the parents with the oldest son as head. This latter stage, ideally, continues on; however, it is frequently broken for a variety of reasons, and each married son departs to establish an independent family. Such new families may begin at any of the three prior stages (Morioka, 1967:601–2).

In the group-interactional facet, Morioka has indicated some of the characteristics that may prevail, though he has not extensively developed this facet of analysis. For the Japanese family, he has devised a further elaboration of the three-stage system to account for the positional occupancy in each of the two basic nuclear families which compose it. He has also indicated part of the normative structure which may arise from the varying kinds of positional occupancy. In addition, he has presented a brief indication of the group-interactional implications of various Chinese joint family compositions, particularly with respect to the characteristics which precipitate the breaking up of the joint family during Stage IV. There is no apparent reason why these analyses cannot be extended further in the way this work has been done for American families.

On the individual-psychological level, Morioka indicates some of the special relationships that develop, particularly between the daughter-in-law and mother-in-law positions in both systems and between the married-brother positions in Stage IV of the Chinese system.

Morioka's primary focus in his analysis is on interactional characteristics of the family. He gives, however, some indication of the transactional implications of his study by referring to the trend in Japan toward conjugal family structure associated with urbanization and with industrialization. This inclination he compares to the tendency to maintain a stem family structure on the part of farmers and other Japanese families who have an economic enterprise handed down from generation to generation (Morioka, 1967:604–5).

Of course, Morioka demonstrates adequately the potentialities for cross-cultural comparisons which the developmental approach has by highlighting the differences between American, Japanese, and Chinese family careers. Except for the slight attention to rural-urban differences in Japan, he does not deal with subcultural differences. Neither does he approach the topic of intrasubcultural differences which may be identified by analyzing differences in urban families according to religion or to socioeconomic status, for example.

Morioka does give some indication of the place of stress as a normal part of the familial career in both China and Japan, primarily with respect to economic matters and to interpersonal stresses arising out of certain patterns of structure which seem more vulnerable than other elements to precipitating dissolution of the family. No treatment of atypical family structures or of atypicality in the characteristics of individual occupants of positions is presented in this particular selection; although in view of the basic method of approaching the familial career in the stem and joint families which Morioka has followed, there is no apparent reason why such analyses may not be accomplished.

Other work on the Japanese family is available. In addition to the extensive bibliography listed by Aldous and Hill (1967:99; 207–12 passim), there are studies by Blood (1967), Vogel (1963), Norbeck (1965), and Goode (1963:321–65) which merit attention. Most of these will not provide explicitly developmental analyses. Since they must dwell on the stem family system of Japan, however, it is possible, using Morioka as a guide, to elicit considerable material for its developmental implications.

Studying the contemporary Chinese family is extremely difficult since the Communist revolution and the subsequent closing off of any major access to Western students as of this writing. There has been some material published, of course; Goode (1967:270–320) cites a great deal. Perhaps, the single most authoritative volume on the postrevolution period is C. K. Yang's (1959) analysis. Goode maintains, however, that despite official Communist doctrine, many of the changes which have occurred in the Chinese family were already well under way before the Communist rise to power. If this contention is the case, Marion J. Levy's (1949; see also Hsu, 1959; Fried, 1959) volume provides an additional major source. Levy's data are drawn from published sources, from informants, and from his own observations during the latter part of World War Two, when he was present in China under "Navy auspices." Most of his data, then, are from the period prior to Communist rule. Again, the necessary focus on the joint family system of China provides the opportunity for abstractions, many of which may be utilized by the developmental analyst.

India provides yet another major non-Western culture in the Asian area. Although it also follows a joint family pattern, it is culturally quite different from China. One article by Collver (1963) deals with an aspect of family development in several Indian villages. This study is a demographic analysis, however, following the pattern of Glick's (1957) work. Because of its brevity, Collver's article gives little detail on the implications of the demographic findings for the interactive or for the transactive patterns of the Indian family career. Collver does point out that the movement to a completely nuclear family system will raise serious problems because of the high mortality rates among parents. This observation contains an important transactive implication for nuclear and extended family. There seems to be no reason why one may not carry out further analysis according to the pattern followed by Morioka in his Chinese study. Of aid in such an attempt are the works of Mandelbaum (1959), of Gore (1965), of Ross (1961), and of Goode (1963:203–69). India provides another opportunity for some subcultural analyses, not only of the varying traditional castes, but also of comparative Hindu and Islamic family patterns. Other religious variations having some importance include Christianity, Sikhism and Jainism. Indeed, India, together with Pakistan, provides a great diversity of subcultures.

Finally, under the subject of major non-Western cultures falls Islam. This case presents a very widespread cultural phenomenon which, as Jeffery (1959) notes, ranges from Morocco to the Philippines and includes "Berbers, Sudanese, Egyptians, Nubians, Albanians, Turks, Syrians, Kurds, Iraquis, Persians, Arabs, Afghans, Indians, Indonsians, Mongols, and Chinese." Goode (1963:87) maintains that little attention has been paid to systematic study of Arabic Islam over the past fifty years. His contention seems to be borne out by my search of the related material, though Hill and Aldous (1967) do cite several titles, perhaps between twenty-five and fifty, with key words such as *Arab, Egypt, Islam, Moslem,* and *Muslim.* In addition, Blitsten (1963:190–220) has attempted a comparison of Moslem and Chinese "corporate" (i.e., joint) family systems. For a person with pertinent interests, there seems to be an adequate base for beginning developmental analysis.

Other non-Western family systems exist, of course. But the ones mentioned certainly will provide ample challenge for application of the developmental theory. Islamic, Hindu, and Chinese systems give adequate opportunity for study of joint family systems, and the Japanese order represent the classic stem family system. In terms of contrast with American family, these systems are clearly the ones most deviant from the small nuclear neolocal pattern.

WESTERN CULTURES

There is, perhaps, far less basic problem with the application of the developmental approach to family systems occurring in cultural settings usually labeled Western. They are all, to a greater or to a lesser extent, conjugal in form. Perhaps, with some exceptions, the greatest difference between them lies in the degree of reliance on ties with extended kin. Beyond this, their differences are probably based in their unique cultural variations on the Western theme. The range is wide between such areas as Southern Europe, the Scandanavian countries, the Soviet Union, France, Spain, Germany, the Netherlands, Poland, the British Isles, the Slavic states of Central Europe, Eurasian Turkey, Canada, Mexico, Central America, the Caribbean, South America, and, of course, the European settlements in a number of South and Central Pacific areas. At the same time *within* each of these places there are major divisions such as the French and English Canadian ones, the varying cultures within the Soviet Union which range from having very European to having very Asian characteristics, and the differences which lie even within the limited geographical areas of the British Isles, Scandanavia, Turkey or the Slavic countries.

All of this means essentially that one must choose his area and seek out data about it. Regarding a great many of these areas, little available material is published in English; however, there has been the establishment of closer international ties since World War Two among behavioral scientists through such organizations as the International Sociological Association and the International Scientific Commission on the Family within the International Union of Family Organizations. In addition, there is increased emphasis on publication of international materials such as that represented by the International Department of the *Journal of Marriage and the Family* and *Current Sociology* published under the auspices of UNESCO. All these trends have increased the possibility of gaining the kind of systematic data which one may desire. There is, indeed, a rather major upsurge in international cooperative research in the behavioral sciences, including the study of the family, based on these and other methods of contact. It is possible to predict that increasingly in the future the developmental theorist may anticipate the opportunity to apply his approach to a variety of Western family settings outside the United States.

At this point the major obstacle to such efforts is financial, since European universities and research institutes are generally quite open to provide bases of operation for American researchers.

Rather than to attempt any kind of general survey of these various cultural settings, I refer the reader to the Aldous-Hill (1967) bibliography and to the selected references listed at the end of this chapter. As mentioned at the outset of this chapter, only a few studies carry an explicit developmental orientation. The opportunity is essentially an open one, therefore, for any one who wishes to enter it, and the potential contributions to the scientific understanding of family behavior are great.

Special attention should go to a particular challenge for the developmental analyst, namely, the opportunity to study family life in collective societies such as the Israeli Kibbutzim. These attempts at a radical restructuring of family life in reaction to a considerably more familistic ideology, are especially fascinating. To trace the family career in the culture of the Kibbutz where, ideally at least, the children never actually reside in the same place as their parents and where the typical roles associated with the provision for maintenance of biological functioning, maintenance of order, division of labor, and the socialization of the children are not part of the positions of the family system, represents a critical test for developmental theory. There are a number of sources for data on this culture; outstanding among them are the works of Spiro (1956, 1968) and Talmon (1965). The Kibbutz provides special interest because it fits none of the three models of family systems discussed: nuclear, stem, or joint. Spiro (1968: 76–79) argues, however, that even the more radical form found in the Kibbutz constitutes a family in terms of the definition we have used. There *are* unique role relationships defined for the husband and wife (though these terms are not used) and for their children. There is also a special term which applies only to this complex of roles and to no other grouping in the Kibbutz. It seems possible, then, to trace the career of these positions and these roles in the manner prescribed by the developmental theory at all three facet levels and both interactionally and transactionally.

UNITED STATES SUBCULTURES

The fifties and the sixties constituted a period in the United States when many subcultures were brought to public consciousness. It was not that these groups had only recently become a part of the society. It was more that the "American dream" of the "melting pot" society was rudely shattered by the growing awareness that, although a number of the older European ethnic groups (the Irish, the Italians, the Germans, the Scandanavians, the Polish, etc.) had been reasonably successful in assimilating themselves, a large minority existed which had not met with the same success. The heightened awareness began with the focus of attention on the black subculture precipitated by the increasingly militant civil rights movement. Aided by the "war on poverty" of the sixties, which revealed other ethnic groups who were becoming progressively more disadvantaged by the widening gap between the poor and the well-to-do, these groups made it impossible to ignore their existence. Thus, black Americans, Mexican-Americans, Puerto Rican Americans, American Indians (*Native Americans*), and Chinese-Americans particularly came into sharp relief. In addition, there was that whole body of the working, as well as the nonworking, poor who were not particularly identified with any ethnic group, but who were seen to be a part of the *culture of poverty*, a term first used by Oscar Lewis.

As may be expected, there was considerable controversy over the legitimacy of the idea of a "culture of poverty" (Roach and Gursslin, 1967; Valentine, 1968; see also the reviews of Valentine's book and his response in *Current Anthropology*, 1969). I do not intend to participate in this particular debate here. We can take as an empirical fact that there is a large body of Americans living in economic circumstances well below the level of the great share of the population, and we can reserve for empirical testing whether or not their family life patterns constitute a unique cultural system.

Other subcultures, which are a part of American life exist, of course, besides the ones identified above. Some of the European ethnic groups still maintain a certain separate cultural identity. The Japanese-Americans, though subjected to the stress of major dislocation during World War Two, have managed to assimilate themselves to a considerable extent. Indeed, they seem to have prospered in spite of or, perhaps, partially because of, their war experience. There remain, nevertheless, significant enclaves of Japanese-Americans in several of the major urban areas of the country. There is the combination ethnic and religious culture of the Jewish American. And there are the more clearly religious subcultures which include large groups such as the Mormons (The Church of Jesus Christ, Latter Day Saints), as well as many smaller sects.

In general, studies of families of subcultural American groups are more readily accessible than are works about the non-American cultures. It is true, nevertheless, that the systematic study of these groups has been subject to some of the fadism in behavioral science research, which I have previously mentioned. Thus, certain groups have received relatively little attention (the Chinese-American, for example), whereas others (the Negro-American) have been more thoroughly studied. I have listed a rather extensive set of references at the end of this chapter. It emphasizes heavily the two groups, consisting of black families and of families in poverty. Again, I refer the reader to the Aldous-Hill (1967) bibliography.

Because of the increasing public attention paid to black Americans over the past two decades as well as because there has been some professional controversy over the proper interpretation of data concerning them, I want to direct some attention to black family life. The controversy arose most specifically out of the Moynihan Report (1965) and his now notorious thesis that, "At the heart of the deterioration of the fabric of Negro society is the deterioration of the Negro family. It is the fundamental source of the weakness of the black community at the present time." This thesis was almost immediately challenged by a number of writers, and there has been a continuing debate on the subject (Rainwater and Yancey, 1967; Billingsley, 1968; Aldous, 1969; Parker and Kleiner, 1969; Staples, 1971). At the heart of the matter is the assertion, by persons who disagree with Moynihan, that there has been a rather consistent, though not necessarily conscious or intentionally malicious, distortion in studies of the black family. Dissenters make two basic and interrelated points about the works: First, they appear to emphasize generally the so-called problem aspects of black family life: crime, delinquency, civil disorder, illegitimacy, desertion, and general instability. Second, they emphasize the alleged deviancy of black family life as the major cause for the problems blacks encounter in American society, rather than seeing the experience of black families in the society as the cause of their deviancy (Billingsley, 1968:198–202; Parker and Kleiner, 1969:500–502).

I am convinced by the scholarly treatment of the data by Billingsley (1968) that the distortions with respect to black family life are real and to a large extent unjustified. Only reading his work will show adequately why I have reached such a conclusion. I can cite the following, however, as the type of evidence which he marshalls: With respect to the matter of black family life being characterized by female heads, he points out that although this situation applies to 25 percent of black families, it does not have relevance to 75 percent (Billingsley, 1968:199). Furthermore, numerically there were only one million black single-parent families, whereas, according to 1966 figures, there were four million white single-parent families. Indeed, when income is taken into account, the differences between black and white families headed by males become greatly reduced (Billingsley, 1968: 14–15). With respect to illegitimacy, Billingsley emphasizes that although 10 percent of black families have experienced it, 90 percent have not. He does not mention that the differential between white and non-white illegitimacy has been narrowing since about the 1950s nor that since 1960 this differential has decreased due to a slight decrease in non-whites coupled with a continuing rise in the rate of white illegitimacy (Clague and Ventura, 1968). Neither did he note the higher likelihood that non-white illegitimate births will be recorded, that whites are more likely to marry on discovery of premarital pregnancy, and that whites probably more frequently have access to abortion as a method of terminating a premarital pregnancy.

But Billingsley goes much beyond statistics in dealing with the Moynihan assertion that the black family is basically an unstable unit. He marshalls his argument to show that it is, first, essentially erroneous to assume that families with what developmental analysts would term a *deficit in structure* are necessarily unstable. Second, he shows that by dealing with the Negro family as a subsystem of the larger social system, much of the difficulty in black family life can be viewed as a result of the problems of the larger social system.

His study, then, generally follows an approach which is quite compatible with developmental theory. He argues for analyzing the family as a social system and for explaining its behavior both with respect to the society of which it is a part and with respect to its own characteristics. Given the fact that normal black family life has been inadequately studied (Billingsley, 1968:197–215), it seems appropriate to observe the importance of obtaining more data on the careers of structurally and normatively typical black families before researchers attempt to understand atypical ones. In this light, it is again interesting to note that the normal structure does not necessarily mean the classic nuclear family, that is, husband, wife, and children only present. Billingsley cites statistics from Paul C. Glick which indicated that in 1953 only 28.6 percent of the white household units fit this classic pattern, and he points out a study by Alan Wilson which showed that in Richmond, California, 45 percent of white families and 49 percent of Negro families were simple nuclear units. Based on 1960 data, Billingsley (1968:18) estimated that about 36 percent of black families were of the simple nuclear type. Billingsley develops a typology of family structures typical of black families, and a number of them also will be typical of white families. The great share of these types include as the basic unit a husband and a wife expanded by the presence of children, other relatives, or non-relatives. The greatest share of black families fall within the types which have the husband-wife present as the basic unit (Billingsley, 1968:16–21). A systematic analysis of black family life careers is long overdue. Nothing in the characteristics of black families or in the characteristics of the theoretical approach appear to prohibit achieving such a goal.

SUMMARY

The chief goal in this chapter has been to show what can be learned by applying the developmental theory to family systems other than the dominant American cultural family system. I have been unable to cite more than a handful of studies which approximate the developmental approach; however, I have attempted to demonstrate that the essential aspects of the theory itself do not prohibit such analyses. As in a number of areas within the dominant American family system, the research is lacking simply because no one has attempted it. I recognize the difficulties in obtaining data on certain systems, because of their inaccessibility or because there is little material from any perspective on them. On the other hand, at least one outstanding case exists of some continuing work from a developmental point of view carried out by Morioka. I believe that this work substantiates my contention that the theory is cross-culturally and comparatively applicable.

A major test of the explanatory power of a theory occurs when it is utilized in areas of behavior which deviate from or which fall outside the dominant culture and when it is applied to cultural settings other than that for which it was originally developed. The systematic application of the developmental approach to non-American family systems and to the subcultural variations within the United States should have at least two consequences. First, it should lead to improving the theory with respect to what the researcher fiinds inadequate about it for explaining the patterns discovered in a given family system. Second, it should expand our knowledge and our understanding of familial behavior throughout human societies. From a pure scientific point of view these goals are worthy. From an applied perspective such accrued knowledge may lead to the improvement in the quality of family life wherever such knowledge is utilized in the development of auxiliary programs by the helping professions.

REFERENCES

Aldous, Joan
> 1969 "Wives' employment status and lower-class men as husband-fathers: support for the Moynihan thesis." *Journal of Marriage and the Family* 31 (August): 469–76.

——, and Reuben Hill
> 1967 *International Bibliography of Research in Marriage and the Family,* 1900–1964. Minneapolis, Minn.: University of Minnesota Press.

Anshen, Ruth N., ed.
> 1959 *The Family: Its Function and Destiny,* rev. ed. New York: Harper and Brothers.

Bernard, Jessie
> 1966 *Marriage and the Family Among Negroes.* Englewood Cliffs, N.J.: Prentice-Hall, Inc.

Billingsley, Andrew
> 1968 *Black Families in White America.* Englewood Cliffs, N.J.: Prentice-Hall, Inc.

BLITSTEN, DOROTHY R.
1963   *The World of the Family.* New York: Random House, Inc.

BLOOD, ROBERT O.
1967   *Love-Match and Arranged Marriage: A Tokyo-Detroit Comparison.* New York: The Free Press.

BRANT, C. S., AND MI MI KHAING
1951   "Burmese kinship and the life cycle." *Southwestern Journal of Anthropology* 7 (Winter): 437–54.

CLAGUE, ALICE J., AND STEPHANIE J. VENTURA
1968   *Trends in Illegitimacy, United States—1940–1965.* Washington, D.C.: Department of Health, Education and Welfare, National Center for Health Statistics.

CLARK, KENNETH B.
1965   *Dark Ghetto.* New York: Harper & Row, Publishers.

COLLVER, ANDREW
1963   "The family cycle in India and the United States." *American Sociological Review* 28 (February): 86–96.

CURRENT ANTHROPOLOGY
1969   "Book review: Culture and Poverty: Critique and Counter-Proposals." *Current Anthropology* 10 (April–June): 181–201.

DELCOURT, J.
1963–64   "Influence of urbanization of the diverse phases of development in the family cycle." *Current Sociology* 12 (1963–64):34–45.

DONALD, HENDERSON H.
1952   *The Negro Freedman.* New York: Abelard-Schuman, Ltd.

EDWARDS, HARRY
1968   "Black Muslim and Negro Christian family relationships." *Journal of Marriage and the Family* 30 (November): 604–11.

FRIED, MORTON H.
1959   "The family in China: the People's Republic." Pp. 146–66 in Ruth N. Anshen (ed.), *The Family: Its Function and Destiny,* rev. ed. New York: Harper and Brothers.

GLICK, PAUL C.
1957   *American Families.* New York: John Wiley & Sons, Inc.

GOODE, WILLIAM J.
1963   *World Revolution and Family Patterns.* New York: The Free Press.

GORE, M. S.
1965   "The traditional Indian family." Pp. 209–31 in M. F. Nimkoff (ed.), *Comparative Family Systems.* Boston: Houghton Mifflin Company.

HAMMEL, E. A.
1961   "The family cycle in a coastal Peruvian slum and village." *American Anthropologist* 63 (October): 989–1005.

Hsu, Frances L. V.
   1959   "The family in China: the classical form." Pp. 123–45 in Ruth N.
           Anshen (ed.), *The Family: Its Function and Destiny*, rev. ed.
           New York: Harper and Brothers.

Jeffery, Arthur
   1959   "The family of Islam." Pp. 201–38 in Ruth N. Anshen (ed.),
           The Family: Its Function and Destiny, rev. ed. New York: Harper
           and Brothers.

Koyama, Takashi
   1959   "Cyclical changes in the family composition." Pp. 67–83 in
           Y. Okada and S. Kitano (eds.), *Ie: Its Structural Analyses*. Tokyo:
           Sobunsha.

Levy, Marion J., Jr.
   1949   *The Family Revolution in Modern China*. Cambridge, Mass.:
           Harvard University Press.

Lewis, Hylan
   1955   *Blackways of Kent*. Chapel Hill, N. C.: University of North
           Carolina Press.

Mandelbaum, David G.
   1959   "The family in India." Pp. 167–87 in Ruth N. Anshen (ed.),
           The Family: Its Function and Destiny, rev. ed. New York: Harper
           and Brothers.

Marenko, A. S.
   1967   *The Collective Family: A Handbook for Russian Parents*. Garden
           City, N. Y.: Doubleday and Company.

Miner, Horace
   1938   "The French Canadian family cycle." *American Sociological Re-
           view* 3 (October): 700–708.

   _____

   1939   *St. Denis, A French Canadian Parish*. Chicago: University of
           Chicago Press.

Morioka, Kiyomi
   1953   "A new approach to the family study: theory and method of
           family life cycle." *Monthly Bulletin of Family Courts* 5 (Febru-
           ary): 66–73 (Japanese).

   _____

   1967   "Life cycle patterns in Japan, China, and the United States."
           Journal of Marriage and the Family 29 (August): 595–606.

Moynihan, Daniel P.
   1965   *The Negro Family: The Case for National Action*. Washington,
           D.C.: U.S. Department of Labor, Office of Planning and Re-
           search.

Murdock, George Peter
   1959   *Africa*. New York: McGraw-Hill Book Company.

NOORDHOEK, J. A.
1969 *Employment*. Vol. I of *Married Women, Family and Work*. Copenhagen: Danish National Institute for Social Research.

NORBECK, EDWARD
1965 *Changing Japan*. New York: Holt, Rinehart & Winston, Inc.

OTTENBERG, SIMON, AND PHOEBE OTTENBERG
1960 *Cultures and Societies of Africa*. New York: Random House, Inc.

PARKER, SEYMOUR, AND ROBERT J. KLEINER
1969 "Social and psychological dimensions of the family role performance of the Negro male." *Journal of Marriage and the Family* 31 (August): 500–506.

PHILLIPS, ARTHUR, ED.
1953 *Survey of African Marriage and Family Life*. London: Oxford University Press.

RADCLIFFE-BROWN, A. R., AND DARYLL FORDE, EDS.
1950 *African Systems of Kinship and Marriage*. London: Oxford University Press.

RAINWATER, LEE
1966 "Crucible of identity: the Negro lower-class family." *Daedalus* 95 (Winter): 172–216.

———, AND WILLIAM L. YANCEY
1967 *The Moynihan Report and the Politics of Controversy*. Cambridge, Mass.: The M.I.T. Press.

ROACH, JACK L., AND ORVILLE R. GURSSLIN
1967 "An evaluation of the concept of 'culture of poverty.'" *Social Forces* 45 (March): 383–92.

ROSS, AILEEN D.
1961 *The Hindu Family in Its Urban Setting*. Toronto: University of Toronto Press.

SCHLESINGER, RUDOLPH
1949 *The Family in the U.S.S.R.* London: Routledge and Kegan Paul, Ltd.

SPIRO, MELFORD E.
1956 *Kibbutz: Venture in Utopia*. Cambridge, Mass.: Harvard University Press.

———
1968 "Is the family universal?—the Israeli case." Pp. 68–79 in Norman W. Bell and Ezra F. Vogel (eds.), *A Modern Introduction to the Family*, rev. ed. New York: The Free Press.

STAPLES, ROBERT
1971 "Towards a sociology of the black family: a theoretical and methodological assessment." *Journal of Marriage and the Family* 33 (February): 119–38.

TALMON, YONINA
    1965   "The family in a revolutionary movement—the case of the Kibbutz
            of Israel." Pp. 259–86 in M. F. Nimkoff (ed.), *Comparative
            Family Systems*. Boston: Houghton Mifflin Company.
VALENTINE, CHARLES A.
    1968   *Culture and Poverty: Critique and Counter-Proposals*. Chicago:
            University of Chicago Press.
VOGEL, EZRA F.
    1963   *Japan's New Middle Class: The Salary Man and His Family in a
            Tokyo Suburb*. Berkeley and Los Angeles: University of California
            Press.
YANG, C. K.
    1959   *The Chinese Family in the Communist Revolution*. Cambridge,
            Harvard University Press.

11

The Challenge
of an Incomplete
Explanation

In the preface to this volume I mentioned that much material was incomplete and inadequate in the discussion of the developmental theory and in the empirical research application of it. Persons who have read the book are now aware of the degree to which that statement was an accurate assessment. We have encountered again and again areas where further work is needed. When I first became acquainted with this theoretical approach about fifteen years ago, it was even less complete. That was one of the basic conditions which attracted me to it. Here was an area of sociological thinking which was not already so well developed and so thoroughly researched that it could be considered a part of the basic "doctrine" of family sociology. Rather, it had more of the status of a heretical position. Its adherents were raising new questions, and were suggesting different approaches to the explanation of family behavior. As a result, the area provided a seductive lure which drew me to it. That lure has continued for me.

As I have presented courses on the developmental approach to family analysis, I have always tried to communicate something of the excitement of dealing with an unsettled area. Over the years, a few more pieces have been added to the puzzle, but the picture is not yet completed. I have invited my students to participate in completing it. This book has simply been an attempt to invite others into that activity. It is possible, of course, that when all of the pieces have been put into place, there will not be a picture at all. It may be that the theory does not explain family behavior in the way that it purports to. That possibility, for me at least, is not at all discouraging. Part of the challenge of scientific exploration is to discover what does not work, as well as what does. If, after the theoretical framework has been developed adequately, the empirical testing of it determines that it cannot meet the test, this finding is important. All that it means is that we must begin at some other point and must move in another direction. But we are not at this point yet. We are still in the process of building the theory, of determining the kinds of methods which will adequately test it, and of designing research studies which will carry out the test. In this final chapter, I would like to review the basic inadequacies which have been observed as a way of identifying the challenge that remains ahead.

THEORETICAL INADEQUACIES

In the early chapters, I developed in some detail the conceptual framework of the theory by identifying three facets of analysis—societal-institutional, group-interactional, and individual-psychological—and by identifying two arenas of family behavior—the interactional and the trans-actional. Each of these areas undoubtedly will undergo future modification and improvement, though some are in greater need of it than others.

Perhaps because family sociologists and sociologists in general have focused so much attention on the societal-institutional aspects of human behavior, this facet seems least in need of further work. The concepts are designed to capture the broad patterns of expectation for familial behavior and appear to perform this function adequately for an entire society or for a subcultural unit of the society. It is also true that this facet of behavior is the most easily inferred from observable behavior. Thus, the high level of generality and the overt quality of this aspect make it the easiest one to handle.

Sociologists also have devoted much effort to the analysis of the group-interactional facet of social behavior. Particularly in the case of the family, however, there remains a certain closed quality to the functioning of groups. It is more difficult to identify the processes carried on and the normative characteristics of these processes. Some basic concepts are designed to capture a great deal of what is known, but the intricate quality of these relationships has not been completely captured yet. It is particularly difficult to identify the behavioral origins of established patterns which can be observed in the various role complexes of the family, even though it is obvious that they are based in some way on the interactional experience of the family group and not on some societal-institutional foundation. As was seen in the analysis of fertility behavior, for example, an explanation based on demographic analysis at the societal-institutional level is inadequate; yet, the group-interactional level of analysis as it has been attempted thus far also leaves much that is unexplained. A need prevails for continued intensive work in improving the conceptual framework for this facet.

Far less well developed than either of the other two facets, however, is the individual-psychological one. The surface has been scratched only barely here. There is no question that the individual actor has a profound impact on the career of the family. We do not have at this point a systematically formulated set of concepts for analyzing the impact. In my judgment, until this facet is more completely conceptualized, we shall continue to leave a major portion of familial behavior unexplained. I am not professing a kind of psychological reductionism but rather I am making an honest recognition that social behavior cannot be fully understood until we have a much more adequate understanding of the contribution of the individual to the group. A major strength of the developmental theory continues to be its recognition of the importance of this facet for shaping the family career. We have yet to see the full benefit which can be derived from a rigorous conceptual development of this area.

Family sociologists have devoted the great bulk of their attention to the interactional arena of family behavior, though this attention has been somewhat unbalanced. A good deal of work has been done on the husband-wife relationships, particularly on marital adjustment. Even here, however, the focus has been more heavily on early marriage than on a systematic tracing of the husband-wife role-complex career. Similarly, certain aspects of the parent-child relationships have been heavily analyzed. We probably have the most information about parents and young children and about parents and adolescents. Here again a systematic treatment of the total parent-child-role-complex career is needed. Far less is known about sibling relationships and about relationships which involve the parents and more than one of the children at the same time. Developmental analyses frequently have lost sight of the importance of children who are not the oldest or the youngest ones. Thus, interactional analysis which attempts to deal with the full family group, rather than only with portions of it, remains to be accomplished. It was also noted that there appeared to be much more work done on socialization, on the division of labor, on certain aspects of recruitment and biological reproduction, and on the maintenance of order areas. We know much less about the maintenance of biological functioning and about the maintenance of meaning with the possible exception of certain aspects of the husband-wife relationship. In spite of the concentrated attention on the interactional arena, then, there is still much theoretical work to do.

The transactional arena remains relatively undeveloped. The great share of work in this area deals with the occupational role of the husband-father and, to a lesser extent, with that of the wife-mother. Transactional roles played in other systems of the society remain to be conceptualized adequately. This fact highlights a general conceptual weakness, existing at a number of points in the developmental theory, that has to do with the bridging concepts necessary to tie together the various areas of behavior.

Not only do we need to devote attention to the bridging between the interactional and the transactional arena, but we need to apply similar effort at several other points. The ties between the individual-psychological and the group-interactional facets and between the group-interactional and the societal-institutional facets also demand more specification. In addition, there is a need to determine the ties which exist between the various "functional" areas identified. Although the overall conceptualization is based on the view of the family as a system, the theory thus far has tended to work with subsystem areas and less often with the way that they relate to one another to constitute a total system.

Identifying the areas of inadequacy in the theoretical formulation, even in this brief manner, provides a somewhat overwhelming feeling. Perhaps, then, it must be said that no individual can possibly expect to accomplish everything indicated. Fortunately, science is a corporate enterprise and, hopefully, individuals may find some challenge in one or more of these areas and may be motivated to devote their efforts to them. My hope is only that those areas which are least well developed may receive some concentrated and systematic attention so that they do not lag so far behind the fields which have received greater attention in the past.

METHODOLOGICAL INADEQUACIES

In this volume I have paid relatively little attention to research methodology, as opposed to research findings. Yet, the findings of a study are only as good as the ability of the researcher to operationalize the theory validly and reliably and to design a research operation that will meet as closely as possible the demands of the theory. This situation is particularly problematic for the developmental theoretical approach on at least two grounds: the first is the ultimate expectation that the data to be gathered will be truly longitudinal in quality. The second is that the data analysis techniques be appropriate to longitudinal data.

In 1964, Reuben Hill published an article about some of the methodological issues facing the developmental approach which focused on the demand for longitudinal data. At that time, he wrote (Hill, 1964:195):

> But following couples from engagement period of wedding through their family life span to the dissolution of the family is fraught with many practical difficulties, not the least of which includes the possibility that

the researcher won't live to see his project completed. There are the difficulties of sampling, of securing the couples' cooperation and commitment over such a long time period, of maintaining contact with the families for a long time, of committing oneself to a study of the necessary duration, and the many other organization and personal changes that lessen the chances of research continuity.

Hill's analysis is still as true today as when he wrote it. His article suggests several alternatives to a strictly longitudinal data gathering design, and each option constitutes some degree of compromise with the resulting loss in quality of the data. The choices include: "1) the synthetic pattern of development constructed from cross-sectional data; 2) retrospective history taking; 3) segmented longitudinal study; 4) segmented longitudinal panels with controls; and 5) the intergenerational panel, combining retrospective histories (backward oriented) and panel interviews forward in time" (Hill, 1964:196). Just as the researcher makes many other decisions, and each one has an impact on the ultimate quality of his data, so he must make a decision in this area as to which alternative will best fit his available resources with the minimal effect on his findings. Hill cites several examples of each kind of approach and discusses the disadvantages they display. Two later references should be cited: Hill's critical analysis of the three-generation research design (1970a) and his final report on the three-generation family study in Minneapolis-St. Paul (1970b).

Hill does not discuss data analysis techniques in any detail in his 1964 article. The developmental theory makes a peculiar demand on the researcher in this area. As has been observed repeatedly, at the heart of the theory is the recognition that present circumstances are to some extent a consequence of past history as well as an anticipation about the future. Thus, analysis of the present assumes some kind of relationship or dependence on the past. In most social research, the analyst compares groups of data from samples which he can assume with some level of confidence are independent of one another. Most statistical techniques carry with them such an assumption, though it is frequently true that the data to which they are applied do not meet the assumption. The issue, then, is joined. What statistical techniques are available to the developmental researcher who begins with an assumption of some level of *dependence* rather than of independence?

At the present time, I envision the most promise in the statistical area to reside in techniques which utilize a stochastic approach. At the risk of oversimplifying and, thus, distorting, the meaning of stochastic statistical processes, I shall identify their central character as follows: Any statistical operation which takes into account the fact that there are several potential alternative Time 2 outcomes to any given set of relationships at Time 1, any statistical operation which assesses the varying probabilities for each of the Time 2 outcomes, which then reassesses the probabilities of later outcomes at Time 3 from the varying Time 2 outcomes, and which continues in such a progression to Time N is essentially a stochastic analysis. A simply presented paradigm of such an approach is illustrated in the Magrabi and Marshall (1965) "game tree" analysis of developmental tasks. More sophisticated versions of this approach are represented in the various attempts to use "Markov chains" in the analysis of social data. I am not prepared to state categorically that the techniques presently available meet the assumptions of developmental theory. I can state that it is this sort of statistical analytical approach which the nature of developmental data indicates, since such an approach explicitly takes into account the influence of the past on the present situation.

I am not entirely comfortable, however, with the heavily quantitative implications of the stochastic statistical operations as I understand them. For certain purposes of analysis, the quantifying of data which is essentially qualitative in nature is justified as long as the analyst is fully conscious of what he may be losing in the process of translating from qualitative to quantitative terms. I argue, nevertheless, for devising methods of data analysis which will allow for an analogous stochastic process for qualitative data. Let me illustrate the problem as I see it. If we begin with a married couple at the establishment of their family of procreation, it is possible to establish the probabilities of their reproductive behavior in terms of the number and the spacing of children by basing such probabilities on the reproductive behavior of couples possessing similar characteristics to theirs. At each birth-order level, these chances can be reassessed. Consequently, a stochastic analysis of their reproductive behavior is possible.

For the developmental analyst, however, this examination is insufficient. What he also will want to do is to develop some manner of carrying out analogous analyses of the qualitative nature of the role sequences and role complexes of the familial career. Depending on how ambitious he may be about the goals which he has set for his analysis, he may wish to examine the impact of several roles from several positions, interactional and transactional, on the familial career over a given period of time. (We shall assume that he is not so ambitious that he wishes to carry out this study for the entire career of the family!) It may be that he can reduce much of this process to quantifiable terms for the analysis and then can reconvert the findings again to qualitative form. To the extent that he can accomplish this step, his only problem appears to be to locate or to devise appropriate statistical operations. The capacity of modern computers seem to be such that, assuming an appropriate program can be written, the complexity and volume of such data should provide no difficulty. The strong probability exists, however, that important portions of his data cannot be quantified in any acceptable manner. In such a situation, he is still faced with the complexity and the volume of his data, but he does not appear to have the abilities of the computer at his disposal. The challenge to the creativity of the researcher is now clear. I cannot point to any examples of research which have met this challenge. In my view, the ultimate promise of the researchability of developmental theory may survive or may die on the basis of whether we can solve this problem.

To summarize, the problems of method related to data gathering appears to be surmountable given adequate resources of time and of money for meeting the demands of the theory. Methodological issues related to the analysis of data gathered in conformity with the demands of the theory appear to remain problematical. The doubts which I have expressed with respect to the ultimate ability of quantitative analysis to provide a solution seem to me to be increasingly shared in the behavioral sciences. Whether it will be possible to derive satisfactory alternatives to quantitative analysis is major concern for the behavioral scientist in the years ahead.

RESEARCH DATA INADEQUACIES

A review of Chapters 5–10 will reveal repeated alternative versions of the statement that "little research which utilizes a developmental theoretical base has been carried out in this area." There should really be little surprise in the recognition of this fact. Concentrated work on the theoretical formulation is little more than fifteen-to-twenty years old. A relatively small core of professionals exist who have devoted even a portion of their efforts to work in the developmental theoretical area. General professional awareness of the approach can probably be traced to the publications of Duvall (1957), Hill and Hansen (1960), and Hill and Rodgers (1964). Methodological problems have been serious; so, although I have been able to point to research which has developmental implications or which seemed to have an implicit, if not explicit, developmental orientation, I really cannot assert that the theory has been put to the test. There are several aspects to this situation.

First in priority, in my view, is the lack of systematic development of research propositions based on the developmental theory even as it now exists in its less than complete form. I believe that we are at a point in the theoretical development of the approach where such systematic work is now indicated. Rather than to take the more generalized approach of identifying a particular area of familial behavior to which we may wish to direct our efforts, it is time to begin by identifying the critical research propositions to be put to the test. We then can identify areas of familial behavior where these propositions may be tested. This procedure will have the effect of enhancing both our theoretical and our empirical research base.

Second, there is still some need for exploratory research, particularly in areas where the theory is not well developed and in areas where we have little empirical knowledge of any kind. The individual-psychological facet and the transactional arena are two such theoretical areas. There are numerous areas in which our empirical knowledge is limited or is non-existent.

Third, there is a general need for explanatory research testing hypotheses derived from the research propositions which should be devised in all of the areas where we have a considerable empirical base. If we are ever to move beyond the current sort of hit-or-miss, eclectic approach to developmental research, we must begin to apply considerably more discipline to our projected research than we have in the past. If we examine almost any area in behavioral science which stands today as well formulated theoretically and as well tested empirically, we can see that it reached this state as a result of such a disciplined effort. Although its early history may have looked very similar to the one of developmental theory, there was a point when a concerted effort occurred—an effort theoretically and empirically based—which carried it to a state of solid scientific integrity.

CONCLUSION

There is something of the evangelist in almost all of us. We want others to see matters as we see them and to be concerned about the issues that concern us. Scientists and academicians in some ways seem to me to be more prone to this orientation than some other groups. Although some of them may be content to live out their lives in the seclusion of their isolated laboratories or their intellectual ivory towers, far more of them have the desire to share widely their intellectual concerns. The frequently maligned propensity to publish is a clear evidence of this inclination. There are many ways to publish other than the journal article, the professional-meeting paper, or a book such as this one. The discussion that takes place in the hallways and in the hotel rooms at professional meetings, the talk over coffee, the debate of the classroom and seminar are all forms of publication. The emotional quality of much of this interchange leaves little doubt about its evangelical fervor.

I admit openly to such a motivation concerning the developmental theoretical approach. For over fifteen years, it has been for me a fascinating intellectual puzzle. In this volume, I have tried to communicate some of my fascination to anyone who will take the time to read these words. The inadequacies which the theory represents in its present form, the ignorance that we have about its empirical support, and the general necessity to find out whether or not it makes any sense at all are all part of its fascination for me. I would like others to share in this experience. If, in spite of all of the shortcomings of my ability to set forth the characteristics of developmental theory, some readers take up the challenge represented by the incomplete state in which it stands today—if, in short, there are some "converts" to the task of developing the theory further, I will have accomplished the goal that I set for myself.

REFERENCES

DUVALL, EVELYN
  1957 *Family Development*. Philadelphia: J. B. Lippincott Company.

HILL, REUBEN
  1964 "Methodological issues in family development research." *Family Process* 3 (March): 186–206.

——
  1970a "The three generation research design: method for studying family and social change." Pp. 536–51 in Reuben Hill and Rene Koenig (eds.), *Families in East and West*. Paris: Mouton.

——
  1970b.*Family Development in Three Generations*. Cambridge, Mass.: Schenkman Publishing Company, Inc.

——, AND DONALD A. HANSEN
  1960 "The identification of conceptual frameworks utilized in family study." *Marriage and Family Living* 22 (November): 299–311.

——, AND ROY H. RODGERS
  1964 "The developmental approach." Pp. 171–211 in Harold Christensen (ed.), *Handbook of Marriage and the Family*. Chicago: Rand McNally & Company.

MAGRABI, FRANCIS M., AND WILLIAM H. MARSHALL
  1965 "Family developmental tasks: a research model." *Journal of Marriage and the Family* 27 (November): 454–61.

RODGERS, ROY H.
  1964 "Toward a theory of family development." *Journal of Marriage and the Family* 26 (August): 262–70.

RODGERS, ROY H.

    1966   "The occupational role of the child: a research frontier in the developmental conceptual framework." *Social Forces* 45 (December): 217–24.

Author Index

Subject Index